THE BEST OF
THE BEST OF
BUSINESS
CARD
DESIGN

rockport

THE BEST OF
THE BEST OF
BUSINESS
CARD
DESIGN

ROCKPORT PUBLISHERS

GLOUCESTER MASSACHUSETTS

First published in the United States of America by

Rockport Publishers, Inc., a member of

Quayside Publishing Group

33 Commercial Street

Gloucester, Massachusetts 01930-5089

Telephone: (978) 282-9590

Fax: (978) 283-2742

www.rockpub.com

ISBN 1-59253-184-9

Cover and Layout design: tabula rasa

Cover image and page 5: T.DeBrocke/Retrofile.com

Grateful acknowledgment is given to Jeannet Leendertse for her work from *The Best of Business Card Design 4* on pages 6–189.

Printed in China

2

Design Firm
  The Riordon Design Group
Art Director
  Ric Riordon
Designer
  Dan Wheaton
Client
  Self-promotion
Software/Hardware
  Adobe Illustrator, Adobe
  Photoshop, QuarkXpress
Paper/Materials
  Beckett Expression
Printing
  Somerset Graphics

3

Design Firm
  Matite Giovanotte
Art Director
  Stefania Adani
Designer
  Stefania Adani
Client
  XT Societá Di Consulenza
Software/Hardware
  Freehand, Macintosh
Paper/Materials
  Fedrigoni Nettuno Bianco Artico
Printing
  2 Colors

2

3

1

Design Firm
  Langer Design
Designer
  Matthias Langer
Client
  Gadebusch Design
Software/Hardware
  QuarkXpress, Freehand,
  Macintosh
Printing
  2 Colors

Design Firm
The Riordon Design Group
Art Director
Ric Riordon
Designer
Dan Wheaton
Client
Chuck Gammage Animation
Software/Hardware
Adobe Photoshop, QuarkXpress
Paper/Materials
Classic Crest
Printing
Somerset Graphics

Design Firm
Sibley Peteet Design
Art Director
Donna Aldridge
Designer
Donna Aldridge
Illustrator
Donna Aldridge
Client
Ray Laskowitz
Software/Hardware
Adobe Illustrator, Macintosh
Paper/Materials
Cougar Opaque Cream
Printing
Millet The Printer

PIECE WORK
PRODUCTIONS

RAY LASKOWITZ
PHOTOGRAPHER
DALLAS, TEXAS
75214·0734

214·941·3678
PWork1121@AOL.com

1

Design Firm
Creative Company

Art Director
Chris Novd

Designer
Chris Novd

Client
Roth Heating & Cooling

Software/Hardware
Macintosh

Paper/Materials
Lustro Dull

Printing
Panther Print

2

Design Firm
Niehinger & Rohsiepe

Art Directors
C. Niehinger, H. Rohsiepe

Designers
C. Niehinger, H. Rohsiepe

Client
Eckart Schuster, Consultant

Software/Hardware
Freehand 8.0, Macintosh

Paper/ Materials
Gmund Die Natuerlichen

Printing
Black, Red, and Silver

1

2

R&M ASSOCIATI GRAFICI
R&M ASSOCIATI GRAFICI

raffaele fontanella   maurizio di somma   **comunicazione visiva**
ore 3   tel.081.870 50 53 fax 870 21 95

raff
80053 castellammare di Stabia   traversa del pescatore 3

Design Firm
R & M Associati Grafici
Art Directors
Di Somma / Fontanella
Client
Self-promotion
Software/Hardware
Adobe Illustrator, Macintosh
Printing
Offset

wasps artists' studios
256 Alexandra Parade
Glasgow G31 3AJ
tel   +44 141 554 2499
fax   +44 141 556 5340
email gillianblack@waspsstudios.org.uk
web   www.waspsstudios.org.uk

Gillian Black
General Manager

Design Firm
   Graven Images Ltd.
Art Director
   Janice Kirkpatrick
Designer
   Colin Raeburn
Client
   Wasps Artists' Studios
Software/Hardware
   Adobe Illustrator, QuarkXpress
Paper/Materials
   Conqueror, Oyster Wove, 300 gsm
Printing
   2 Color Litho

1

Design Firm
  J. Gail Bean, Graphic Design
Art Director
  J. Gail Bean
Designer
  J. Gail Bean
Illustrator
  J. Gail Bean
Client
  Self-promotion
Software/Hardware
  Adobe Illustrator 7.0, Macintosh
Paper/Materials
  Cougar 80 lb. Natural Smooth
Printing
  Rainbow Printing, Marietta GA;
  2 Color

2

Design Firm
  Dean Johnson Design
Art Director
  Bruce Dean
Designer
  Bruce Dean
Illustrator
  Bruce Dean
Client
  Tod Martens Photography

1

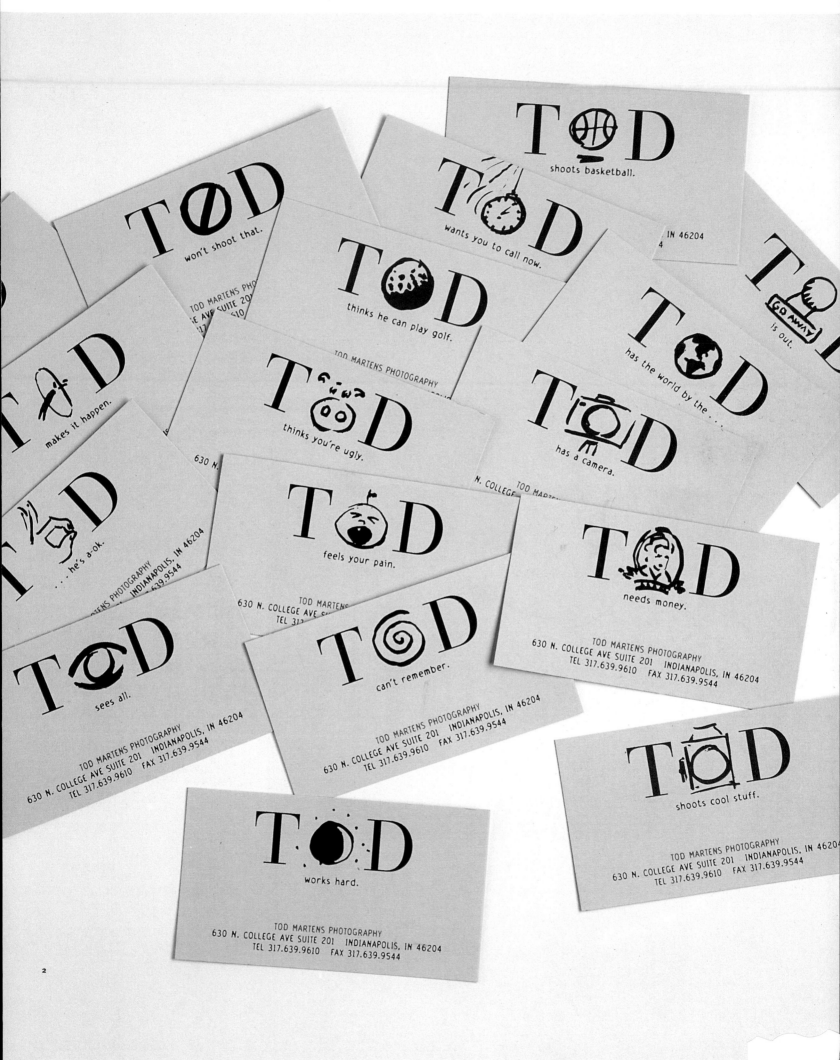

Design Firm
Treehouse Design
Art Director
Tricia Rauen
Designer
Tricia Rauen
Client
Salon Blu
Software/Hardware
Adobe Illustrator
Paper/Materials
Strathmore Elements
Printing
Blair Graphics

SALON **blu**

Dino Gugliuzza

2510 Main Street
Suite D
Santa Monica
California 90405

310.392.3331 *tel*
310.392.4811 *fax*

1

2

1
Design Firm
    Langer Design
Designer
    Matthias Langer
Client
    Thorsten Pohl, Cutter & Editor
Software/Hardware
    QuarkXpress, Adobe Photoshop,
    Macintosh
Printing
    2 Colors

2
Design Firm
    Michael Kimmerle·Art
    Direction + Design
Art Director
    Michael Kimmerle
Designer
    Michael Kimmerle
Illustrator
    Michael Kimmerle
Client
    Performa
Software/Hardware
    QuarkXpress, Macintosh
Paper/Materials
    Naturals, König 650 glm2
Printing
    Siebdruck, Screen Printing

3
Design Firm
    Castenfors & Co.
Art Director
    Jonas Castenfors
Designer
    Jonas Castenfors
Client
    Inredningsbyrån Inte & Co.
Software/Hardware
    QuarkXpress
Paper/Materials
    Skandia
Printing
    Elfströms Tryckeri

3

PAOLA OCONE

Via Varano 72

80054 Gragnano (Na)

TELEFONO 081. 8712322

1

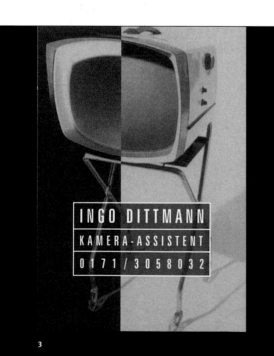

3

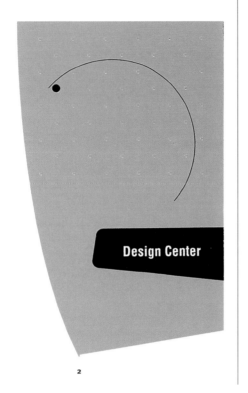

Design Center

Vanessa J. Mathwig
Marketing Manager

Design Center, Inc.
15119 Minnetonka Boulevard
Minnetonka, MN 55345 USA
Tel: (612) 933 9766
Fax: (612) 933 1562

Email: dc@design-center.com
Web: design-center.com

2

INGO DITTMANN • KAMERA-ASSISTENT • 0171/3058032

3
Design Firm
    Langer Design
Designer
    Matthias Langer
Client
    Ingo Dittmann,
    Camera Assistant
Software/Hardware
    QuarkXpress, Adobe Photoshop,
    Macintosh
Printing
    2 Colors

1
Design Firm
  Opera Grafisch Ontwerpers
Art Directors
  Ton Homburg, Marty Schoutsen
Designers
  Sappho Panhuysen,
  Ton Homburg
Client
  Rijksmuseum Voor Volkenkunde
Software/Hardware
  QuarkXpress, Macintosh
Paper/Materials
  Chambord
Printing
  Drukkerij Oomen Breda

2
Design Firm
  Case
Designer
  Kees Wagenaars
Client
  Self-promotion
Software/Hardware
  QuarkXpress
Paper/Materials
  Pecunia
Printing
  PMS 392

RIJKSMUSEUM voor
VOLKENKUNDE
LEIDEN **National Museum of Ethnology**

Steenstraat 1
Postbus 212
2300 AE Leiden
The Netherlands

drs. Herman de Boer
head of exhibitions

T +31 (0)71 5168 800
F +31 (0)71 5128 437
herman@rmv.nl

1

case

Kees Wagenaars

Baronielaan 78 4818 RC Breda
t 076 5215187 f 076 5217457
e kwcase@knoware.nl

2

Design Firm
  Design Center
Art Director
  John Reger
Designer
  Cory Docken
Client
  Ncell Systems
Software/Hardware
  Freehand, Macintosh
Paper/Materials
  Strathmore Writing
Printing
  Pro-Craft

BileniaTech

Noah Prywes
CEO. CCCC - General Partner

BileniaTech, LP
2400 Chestnut Street
Philadelphia. PA
19103-4316

Voice 215.854.0555
ext. 211
Fax   215.854.0665
Prywes@BileniaTech.com
www.BileniaTech.com

1

billennium
Year 2000 COBOL Software Factory

billennium.lp
tony newshel
general manager

2300 chestnut street
philadelphia pa
19103

voice 215.854.0555
fax   215.854.0665
newshel@billenn.com
http://www.billenn.com

2

Patrick M. Baldasare
President & CEO

@RISK
SolutionsThroughDataMining

web www.atRiskInc.com e-mail PBaldasare@atRiskInc.com
Tel 610.296.0800 x701   Fax 610.296.8181
1205 Westlakes Drive Suite 180 • Berwyn • PA • 19312

SolutionsThroughDataMining

3

1

Design Firm
LF Banks + Associates
Art Director
Lori F. Banks
Designer
John German
Client
BileniaTech, LP
Software/Hardware
Freehand
Paper/Materials
Neenah Classic Columns
Printing
RoyerComm Corporation

2

Design Firm
LF Banks + Associates
Art Director
Lori F. Banks
Designer
John German
Client
Billennium, LP
Software/Hardware
Freehand
Paper/Materials
Neenah Classic Columns
Printing
Fern Hill Printing Co.

3

Design Firm
LF Banks + Associates
Art Director
Lori F. Banks
Designer
John German
Client
@Risk, Inc.
Software/Hardware
Freehand, Adobe Photoshop
Paper/Materials
Neenah Classic Columns
Printing
Quality Lithographing Co.

Design Firm
  LF Banks + Associates
Art Director
  Lori F. Banks
Designer
  Lori F. Banks
Client
  Self-promotion
Software/Hardware
  Freehand
Paper/Materials
  Grafika Lineal
Printing
  Quality Lithographing Co.

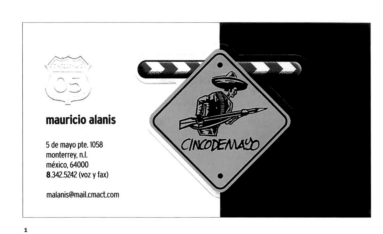

1

Design Firm
Cincodemayo Design
Art Director
Mauricio H. Alanis
Designer
Mauricio H. Alanis
Client
Self-promotion
Software/Hardware
Freehand 7.0, Macintosh
Paper/Materials
Magnomatt
Printing
5DM Offset Printing

1

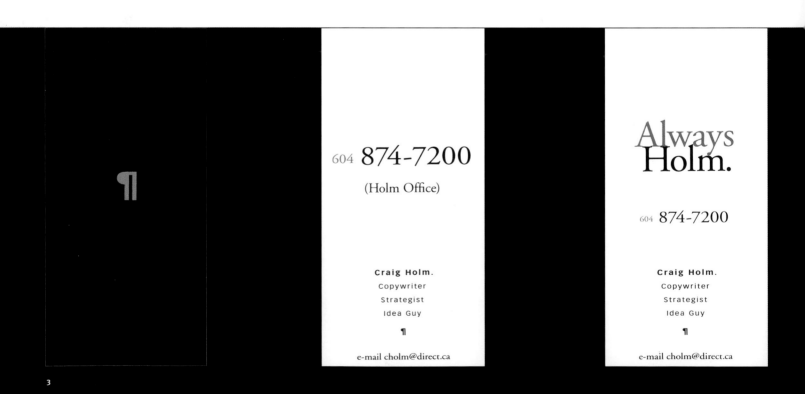

604 **874-7200**

(Holm Office)

Craig Holm.
Copywriter
Strategist
Idea Guy

¶

e-mail cholm@direct.ca

Always
Holm.

604 **874-7200**

Craig Holm.
Copywriter
Strategist
Idea Guy

¶

e-mail cholm@direct.ca

3

LAURIE OKAMURA
QUEEN BEE

THE HIVE DESIGN STUDIO
10 JACKSON STREET, SUITE 204
LOS GATOS, CALIFORNIA 95032
PHONE 408.354.2961
FAX 408.354.3682
EMAIL: ELCY@AOL.COM

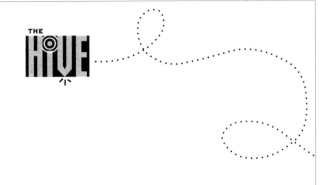

2

2
Design Firm
The Hive Design Studio
Art Directors
Laurie Okamura, Amy Stocklein
Designers
Laurie Okamura, Amy Stocklein
Client
Self-promotion
Software/Hardware
Adobe Illustrator, Macintosh
Paper/Materials
Cranes Crest
Printing
Mission Printers

Call Holm
More Often.

604 874-7200

Craig Holm.
Copywriter
Strategist
Idea Guy

¶

e-mail cholm@direct.ca

Call Me.
I'm Holm.

604 874-7200

Craig Holm.
Copywriter
Strategist
Idea Guy

¶

e-mail cholm@direct.ca

3
Design Firm
Big Eye Creative
Art Directors
Perry Chua, Dann Ilicic
Designer
Perry Chua
Copy writer
Craig Holm
Client
Craig Holm
Software/Hardware
Adobe Illustrator
Paper/Materials
Potlatch McCoy
Printing
Clarke Printing

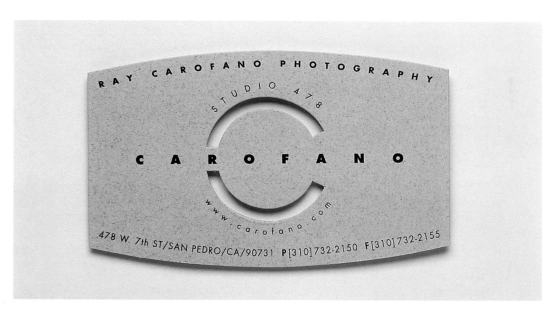

Design Firm
    D Zone Studio, Inc.
Designer
    Joe L. Yule
Client
    Ray Carofano Photography
Software/Hardware
    Adobe Illustrator, QuarkXPress
Paper/Materials
    Fraser Passport Cover
Printing
    1/o Black

Design Firm
  Elizabeth Resnick Design
Art Director
  Elizabeth Resnick
Designer
  Elizabeth Resnick
Client
  Design Times Magazine
Software/Hardware
  QuarkXpress 3.32, Macintosh
Paper/Materials
  Mohawk Superfine Natural
Printing
  Alpha Press, Waltham, MA

830 EAST FIRST · WICHITA, KS 67202

Tel 316-267-4800 · *Fax* 316-267-4840

RESERVATIONS 888-CANDLEWOOD EXT. 521222

W W W . H O T E L A T O L D T O W N . C U M

Barbara Waitt   **DIRECTOR OF SALES**

Delivering Exceptional Value®

HOTEL AT OLDTOWN

Operated By Candlewood Hotel Company

Design Firm
  Greteman Group
Art Director
  Sonia Greteman
Designers
  James Strange, Garrett Fresh
Client
  Hotel at Oldtown
Software/Hardware
  Freehand
Paper/Materials
  Astroparche Cream
Printing
  Offset

1

804.329.0661

C. BENJAMIN DACUS

bendacus@richmond.infi.net

1

2

DAVID RICCARDI

The CONTINENTAL

8400 WILSHIRE BLVD.

BEVERLY HILLS, CA 90211

323.782.9717

2

3

1
Design Firm
Zeigler Associates
Art Director
C. Benjamin Dacus
Designer
C. Benjamin Dacus
Client
C. Benjamin Dacus
Software/Hardware
QuarkXpress
Paper/Materials
French Construction
Printing
Offset, Pine Tree Press, Richmond, VA

2
Design Firm
[i]e design
Art Director
Marcie Carson
Designers
Cya Nelson, David Gilmour
Client
The Continental
Software/Hardware
Adobe Illustrator, Macintosh
Paper/Materials
French Construction
Printing
3 Metallic PMS

3
Design Firm
José J. Dias da S. Junior
Art Director
José J. Dias da S. Junior
Designer
José J. Dias da S. Junior
Client
The Cigar Place
Software/Hardware
Corel Draw, PC
Paper/Materials
Unpolished Couche 180 g
Printing
2 Color (Black & Pantone 1385)

DE ZONNEHOF
centrum voor moderne kunst

Zonnehof 4a • Postbus 699 • 3800 AR Amersfoort
T 033 4633034 **F** 033 4652691
E zonnehof@worldonline.nl

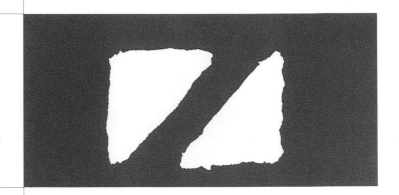

DE ZONNEHOF
centrum voor moderne kunst

TINNEKE SCHOLTEN
medewerker artotheek

Zonnehof 4a • Postbus 699 • 3800 AR Amersfoort
T 033 4633034 **F** 033 4652691
E zonnehof@worldonline.nl

Design Firm
Opera Grafisch Ontwerpers
Art Directors
Ton Homburg, Marty Schoutsen
Designer
Marty Schoutsen
Client
De Zonnehof
Software/Hardware
QuarkXpress, Macintosh
Paper/Materials
Oxford 250 gr.
Printing
Drukkery̌ Printing

1

Design Firm
Vestígio

Art Director
Emanuel Barbosa

Designer
Emanuel Barbosa

Client
Emanuel Barbosa Design

Software/Hardware
Freehand, Macintosh

Paper/Materials
Torras Paper

2

Design Firm
The Weller Institute for the
Cure of Design, Inc.

Art Director
Don Weller

Designer
Don Weller

Illustrator
Don Weller

Client
Park City Museum

Software/Hardware
Photoshop, QuarkXpress

b

**Emanuel
Barbosa
Design**

Rua da Vassada, 1682
Milheirós
4470 Maia
Tel. 02 - 9011868
Portugal

1

PARK CITY MUSEUM

Marianne Cone
Director

528 Main St.
P.O. Box 555
Park City, UT 84060
(801)649-0375

2

Alexander Stone & Co.
solicitors

Anita K Salwan

4 west regent street, glasgow G2 1RW
tel: +44 (0) 141 332 8611
fax: +44 (0) 141 332 5482
e-mail: mailbox@alexanderstone.co.uk

1

Heads Inc.
176 Thompson Street #2D New York, NY 10012
T+F 212 533 8693

So Takahashi

PMS 5743

2

1
Design Firm
Graven Images Ltd.
Art Director
Mandy Nolan
Designer
Colin Raeburn
Client
Alexander Stone & Co. Solicitors
Software/Hardware
QuarkXpress. Macintosh
Paper/Materials
Conqueror, Brilliant White, 300 gsm
Printing
3 Color Litho

2
Design Firm
Heads Inc.
Art Director
So Takahashi
Designer
So Takahashi
Client
Self-promotion
Software/Hardware
QuarkXpress
Printing
GM Imaging

Design Firm
   400 Communications Ltd.
Art Director
   Peter Dawson
Designer
   Peter Dawson
Client
   Print & Design Limited
Software/Hardware
   QuarkXpress, Macintosh
Printing
   2 Color Litho

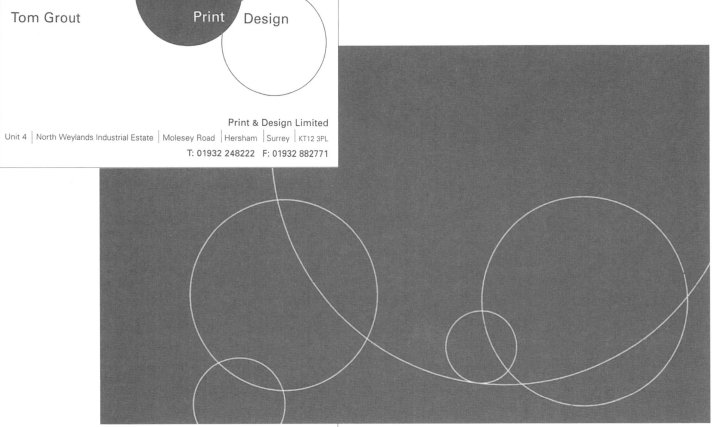

Tom Grout   Print   Design

Print & Design Limited

Unit 4 | North Weylands Industrial Estate | Molesey Road | Hersham | Surrey | KT12 3PL

T: 01932 248222 F: 01932 882771

1

1
Design Firm
  Second Floor
Art Director
  Warren Welter
Designer
  Lori Powell
Illustrator
  Lori Powell
Client
  Hotel Monaco/Kimpton Group
Software/Hardware
  QuarkXpress, Adobe
  Illustrator, iMac
Printing
  Hatcher Press

2
Design Firm
  Wallace/Church
Art Director
  Stan Church
Designer
  Wendy Church
Illustrator
  Lucian Toma
Client
  The Axis Group, Llc.
Software/Hardware
  Adobe Photoshop,
  Adobe Illustrator

3
Design Firm
  Bruce Yelaska Design
Art Director
  Bruce Yelaska
Designer
  Bruce Yelaska
Client
  Self-promotion
Software/Hardware
  Adobe Illustrator
Paper/Materials
  Strathmore Writing Wove
Printing
  Offset - Vision Printing

4
Design Firm
  Inox Design
Art Director
  Mauro Pastore
Designer
  Mauro Pastore
Client
  Free Pass
Software/Hardware
  Adobe Photoshop,
  QuarkXpress,
  Adobe Illustrator
Printing
  Offset, 2 Colors

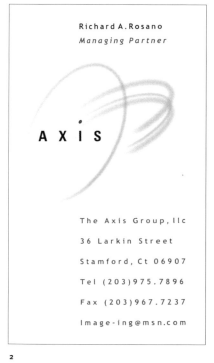

Richard A. Rosano
Managing Partner

A X I S

The Axis Group, llc

36 Larkin Street

Stamford, Ct 06907

Tel (203)975.7896

Fax (203)967.7237

Image-ing@msn.com

2

BRUCE YELASKA DESIGN

1546 Grant Avenue

San Francisco, California 94133

tel / 415.392.0717

fax / 415.397.1174

bruceyelaska@yelaskadesign.com

www.yelaskadesign.com

BRUCE YELASKA

3

F R E E · P A S S

FREE PASS s.r.l.
Via Cornegliano 1
20097 S. Donato Mil.se (MI)
C.F. e P.IVA 12129030156
Tel. & Fax 02/556.01.814

4

Design Firm
twenty2product
Art Director
Terry Green
Designer
Terry Green
Client
Self-promotion
Software/Hardware
Freehand
Paper/Materials
Simpson Protocol,
Westvaco Glassine
Printing
Valencia Printing

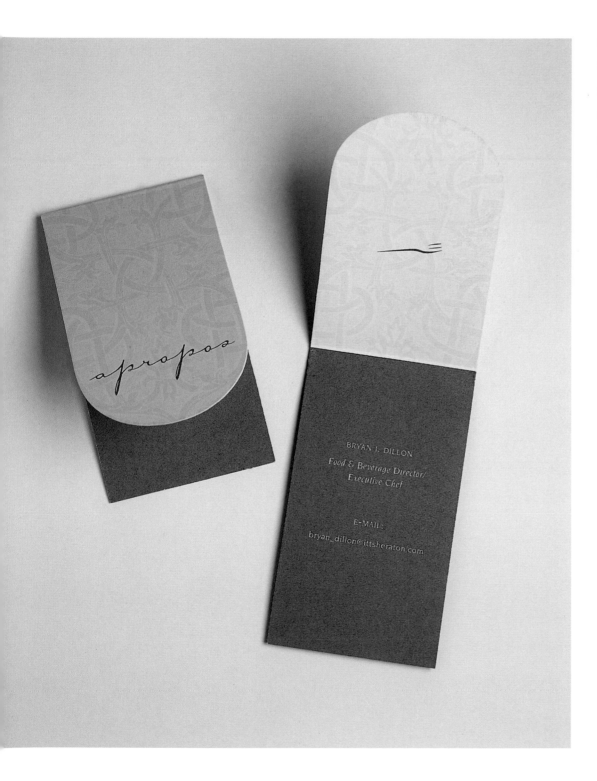

Design Firm
  Harris Design
Art Director
  Toni Harris-Hadad
Designer
  Toni Hadad
Client
  Apropos
Software/Hardware
  QuarkXpress, Adobe Photoshop,
  Adobe Illustrator 8
Printing
  Offset, 2 PMS, die cut

apropos

BRYAN I. DILLON
Food & Beverage Director/
Executive Chef

E-MAIL:
bryan_dillon@ittsheraton.com

Rick Vermeulen

Via Vermeulen
William Boothlaan 4
3012 VJ Rotterdam
The Netherlands
Tel: + 31 (0)10 - 213.27.80
Fax: + 31 (0)10 - 213.47.22
e-mail: viarick@ipr.nl

1

perdura
Stahl- und Anlagentechnik Michael Rammelmann

Dipl.-Ing. Michael Rammelmann
Geschäftsführer

Industriestraße 7
D-59457 Werl
Tel. 0 29 22 · 86 51 86
Fax 0 29 22 · 86 51 88
mobil 01 73 · 2 72 89 32
e-mail perdura-werl@t-online.de

2

1
Design Firm
  Via Vermeulen
Art Director
  Rick Vermeulen
Designer
  Rick Vermeulen
Photographer
  Monica Nouwens
Client
  Self-promotion

2
Design Firm
  graphische formgebung
Art Director
  Herbert Rohsiepe
Designer
  Herbert Rohsiepe
Client
  Perdura
Software/Hardware
  Freehand 8.o, Macintosh
Printing
  Blue, Black, & Silver

83 COLUMBIA ST. SUITE 400, SEATTLE, WA 98104

TEL 206·682·3685   FAX 206·682·3867

HAMMERQUIST & HALVERSON

CAROL DAVIDSON

E-MAIL carol@hammerquist.net

Design Firm
  Hornall Anderson Design Works
Art Director
  Jack Anderson
Designers
  Jack Anderson, Mike Calkins
Illustrator
  Mike Calkins
Client
  Hammerquist & Halverson
Software/Hardware
  Freehand, Macintosh
Paper/Materials
  Mohawk Navaho

en digitized written spoken

tized spoken digitized writt

en digitized written spoken

tized written spoken digitiz

ten spoken digiti

en digitized writt

ROBIN SHEPHERD
creative communications

18576 TWIN CREEKS ROAD
MONTE SERENO, CA 95030
PHONE: 408.354.2441
FAX: 408.354.3181
EMAIL: rswriter@flash.net
WEB: www.greatwords.com

WORDS WITH IMPACT

Design Firm
    The Hive Design Studio
Art Directors
    Laurie Okamura, Amy Stocklein
Designers
    Laurie Okamura, Amy Stocklein
Illustrator
    Pete Caravalho
Client
    Robin Shepherd
Software/Hardware
    Adobe Illustrator, Macintosh
Paper/Materials
    Strathmore
Printing
    Mission Printers

Design Firm
  Big Eye Creative
Art Director
  Perry Chua
Designers
  Perry Chua, Nancy Yeasting
Client
  Clarke Printing
Software/Hardware
  Adobe Illustrator
Paper/Materials
  Starwhite Vicksburg
Printing
  Clarke Printing

changing the way you think about printing.

sean clarke

C L A R K E **C** P R I N T I N G

105-366 east kent avenue s.
vancouver bc v5x 4n6
tel **604** 327.2213 fax 327.2240

sean clarke

C L A R K E **C** P R I N T I N G

105-366 east kent avenue s.
vancouver bc v5x 4n6
tel **604** 327.2213 fax 327.2240

1
Design Firm
   H3/Muse
Designer
   Harry M. Forehand III
Client
   Jeff Forehand
Software/Hardware
   Macintosh
Printing
   Local Color, Santa Fe

2
Design Firm
   H3/Muse
Designer
   Harry M. Forehand III
Client
   Orotund Turmoil
Software/Hardware
   Macintosh
Printing
   Local Color, Santa Fe

1

2

Design Firm
H3/Muse
Designer
Harry M. Forehand III
Client
Tim Forehand
Software/Hardware
Macintosh
Printing
Local Color, Santa Fe

Design Firm
  Atelier Tadeusz Piechura
Art Director
  Tadeusz Piechura
Designer
  Tadeusz Piechura
Client
  TVP - LODZ
Software/Hardware
  Corel 7, Pentium 200
Printing
  Offset

Design Firm
Atelier Tadeusz Piechura
Art Director
Tadeusz Piechura
Designer
Tadeusz Piechura
Client
Photo Studio,
Jacek Jakub Marczewski
Software/Hardware
Corel 7, Pentium
Printing
Laser Printer, 2nd Edition,
New Version

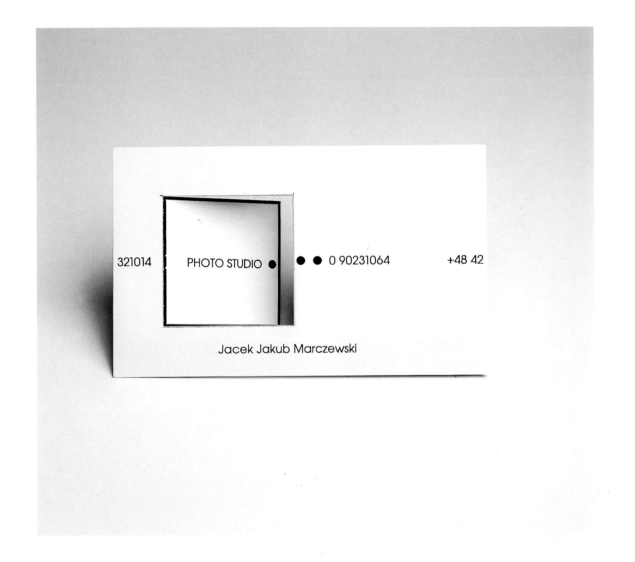

De Elleboogkerk Postbus 699 / NL - 3800 AR Amersfoort
Langegracht 36 / T 033 461 40 88 / F 033 464 05 50
armando.museum@worldonline.nl

ARMANDOMUSEUM

Paul Coumans / Directeur

De Elleboogkerk Postbus 699 / NL - 3800 AR Amersfoort
Langegracht 36 / T 033 461 40 88 / F 033 464 05 50
armando.museum@worldonline.nl

ARMANDOMUSEUM

Henk Panjer / Beheerder

De Elleboogkerk Postbus 699 / NL - 3800 AR Amersfoort
Langegracht 36 / T 033 461 40 88 / F 033 464 05 50
armando.museum@worldonline.nl

ARMANDOMUSEUM

Miriam Windhausen / Conservator

Design Firm
  Opera Grafisch Ontwerpers
Art Directors
  Ton Homburg, Marty Schoutsen
Designers
  Sappho Panhuysen,
  Marty Schoutsen
Client
  Armando Museum
Software/Hardware
  QuarkXpress, Macintosh
Paper/Materials
  Distinction Prestige
Printing
  Drukkerij Printing Amersfoort

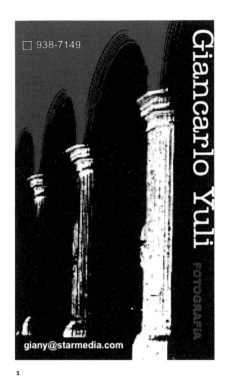

938-7149

Giancarlo Yuli

FOTOGRAFIA

giany@starmedia.com

1

1
Design Firm
  S & S Design
Art Director
  Mónica Sánchez Farfán
Designer
  Mónica Sánchez Farfán
Photographer
  Giancarlo Yuli
Client
  Giancarlo Yuli, Photographer
Software/Hardware
  Adobe Photoshop 5.0,
  QuarkXpress 4.0, Zbmaptiva
Paper/Materials
  White Fine Cardboard
Printing
  Valdez Printers

2
Design Firm
  400 Communications Ltd.
Art Director
  Peter Dawson
Designer
  Peter Dawson
Client
  Opus Furniture Limited
Software/Hardware
  QuarkXpress, Macintosh
Printing
  2 Special Colors

Jonathan Crabtree

Opus Furniture Limited

5 Sandy's Row London E1 7HW
Telephone: +44 (0)171 247 2224 Fax: +44 (0)171 247 1168

Opus

2

ifa ▌ Institute for Foreign
Cultural Relations

ifa ▌ Institut für Auslandsbeziehungen e. V.

Postfach 10 24 63
70177 Stuttgart

Charlottenplatz 17
70173 Stuttgart

Tel. 0711 / 22 25-0
Fax 0711 / 2 26 43 46

e-mail: info@ifa.de
http://www.ifa.de

P. O. Box 10 24 63
D-70020 Stuttgart

Charlottenplatz 17
D-70173 Stuttgart

Tel. 0049-711 / 22 25-0
Fax 0049-711 / 2 26 43 46

e-mail: info@ifa.de
http://www.ifa.de

1

1
Design Firm
  Michael Kimmerle·Art
  Direction + Design
Art Director
  Michael Kimmerle
Designer
  Michael Kimmerle
Client
  Institut für
  Auslandsbeziehungen e. V.
Software/Hardware
  QuarkXpress, Macintosh
Paper/Materials
  Diplomat
Printing
  Offset

2
Design Firm
  R & M Associati Grafici
Art Director
  Di Somma/Fontanella
Client
  Self-promotion
Software/Hardware
  Adobe Illustrator, Macintosh
Printing
  Offset

MAURIZIO DI SOMMA
80053 CASTELLAMMARE DI STABIA_ITALIA
TRAVERSA DEL PESCATORE 3
RAFFAELE FONTANELLA
R&MASSOCIATIGRAFICI
COMUNICAZIONE VISIV
TELEFONO +39 081 870 50 53_FAX 0818702195

2

Design
    Firm Stang
Designer
    Stang Gubbels
Client
    Self-promotion
Software/Hardware
    QuarkXpress, Macintosh
Paper/Materials
    Graniet
Printing
    Offset

scott price

consultant

tel 214.265.7290
fax 214.691.0137
6060 n. central expwy
suite number 560
dallas tx 75206
scott@monsterbit.com

price

marketing communications

Design Firm
Joy Price
Designer
Joy Price
Client
Scott Price, Price Marketing
Communications
Software/Hardware
Adobe Illustrator, Macintosh
Printing
Digitally Printed on
Chromapress System;
Corners Trimmed by Hand;
Punched by Hand

Design Firm
Spectrum Graphics Studio
Designer
Joanne Spangler
Illustrator
Joanne Spangler
Client
Ali Wilson, Ali Wilson Massage
Software/Hardware
Adobe Illustrator 8.0
Paper/Materials
Wausau Royal Fiber, Balsa 80 lb. Cover
Printing
Spectrum Printers; 3 PMS: Bronze 876, Yellow 124, Orange 718

MARKETING BRAINS
creative soul

CREATIVE COMPANY

3276 Commercial St SE Suite 2
Salem Oregon 97302
l 503.363.4433 Fax 503.363.6817
www.creativeco.com

creative CULMINATOR

MIKE PEMBERTON
mikeyp@creativeco.com

Design Firm
Creative Company
Art Director
Matt Davis
Designer
Matt Davis
Client
Self-promotion
Software/Hardware
Macintosh
Paper/Materials
Strobe Dull Cover
Printing
K.P. Corporation

1
Design Firm
Bruce Yelaska Design
Art Director
Bruce Yelaska
Designer
Bruce Yelaska
Client
Bikram's Yoga College of India
Software/Hardware
Adobe Illustrator
Paper/Materials
Strathmore Writing Wove
Printing
Offset, Vision Printing

2
Design Firm
Kan & Lau Design Consultants
Art Director
Kan Tai-Keung
Designers
Kan Tai-Keung, Lam Wai Hung
Client
Friends of Mine Group Limited
Software/Hardware
Freehand 8.0
Paper/Materials
300 gsm High White Wove
(Conqueror)
Printing
Offset

Robin Schmidt
Director

1816 Magnolia Ave.
Burlingame, CA 94010
Tel: 650.552.9642 (YOGA)
www.bikramyoga.com

1

友 福 集 團 有 限 公 司
FRIENDS *of* MINE GROUP LIMITED

Unit 302, 3/F
38 Russell Street
Causeway Bay, Hong Kong
Tel (852) 2545 3635
Fax (852) 2970 2226

Eva S. W. Fung
Assistant to Managing Director
Mobile Phone 9473 2350

友 福 集 團 有 限 公 司
FRIENDS *of* MINE GROUP LIMITED

香 港 銅 鑼 灣
羅 素 街 38 號 3 樓 302 室
電 話 (852) 2545 3635
傳 真 (852) 2970 2226

馮 瑞 華
董 事 總 經 理 助 理

手 提 電 話 9473 2350

2

1

1
Design Firm
   Inox Design
Art Director
   Mauro Pastore
Designer
   Mauro Pastore
Client
   FA.MA.
Software/Hardware
   Adobe Illustrator, QuarkXpress
Printing
   Offset, 3 & 1 Color

afterhours

pt Grafika Estetika Atria
Jalan Merpati Raya 45, Jakarta 12870, Indonesia
tel +62 21 8306819   fax +62 21 8290612
e.mail info@afterhours.co.id

afterhours

2

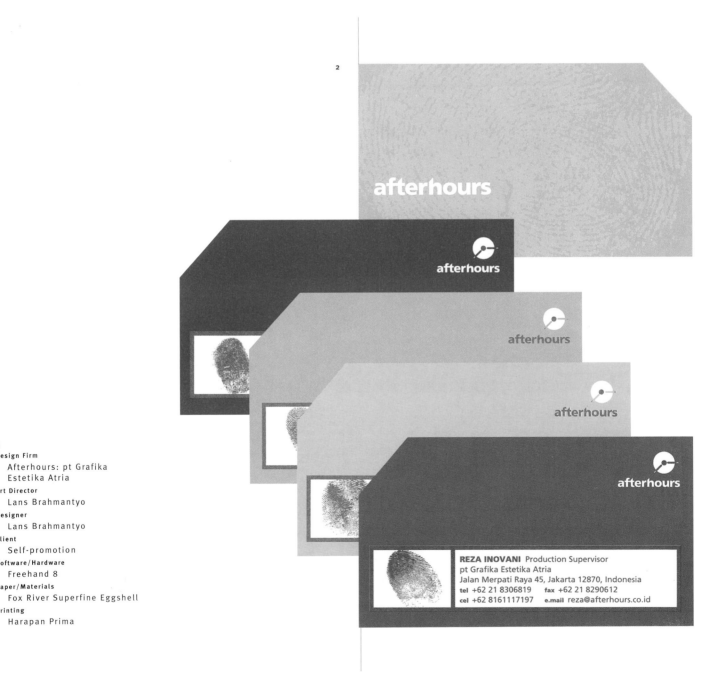

2

Design Firm
Afterhours: pt Grafika
Estetika Atria

Art Director
Lans Brahmantyo

Designer
Lans Brahmantyo

Client
Self-promotion

Software/Hardware
Freehand 8

Paper/Materials
Fox River Superfine Eggshell

Printing
Harapan Prima

Design Firm
Inox Design
Art Director
Masa Magnoni
Designer
Mauro Pastore
Illustrator
Masa Magnoni
Client
Laura Bisaro
Software/Hardware
Adobe Illustrator
Printing
Offset, 1 Color

1
Design Firm
  400 Communications Ltd.
Art Director
  David Coates
Designer
  David Coates
Illustrator
  David Coates
Client
  Self-promotion
Software/Hardware
  QuarkXpress, Adobe Photoshop,
  Macintosh
Paper/Materials
  300 gsm
Printing
  1 Special, Process Blue

2
Design Firm
  Troller Associates
Art Director
  Fred Troller
Designer
  Fred Troller
Client
  Primo
Paper/Materials
  Strathmore, Bristol
Printing
  Offset

David Coates
graphic designer

m 0958 503348 t 0181 547 2356
34a Southsea Road Kingston upon Thames Surrey KT1 2EH

1

John M. Tremaine
President

114 Washington Street
South Norwalk CT 06854
203.866.4321

2

Finance Manager
Bomie S.Y. Chan

 FRUITO RICCI

[Office]
Unit 302, 3/F., 38 Russell Street, Causeway Bay, Hong Kong
Tel 2545 3635   Fax 2970 2226

[Shop]
Shop 7C, G/F., Site 1, Whampoa Garden, Hunghom, Kowloon
Tel 2363 8618, 2363 8622   Fax 2363 8210

[寫字樓]
香港銅鑼灣羅素街38號3樓302室
電話 2545 3635   傳真 2970 2226

[店 舖]
九龍紅磡黃埔花園第一期商場7C
電話 2363 8618, 2363 8622   傳真 2363 8210

Design Firm
    Kan & Lau Design Consultants
Art Directors
    Kan Tai-Keung, Eddy Yu Chi Kong
Designers
    Eddy Yu Chi Kong, Lam Wai Hung
Illustrator
    Eddy Yu Chi Kong
Client
    Fruito Ricci Holdings Co. Ltd.
Software/Hardware
    Freehand 8.0
Paper/Materials
    (Wiggins Teape) Zanders CX700,
    White 250 gsm
Printing
    Offset

Design Firm
  Kan & Lau Design
  Consultants
Art Director
  Freeman Lau Siu Hong
Designer
  Stephen Lau
Client
  Hong Kong Institute of
  Contemporary Culture
Software/Hardware
  Freehand 7.0
Paper/Materials
  260 gsm Art Card
Printing
  Offset 3 x 2 (spot) C

hki
cc

HONG KONG

INSTITUTE OF

CONTEMPORARY

CULTURE

danny yung 榮念曾

artistic director

香港當代
文化中心
HONG KONG

INSTITUTE OF

CONTEMPORARY

CULTURE

- tel no   852-2358-6146
- fax no   852-2358-3516
- e-mail   payung-@usthk.ust.hk

- c/o 40/F bank of china tower
  1 garden road hong kong
- tel no   852-2867-1306
- fax no   852-2810-6398

1

1
Design Firm
R & M Associati Grafici
Art Director
Di Somma/Fontanella
Client
Dario Diogene
Software/Hardware
Adobe Illustrator, Macintosh
Printing
Offset

2
Design Firm
Kan & Lau Design Consultants
Art Director
Freeman Lau Siu Hong
Designer
Freeman Lau Siu Hong
Client
Cheung Yee
Software/Hardware
Freehand 7.0 C
Paper/Materials
Gulliver 197 gsm - CL170 1
Printing
Offset

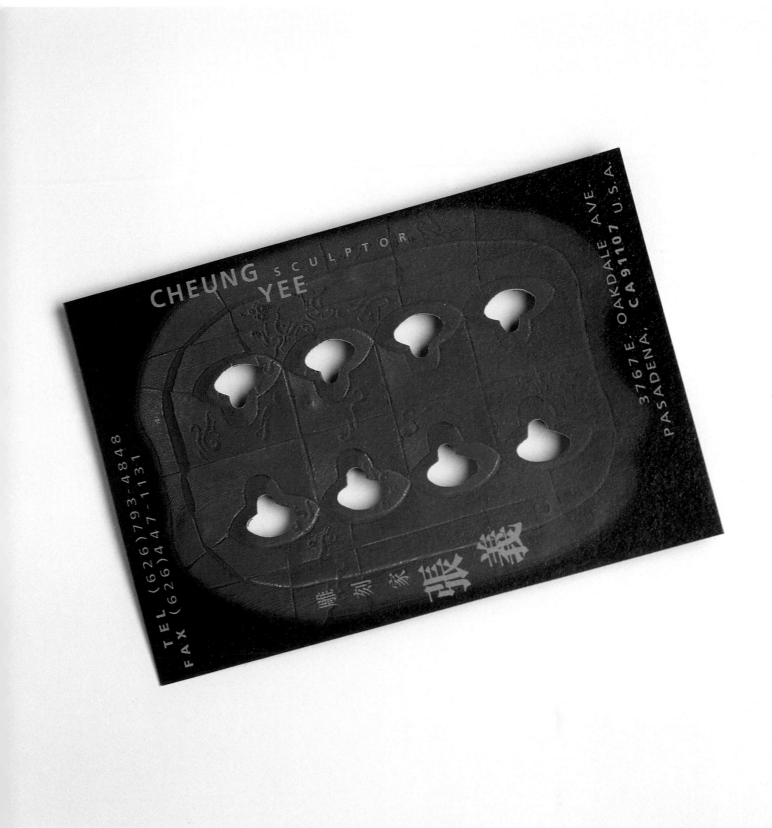

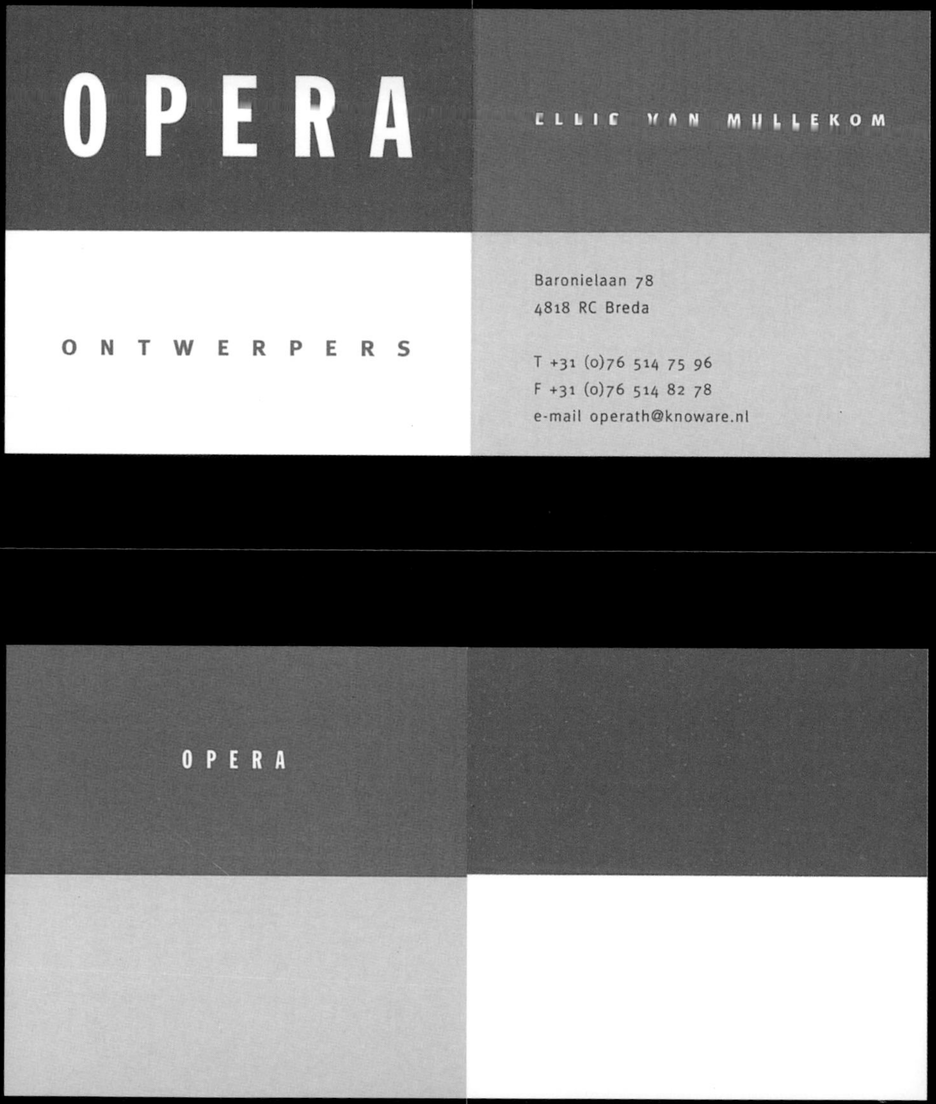

OPERA

ELLIE VAN MULLEKOM

ONTWERPERS

Baronielaan 78
4818 RC Breda

T +31 (0)76 514 75 96
F +31 (0)76 514 82 78
e-mail operath@knoware.nl

OPERA

1

1
Design Firm
  Opera Grafisch Ontwerpers
Art Directors
  Marty Schoutsen, Ton Homburg
Designers
  Stefanie Rôsch, Ton Homburg
Client
  Opera Ontwerpers
Software/Hardware
  QuarkXpress, Macintosh
Paper/Materials
  Conqueror Vergé
Printing
  Plantijn Casparie Breda

HOBOKEN

GRAND CAFÉ (H) HOBOKEN BV WESTZEEDIJK 343 3015 AA ROTTERDAM
TELEFOON: 010. 225 05 60 FAX: 010. 225 04 42

ONDERDEEL VAN MÂITRE FRÉDÉRIC CATERING & EVENTS
VOOR RESERVERINGEN KUNT U BELLEN 010. 522 03 40

2

2
Design Firm
  Stang
Art Director
  Stang Gubbels
Designer
  Anneke Van Der Stelt
Client
  Grand Café Hoboken
Software/Hardware
  QuarkXpress, Macintosh
Paper/Materials
  Mat Mc
Printing
  Offset

Design Firm
be
Art Director
Will Burke
Designers
Eric Read, Yusuke Asaka
Client
Self-promotion
Software/Hardware
Adobe Photoshop, Adobe
Illustrator, Macintosh

William V Burke

E will_burke@beplanet.com
T 415 451 3530
F 415 451 3532

1323 Fourth Street
San Rafael · CA · 94901-2809

be.next

Angela Hildebrand

E angela_hildebrand@beplanet.com
T 415 451 3530
F 415 451 3532

1323 Fourth Street
San Rafael · CA · 94901-2809

be.next

Eric J Read

E eric_read@beplanet.com
T 415 451 3530
F 415 451 3532

1323 Fourth Street
San Rafael · CA · 94901-2809

be.next

Carissa E Guirao

E carissa_guirao@beplanet.com
T 415 451 3530
F 415 451 3532

1323 Fourth Street
San Rafael · CA · 94901-2809

be.next

Rupert Goddard

21 Station Road
Barnes
London SW13 0LJ

Telephone (020) 8 939 6100
Facsimile (020) 8 939 6109
Mobile 07971 884 470
ISDN (020) 8 939 6112
Website www.cairnes.co.uk
EMail rupert.goddard@cairnesdesign.co.uk

cairnes

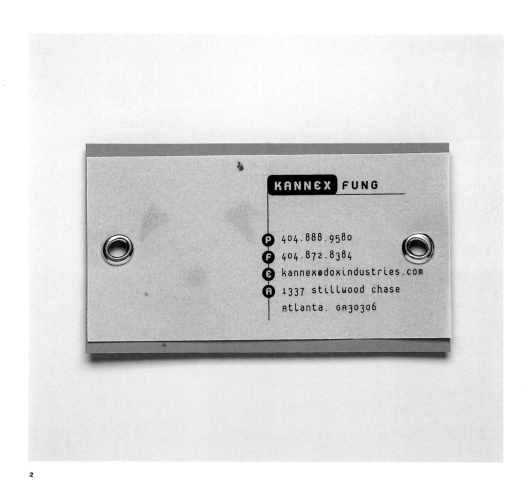

2

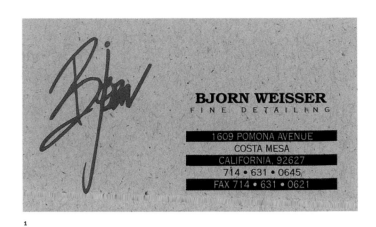

1

HAIR STYLIST

KH

SALON MEI

PAN AM BUILDING

1600 KAPIOLANI

SUITE 222

TEL: 955.1600

PGR: 267.0773

2

1
Design Firm
   Aloha Printing
Art Director
   James Picquelle
Designer
   James Picquelle
Client
   BJorn Weisser Fine Detailing
Software/Hardware
   Corel Draw
Printing
   Offset Sheet Fed Press

2
Design Firm
   Voice Design
Art Director
   Clifford Cheng
Designer
   Clifford Cheng
Client
   Keri Hauser, Hair Stylist
Software/Hardware
   Freehand, Macintosh
Printing
   Offset, 2 Color

HSB

Hengst Streff Bajko Architects

HSB

Kevin Hengst, AIA

1250 Old River Road
Suite 201
Cleveland Ohio 44113-1243
e-mail: hsb@cyberdrive.net
216 586 0440 f
216 586 0229 t

Design Firm
   Nesnadny + Schwartz
Art Directors
   Timothy Lachina,
   Michelle Moehler,
   Gregory Oznowich
Designers
   Timothy Lachina,
   Michelle Moehler,
   Gregory Oznowich
Client
   Hengst Streff Bajko Architects
Software/Hardware
   QuarkXpress
Paper/Materials
   Mohawke Superfine White
   Eggshell 80 lb., Mohawke
   Superfine White Eggshell 70 lb.
Printing
   Master Printing

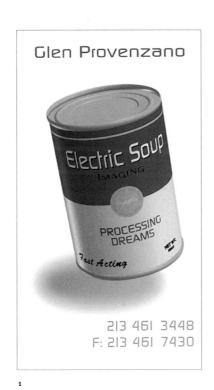

Glen Provenzano

Electric Soup
IMAGING

PROCESSING
DREAMS

Fast Acting

213 461 3448
F: 213 461 7430

1

peter j. urban
760.737.9397
phone/fax

urbangraphic

1148 Felicita Lane
Escondido, CA 92029-6626

2

1
Design Firm
   Media Bridge
Art Director
   Christopher Sullivan
Designer
   Mark Goss
Client
   Electric Soup
Software/Hardware
   Adobe Illustrator

2
Design Firm
   Urbangraphic
Art Director
   Peter Urban
Designer
   Peter Urban
Illustrator
   Peter Urban
Client
   Self-promotion
Software/Hardware
   Adobe Photoshop,
   Adobe Illustrator
Paper/Materials
   Chromecoat
Printing
   4 Color Process

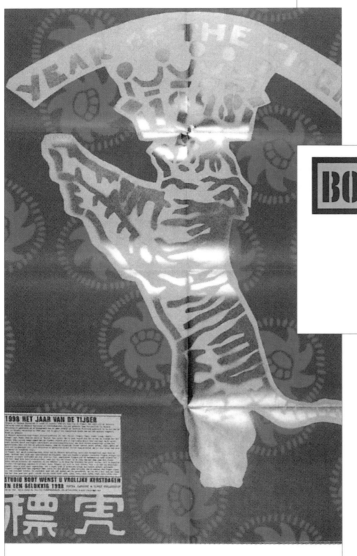

studio Boot · Brede Haven 8a
5211 Tl 's-Hertogenbosch
Tel.073-6143593 · Fax 073-6133190
ISDN 073-6129865 · bootst@wxs.nl

graphic design
Studio Boot

Design Firm
 Studio Boot
Art Directors
 Petra Janssen, Edwin Vollebergh
Designers
 Petra Janssen, Edwin Vollebergh
Illustrator
 Studio Boot
Client
 Self-promotion
Paper/Materials
 MC on 3mm.Grey Board
Printing
 Full Color and Laminate

Design Firm
Cooper-Hewitt, National
Design Museum

Art Director
Jen Roos

Designer
Jen Roos

Client
Self-promotion

Software/Hardware
QuarkXpress 4.04,
Adobe Photoshop

Paper/Materials
100 lb. Mohawk Navajo
Brilliant White

Printing
Aristographics

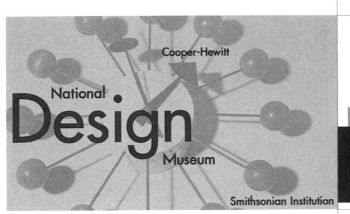

OLIVER HUMMEL
Assistant Manager

Design Museum Shop

National **Design** Museum

hummeol@ch.si.edu

2 EAST 91ST STREET
NEW YORK, NEW YORK 10128-9990

T   212 849 8353
F   212 849 8357

DIANNE H. PILGRIM
Director

National **Design** Museum

pilgrdi@ch.si.edu

2 EAST 91ST STREET
NEW YORK, NEW YORK 10128-9990

T   212 849 8370
F   212 849 8367

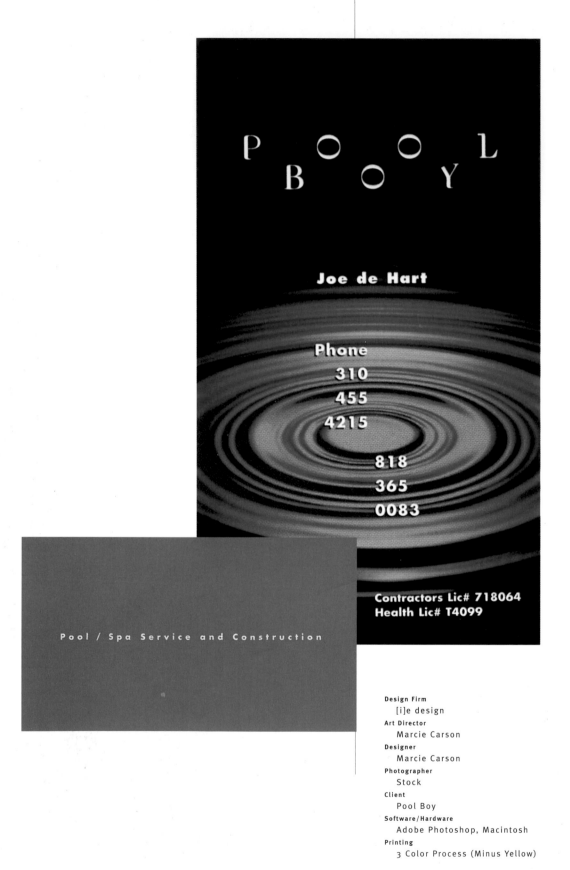

P O O L
B O O Y

Joe de Hart

Phone
310
455
4215

818
365
0083

Contractors Lic# 718064
Health Lic# T4099

Pool / Spa Service and Construction

Design Firm
  [i]e design
Art Director
  Marcie Carson
Designer
  Marcie Carson
Photographer
  Stock
Client
  Pool Boy
Software/Hardware
  Adobe Photoshop, Macintosh
Printing
  3 Color Process (Minus Yellow)

PHYSIOTHERAPIE CANERI

AMBULANTE REHA

CRYO-POINT –110°C

Francois Caneri
Physiotherapeut

Kriegsbergstraße 28
70174 Stuttgart

Tel. 0711/163 56-0
Fax 0711/163 56-13

Design Firm
Michael Kimmerle·Art
Direction + Design
Art Director
Michael Kimmerle
Designer
Michael Kimmerle
Illustrator
Michael Kimmerle
Client
Pro-moto
Software/Hardware
Freehand, Macintosh
Paper/Materials
Diplomat 250 glm2
Printing
Offset

1
Design Firm
Inox Design
Art Director
Masa Magnoni
Designer
Masa Magnoni
Illustrator
Masa Magnoni
Client
Ca' Del Moro
Software/Hardware
Adobe Illustrator, QuarkXpress
Paper/Materials
Fibrone 2 mm.
Printing
Offset, 2 Colors

2
Design Firm
Visser Bay Anders Toscani
Art Director
Hilde Lottuis
Designer
Hilde Lottuis
Client
Self-promotion
Paper/Materials
Hello Silk 300 grams

1

Hartmut A. Raiser

N U M E R O
I n t e r i o r
D E S I G N
Olgastrasse 15
7000 Stuttgart 1
No 0711·235757
Fax 0711·293035

Design Firm
   Michael Kimmerle·Art
   Direction + Design
Art Director
   Michael Kimmerle
Designer
   Michael Kimmerle
Illustrator
   Michael Kimmerle
Client
   Numero·Interior Design
Software/Hardware
   Freehand, Macintosh
Paper/Materials
   Conqueror, Römerturm 200
   glm2
Printing
   Offset, Prägefolie, Stamping

1
Design Firm
   Michael Kimmerle·Art
   Direction + Design
Art Director
   Michael Kimmerle
Designer
   Michael Kimmerle
Illustrator
   Michael Kimmerle
Client
   Antora Selection
Software/Hardware
   Freehand, Macintosh
Paper/Materials
   Conqueror, Römerturm 250 glm2
Printing
   Offset

2
Design Firm
   Ringo W.K. Hui
Art Director
   Ringo W.K. Hui
Designer
   Ringo W.K. Hui
Client
   Pal Pang 100% Mode
Software/Hardware
   Freehand 8.0
Paper/Materials
   Esse, White Green Texture 216 gsm
Printing
   1 Color, 0 Color

1

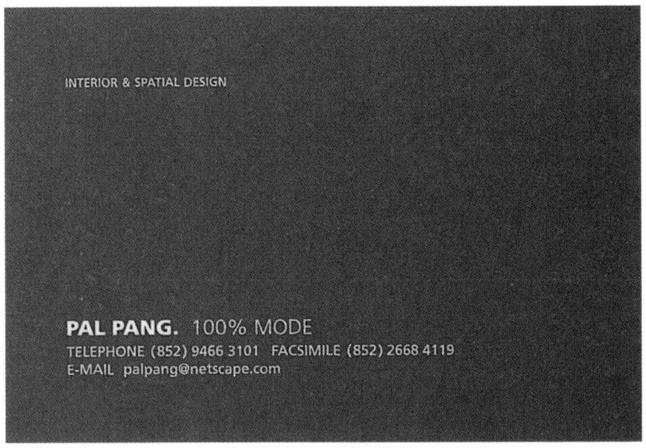

2

Earth Greens

TODD KOONS

HARBINGER

1129 HARKINS RD
SALINAS, CA 93901
TEL: 408.424.7063
FAX: 408.424.0740

1

1

Design Firm
   The Hive Design Studio
Art Directors
   Laurie Okamura, Amy Stocklein
Designers
   Laurie Okamura, Amy Stocklein
Illustrator
   Pete Caravalho
Client
   Misionero Vegetables
Software/Hardware
   Adobe Illustrator, Macintosh
Paper/Materials
   Strathmore
Printing
   Mission Printers

2

Design Firm
   [i]e design
Art Director
   Marcie Carson
Designer
   David Gilmour
Illustrator
   Mirjam Selmi
Client
   Sunset Sound
Software/Hardware
   Adobe Illustrator, Adobe
   Photoshop, Macintosh
Paper/Materials
   Star White Vicksburg
Printing
   3 PMS, o PMS

Paul Camarata
President

6650 Sunset Boulevard
Hollywood, CA 90028

Tel 323/469-1186
Fax 323/465-5579

2

Design Firm
  Studio Boot
Art Directors
  Petra Janssen,
  Edwin Vollebergh
Designers
  Petra Janssen,
  Edwin Vollebergh
Illustrator
  Studio Boot
Client
  Sacha Shoes
Paper/Materials
  Sulfaat Karton
Printing
  2 colors, offset
  and perforation

Gespecialiseerd in het maken van:

• historische kleding

• theater- en showbizzkleding

• promotiepakken

• fantasie- en dierenkostuums

• hoeden en maskers

Liesbeth Verbeek P. Kerssemakersdreef 3

4904 WE Oosterhout t/f 0162 429 863 LIZ-ART@hetnet.nl

1

1
Design Firm
Case
Designer
Kees Wagenaars
Client
Lizard

2
Design Firm
Bettina Huchtemann Art-Direction
& Design
Designer
Bettina Huchtemann
Illustrator
Bettina Huchtemann
Client
Frank Aschermann·Photography
Software/Hardware
QuarkXpress
Paper/Materials
Countryside
Printing
Offset, Steel-Engraving, Embossing

3
Design Firm
Belyea
Art Director
Patricia Belyea
Client
Meredith & crew

2

Meredith Robinson
technology marketing consultant

15127 NE 24th Street
Suite 466
Redmond, WA 98052

tel **206.369.3274**
fax 425.881.3959
meredith@mcrew.com

Meredith Robinson
principal

15127 NE 24th Street
Suite 466
Redmond, WA 98052

tel **206.369.3274**
fax 425.881.3959
meredith@mcrew.com

Meredith Robinson
designer

15127 NE 24th Street
Suite 466
Redmond, WA 98052

tel **206.369.3274**
fax 425.881.3959
meredith@mcrew.com

Meredith Robinson
columnist/writer

15127 NE 24th Street
Suite 466
Redmond, WA 98052

tel **206.369.3274**
fax 425.881.3959
meredith@mcrew.com

3

Michael Kimmerle

Ostendstraße 106

70188 Stuttgart

Fon 0711 · 48 10 26

Fax 0711 · 48 10 60

Mi@Kimmerle.de

www.Kimmerle.de

ART

▲

Direction

✚

Design

Design Firm
Michael Kimmerle·Art
Direction + Design
Art Director
Michael Kimmerle
Designer
Michael Kimmerle
Illustrator
Michael Kimmerle
Client
Self-promotion
Software/Hardware
Freehand, Macintosh
Paper/Materials
Ricarta 260 glm2
Printing
Offset

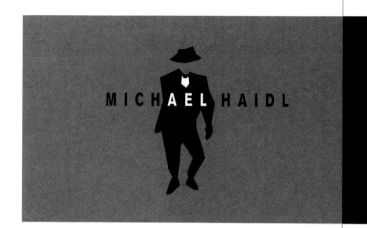

1

Altamiro Machado
Gestor de Projectos

Estudos de
Desenvolvimento
Económico e Social, Lda.

Av. Central, 45
Tel. 053. 616510/906
Fax 053. 611872
4710 Braga
Portugal

2

1
Design Firm
   Michael Kimmerle·Art
   Direction + Design
Art Director
   Michael Kimmerle
Designer
   Michael Kimmerle
Illustrator
   Michael Kimmerle
Client
   Michael Haidl
Software/Hardware
   Freehand, Macintosh
Paper/Materials
   Diplomat/Karton 250 glm2
Printing
   Offset

2
Design Firm
   Vestígio
Art Director
   Emanuel Barbosa
Designer
   Emanuel Barbosa
Client
   Vector XXI
Software/Hardware
   Freehand, Macintosh
Paper/Materials
   Torras Paper

1

Design Firm
  "That's Nice" l.l.c.
Art Director
  Nigel Walker
Designer
  Michael McDevitt
Client
  United Nations Population Fund
Software/Hardware
  Quark XPress, Adobe
  Photoshop, Macintosh
Paper/Materials
  Potlach Silk 80 lb.
Printing
  3/2 PMS

2

Design Firm
  Inkwell Publishing Co.
Art Director
  Jimmy Hilario
Designer
  Jimmy Hilario
Client
  University of Asia and the Pacific
Software/Hardware
  Freehand 8, Adobe Photoshop 5,
  Macintosh
Paper/Materials
  Gilclear Heavy Cream 150 gsm
Printing
  Offset

2

DENNIS IRWIN ILLUSTRATION
1251 COLLEGE AVENUE PALO ALTO, CA 94306
650.856.0780 dei2465@fhda.edu

1

1

Design Firm
Dennis Irwin Illustration

Art Director
Dennis Irwin

Designer
Dennis Irwin

Illustrator
Dennis Irwin

Client
Self-promotion

Printing
Linotext Printing

2

Design Firm
Studio Boot

Art Directors
Petra Janssen, Edwin Vollebergh

Designers
Petra Janssen, Edwin Vollebergh

Illustrator
Studio Boot

Client
Sacha Shoes

Paper/Materials
Sulfaat Karton

Printing
2 colors, offset and perforation

PATRICIA BRADY-DANZIG

S O P R A N O

POST OFFICE BOX **683**
SOUTH ORANGE, N.J. 07079
201.761.0041 | FAX: 201.763.7365

3

SACHA SHOES

TERMEE
SAAL VAN ZWANENBERGWEG 10
5026 RN TILBURG
THE NETHERLANDS
PHONE: +31(0)13 4631115
FAX: +31(0)13 4639091
MOBILE: +31 (0)6 53125641
E-MAIL: sacha@sacha.nl
VAT. nr.: NL 007851509 B03

伯特・特米尔
董事長

sacha°

SACHA SHOES

TERMEER SCHOENEN BV
SAAL VAN ZWANENBERGWEG 10
5026 RN TILBURG
THE NETHERLANDS
PHONE: +31(0)13 4631115
FAX: +31(0)13 4639091
MOBILE: +31 (0)6 53125641
E-MAIL: sacha@sacha.nl
VAT. nr.: NL 007851509 B03

BERT TERMEER
PRESIDENT

sacha°

2

3
Design Firm
  Josh Klenert
Designer
  Josh Klenert
Photographer
  Josh Klenert
Client
  Patricia Brady-Danzig
Software/Hardware
  QuarkXpress, Adobe Photoshop,
  Adobe Illustrator, Printing
  2 Color

SCOTT STOLL

PHOTOGRAPHY

5013 Pacific Highway East #20

Tacoma, Washington 98424

[253]896-0133

1

1
Design Firm
  Belyea
Art Director
  Patricia Belyea
Client
  Scott Stoll Photography

2
Design Firm
  Cisneros Design
Designer
  Harry M. Forehand III
Photographer
  William Rotsaert
Client
  Leapfrog Integrated
  Technology Solutions
Software/Hardware
  Macintosh
Printing
  Aspen Printing,
  Albuquerque

LEAPFROG
INTEGRATED TECHNOLOGY SOLUTIONS

LEAPFROG

2050 Botulph Rd. Suite B | Santa Fe, New Mexico 87505
505.988.9279 | Fax 505.988.3101
e-mail LJRice@ix.netcom.com

2

belyea

Patricia Belyea
PRINCIPAL

patricia@belyea.com

1250 Tower Building
1809 Seventh Avenue
Seattle, WA 98101

206.**682.4895**
FAX 206.623.8912
WEB belyea.com

marketing

communication

design

Design Firm
  Belyea
Art Director
  Patricia Belyea
Client
  Self-promotion

Design Firm
  Sb Design-Brazil
Designer
  Ricardo Bastos
Client
  Tortaria-Sweet Shop
Software/Hardware
  Corel Draw, PC
Paper/Materials
  Couché, Dull, 180 gr
Printing
  Offset

Fernando Gomes, 114/A · Moinhos de V.
CEP 90510-010 · Porto Alegre · RS
Fones:(051)395·5599/395·3639

1

2

3

1
Design Firm
Inox Design
Art Director
Mauro Pastore
Designer
Mauro Pastore
Client
Luca Benetti
Software/Hardware
Adobe Illustrator
Printing
Offset, 2 Colors

2
Design Firm
Izak Podgornik
Designer
Izak Podgornik
Illustrator
Izak Podgornik
Client
Self-promotion
Software/Hardware
Corel Draw 7, PC
Paper/Materials
Cordenons Venicelux
300 glm2
Printing
2 PMS Colors,
Plastic Coating

3
Design Firm
R & M Associati Grafici
Art Director
Di Somma/Fontanella
Client
Artemedia
Software/Hardware
Adobe Illustrator,
Macintosh
Printing
Offset

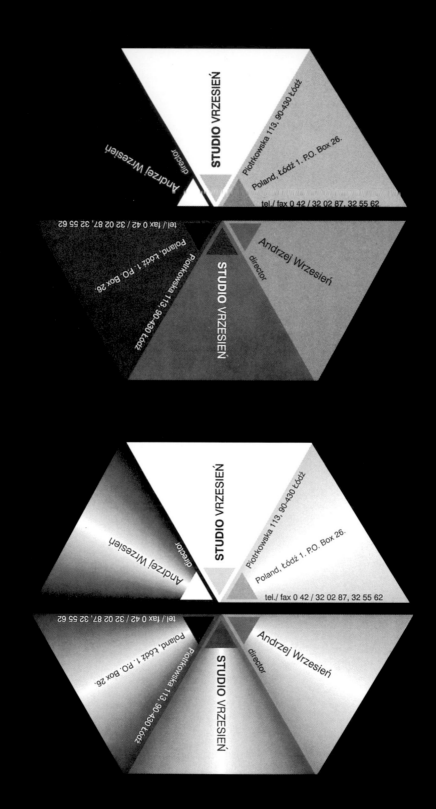

1
Design Firm
   Atelier Tadeusz Piechura
Art Director
   Tadeusz Piechura
Designer
   Tadeusz Piechura
Client
   Studio Vrzesien
Software/Hardware
   Corel 7
Printing
   Offset

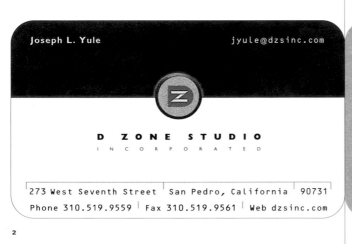

2

2
Design Firm
   D Zone Studio Inc.
Designer
   Joe L. Yule
Client
   Self-promotion
Software/Hardware
   QuarkXpress, Adobe Illustrator
Paper/Materials
   130 lb. Classic Crest -
   Solar White
Printing
   4 Color, Clear Foil, Emboss

Design Firm
  Manhattan Transfer
Art Director
  Micha Riss
Designer
  Patrick Asuncion
Client
  Self-promotion
Software/Hardware
  Adobe Illustrator, Macintosh
Paper/Materials
  Plastic
Printing
  Digicard

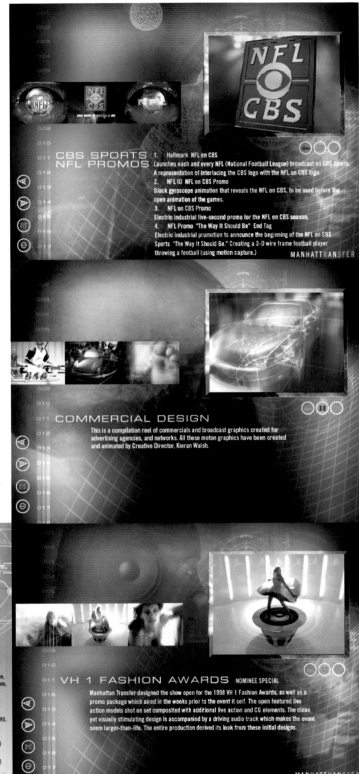

CBS SPORTS NFL PROMOS

1. Hallmark NFL on CBS
Launches each and every NFL (National Football League) broadcast on CBS Sports. A representation of interlacing the CBS logo with the NFL on CBS logo.
2. NFL ID NFL on CBS Promo
Black gyroscope animation that reveals the NFL on CBS, to be used before the open animation of the games.
3. NFL on CBS Promo
Electric industrial five-second promo for the NFL on CBS season.
4. NFL Promo "The Way It Should Be" End Tag
Electric industrial promotion to announce the beginning of the NFL on CBS Sports "The Way It Should Be." Creating a 3-D wire frame football player throwing a football (using motion capture.)

MANHATTRANSFER

COMMERCIAL DESIGN

This is a compilation reel of commercials and broadcast graphics created for advertising agencies, and networks. All these motion graphics have been created and animated by Creative Director, Kieran Walsh.

VH 1 FASHION AWARDS NOMINEE SPECIAL

Manhattan Transfer designed the show open for the 1998 VH 1 Fashion Awards, as well as a promo package which aired in the weeks prior to the event it self. The open featured live action models shot on set composited with additional live action and CG elements. The clean yet visually stimulating design is accompanied by a driving audio track which makes the event seem larger-than-life. The entire production derived its look from these initial designs.

MANHATTRANSFER

micha RISS CREATIVE DIRECTOR

In 1982, Micha Riss designed imagery for record companies and music publications, among them, the VHS cover for the Rolling Stones "25x5". Since 1984, Micha has been designing for television. He worked on numerous sports, news and entertainment events, including SuperBowl, Olympics, NBA, NCAAHoops, US Open Tennis, and The Masters. As of 1990 Micha has focused on total brand identity for television entities.

PROJECTS
CBS, VH-1, ESPN, SCI-FI, Kodak, Merrill Lynch, Museum of Natural History, CNN, Cartoon Network, WGBH (PBS station), HBO, USA Network, Fox, Life Magazine and Sony Music.

AWARDS
• EMMY award, 1994 Winter Olympics on CBS.
• PROMAX award, 1998 Olympic Downhill Promo on CBS.
• ITS MONITOR award, 1998 Olympic Downhill Promo on CBS.
• TELLY award, 1999 Inside the NFL on HBO.

PUBLICATIONS
Life Magazine, Daily News, Computer Graphics World, Digital Photo Illustration, Graphic Design, Click, Leonardo, AdvertisingAge / Creativity, HOW, Art Direction, Design Journal, Backstage, Videography, Video Magazine, Millimeter, Post Magazine, SPIN, Musician, Billboard, International Musician, and Rock Photo.

EDUCATION
TV Graphic Design Instructor in School of Visual Arts, New York City, since 1993. BFA Computer Graphics, New York Institute of Technology, New York City

MANHATTRANSFER

Petter Frostell Graphic Design

Roslagsgatan 34
SE-113 55 Stockholm, Sweden
Telephone +46 8 442 94 91
Facsimile +46 8 442 94 99
petter.frostell@telia.com

1

e
Credit.com

Mark S. Hayward
National Account Manager
mark@ecredit.com

www.ecredit.com
1000 Mansell Exchange West, Suite 250   Alpharetta, GA 30022
phone: (770) 645 5257   fax: (770) 645 5258

2

glauer@crescentnets.com

CRESCENT
networks

GREGORY LAUER, PH.D.
founder,
director of product marketing

201 riverneck road   chelmsford, ma 01824
t 978 244 9002 x206   c 978 884 4734
f 978 244 9211

3

1
Design Firm
  Petter Frostell Graphic Design
Designer
  Petter Frostell
Client
  Self-promotion
Software/Hardware
  Adobe Illustrator, Macintosh
Paper/Materials
  Scandia 2000
Printing
  Elfströms Tryckeri

2
Design Firm
  Stewart Monderer Design, Inc.
Art Director
  Stewart Monderer
Designer
  Aime Lecusay
Client
  eCredit.com
Software/Hardware
  Adobe Illustrator,
  QuarkXpress, Macintosh
Paper/Materials
  Gilbert Neutech
Printing
  2 Match Colors

3
Design Firm
  Stewart Monderer Design, Inc.
Art Director
  Stewart Monderer
Designer
  Aime Lecusay
Client
  Crescent Networks, Inc.
Software/Hardware
  Adobe Illustrator,
  QuarkXpress, Macintosh
Paper/Materials
  Monadnock Astrolite
Printing
  2 Match Colors

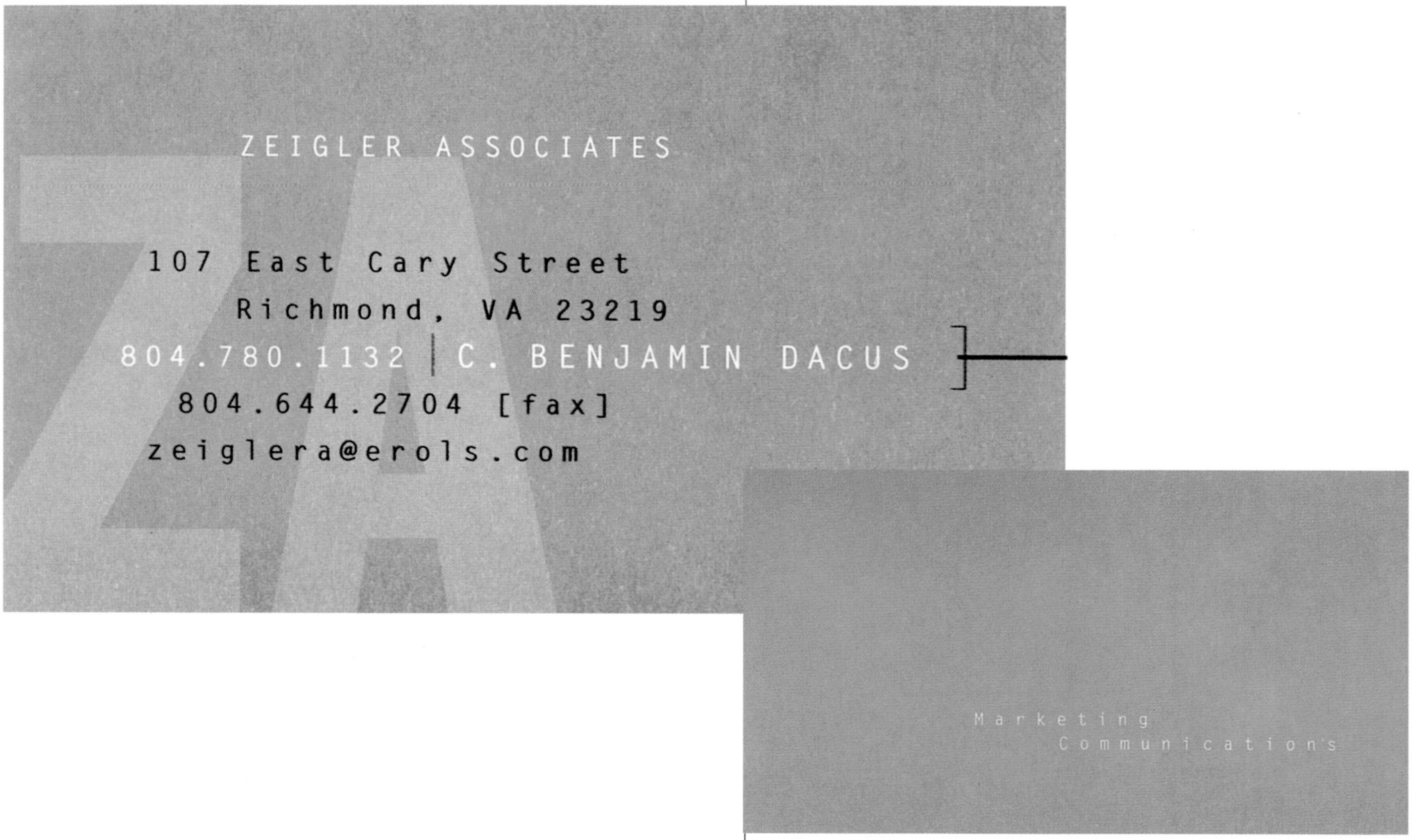

ZEIGLER ASSOCIATES

107 East Cary Street
Richmond, VA 23219
804.780.1132 | C. BENJAMIN DACUS
804.644.2704 [fax]
zeiglera@erols.com

Marketing
Communications

Design Firm
Zeigler Associates
Art Director
C. Benjamin Dacus
Designer
C. Benjamin Dacus
Client
Self-promotion
Software/Hardware
QuarkXpress
Paper/Materials
French Butcher
Printing
Offset; Business Press,
Richmond, VA

Doug Bamford
Marketing

Space Needle
Live The View

203 6th Avenue North
Seattle, WA 98109-5005 ,
Main: (206) 443-9700
Direct: (206) 443-2161, ext.1432
Fax: (206) 441-7415
E-mail: doug@bamford.com

1
Design Firm
  Hornall Anderson Design Works
Art Director
  Jack Anderson
Designers
  Mary Hermes, Gretchen Cook,
  Andrew Smith
Client
  Space Needle
Software/Hardware
  Freehand, Macintosh
Paper/Materials
  Fox River Confetti

 personify

www.personify.com
50 Osgood Place, Suite 100
San Francisco, California 94133

T 415 / 782 2050
F 415 / 544 0318

personify

[EILEEN HICKEN GITTINS]
ceo

415 / 782 2055
egittins@personify.com

2
Design Firm
  Hornall Anderson Design Works
Art Director
  Jack Anderson
Designers
  Jack Anderson, Debra
  McCloskey, Holly Finlayson
Illustrator
  Holly Finlayson
Client
  Personify
Software/Hardware
  Freehand, Macintosh
Paper/Materials
  Regalia

Design Firm
Hornall Anderson Design Works
Art Director
Jack Anderson
Designers
Jack Anderson, Heidi Favour,
Margaret Long
Client
Mahlum Architects
Software/Hardware
Freehand, Macintosh
Paper/Materials
Mohawk Superfine Recycled,
White

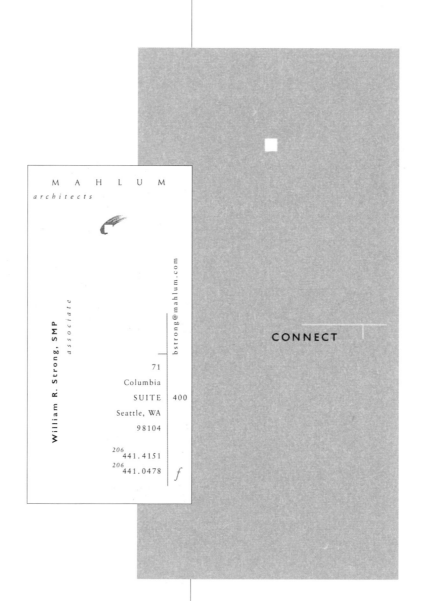

CONNECT

Design Firm
  Visual Marketing Associates
Art Directors
  Jason Selke, Tracy Meiners,
  Ken Botts
Designer
  Jason Selke
Photographer
  Quigley
Client
  C/ND Snowboard Apparel
Software/Hardware
  Freehand 8.0
Paper/Materials
  French Frostone
Printing
  Patented Printing

TODD STURZA
PRESIDENT

33 MIMOSA COURT
QUAKERTOWN, PA
18951

215.538.3454

www.cynd.com
cyndman@worldnet.att.net

CYND
SNOWBOARD APPAREL

Design Firm
    Form Studio
Art Director
    Jeffrey Burk
Designer
    Jeffrey Burk
Client
    Self-promotion
Software/Hardware
    Strata Studio Pro, Adobe
    Photoshop, Freehand
Paper/Materials
    Havana, Perla 111 lb. Cover
Printing
    Lithography, Letter Press

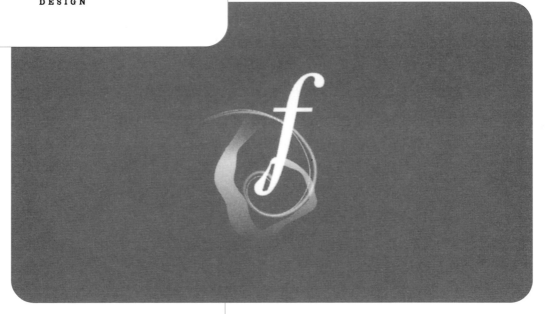

FORM STUDIO INC.
2900 First Ave P501 Seattle, WA 98121
JEFFREY BURK
TEL 206.448.0275 FAX 206.448.0277
EMAIL jeffrey@formstudio.com WEB www.formstudio.com
PRINT IDENTITY INTERNET
DESIGN

1

1

Design Firm
O2 Design

Art Director
Peter Dawson

Designer
Peter Dawson

Client
Self-promotion

Software/Hardware
QuarkXpress, Adobe Photoshop, Macintosh

Paper/Materials
Federal Tait Presentation 300 gsm

Printing
2 Specials and Die cuts

2

Design Firm
Pfeiffer plus Company

Art Director
Jerry Bliss

Designers
Terry Bliss, Katy Fischer

Illustrators
Terry Bliss, Katy Fischer

Client
Self-promotion

Software/Hardware
Adobe Illustrator 8.0, QuarkXpress 4.0

Paper/Materials
Mohawk Superfine 80 lb. Bright White Cover

Printing
Reprox

O₂ Design

West Point
36-37 Warple Way
London W3 0RG

Tel: 0181 746 0333
Fax: 0181 746 1110

Design Firm
    Becker Design
Art Director
    Neil Becker
Designers
    Neil Becker, Mary Eich
Client
    tesserae
Software/Hardware
    QuarkXpress, Adobe Illustrator

t e s s e r a e

custom tables • fireplace facades
lamps • mirrors • frames • planters

mosaics for life

Tammy Leiner
414.385.0320

Design Firm
   Total Creative, Inc.
Art Director
   Rod Dyer
Designer
   John Sabel
Illustrator
   John Sabel
Client
   Farrier's Nature
Software/Hardware
   Adobe Illustrator, Macintosh

FARRIER'S NATURE
354 HUNTLEY DRIVE
WEST HOLLYWOOD
CALIFORNIA 90048
TEL: 310.289.7701
FAX: 310.289.7719

DENNIS FARRIER

Design Firm
Greteman Group
Art Director
Sonia Greteman
Designer
James Strange
Client
Self-promotion
Software/Hardware
Freehand
Paper/Materials
Light Spec Snow
Printing
Offset

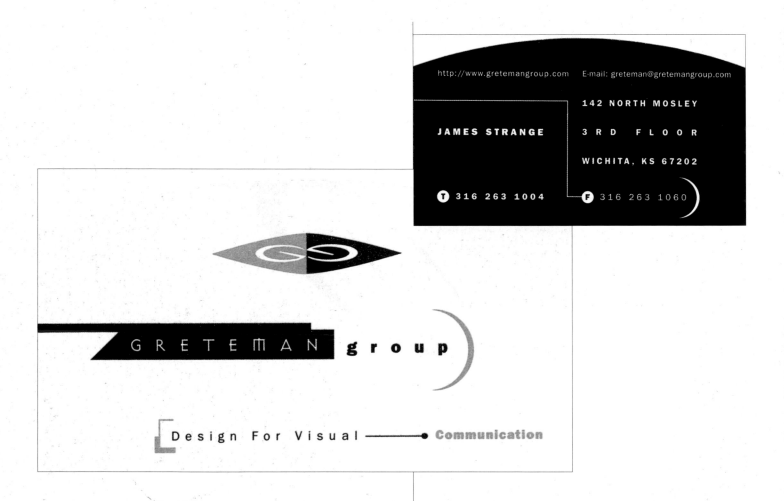

1
Design Firm
Greteman Group
Art Directors
Sonia Greteman, James Strange
Designer
James Strange
Client
Russell Communications
Software/Hardware
Freehand
Paper/Materials
Strathmore Elements
Printing
Offset

2
Design Firm
Dean Johnson Design
Art Directors
Scott Johnson, Bruce Dean
Designers
Scott Johnson, Bruce Dean,
Pat Prather
Client
Expidant

Design Firm
   Opera Grafisch Ontwerpers
Art Directors
   Ton Homburg, Marty
   Schoutsen
Designer
   Sappho Panhuysen
Client
   Werk 3
Software/Hardware
   QuarkXpress, Macintosh
Paper/Materials
   Biotop

Bianca Locker

Rambaldistrasse 27   T +49 (0)89 957 20 172   ISDN +49 (0)89 957 20 173
D - 81929 München   F +49 (0)89 957 20 174   e-mail: design@werk3.ccn.de

1
Design Firm
   Studio Boot
Art Directors
   Petra Janssen, Edwin Vollebergh
Designers
   Petra Janssen, Edwin Vollebergh
Illustrator
   Studio Boot
Client
   Pieksma bv.
Paper/Materials
   Sulfaat Karton
Printing
   Offset, 3 colors

Pieksma bv.
sinds 1889
Medische divisie

Frank Rooijakkers
Achtergracht 27
1017 WL Amsterdam
T.020-6237754 F.020-6245203
privé 020-6937612

Helen Brennan

Sir John Lyon House
5 High Timber Street
Blackfriars
London
EC4V 3NX

tel +44 (0)207 2484945
fax +44 (0)207 2484946
mob +44 (0)467 785786
helen@chameleonmkg.com

chameleon marketing communications

Sir John Lyon House 5 High Timber Street Blackfriars London **EC4** V 3NX

Paul Burgess
T +44 (0)171 420 7700
F +44 (0)171 420 7701
m 0976 607126
paulb@wilsonharvey.co.uk

Wilson Harvey
Contagious Marketing and Design

1

Uday Radia

lighthouse

• Sir John Lyon House
5 High Timber Street
London
EC4V 3NX

• t 020 7420 7714
f 020 7420 7723

• e uradia@lighthousepr.com
www.lighthousepr.com

2

Anthony Berry

AC Networks
12 Astra Drive
Gravesend
Kent
DA12 4PY

Tel 01474 350890
Fax 01474 320400

3

Design Firm
  Studio Boot
Art Directors
  Petra Janssen, Edwin Vollebergh
Designers
  Petra Janssen, Edwin Vollebergh
Illustrator
  Studio Boot
Client
  The Framehouse
Paper/Materials
  Plastic Phone Card
Printing
  Silkscreen, 3 colors

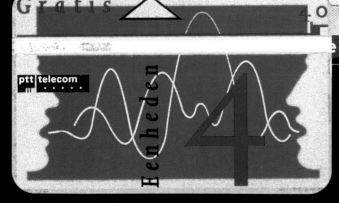

Design Firm
   Studio Boot
Art Directors
   Petra Janssen, Edwin Vollebergh
Designers
   Petra Janssen, Edwin Vollebergh
Illustrator
   Studio Boot
Client
   Self-promotion
Paper/Materials
   MC on 3mm Grey Board
Printing
   Full Color and Laminate

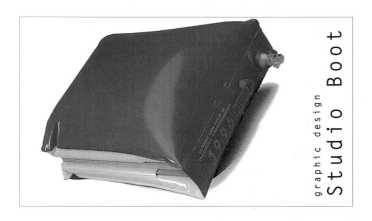

HermanMiller

for Healthcare

HermanMiller

HermanMiller

for the Home

HermanMiller

Internationa

www.hermanmiller.c

www.hermanmiller.c

for Government

Capital Corp

€$£
¢¥

www.hermanmiller.com

www.hermanmiller.com

Raymond Kennedy AMA
General Manager
Herman Miller for the Home

HermanMiller

ray_kennedy@hermanmiller.com
616 654 8329   TELEPHONE
616 654 5817   FAX
616 560 4441   CELLULAR
616 447 9594   HOME OFFICE

LOCATION
375 West 48th Street
Holland MI 49423-5341

US MAIL
Herman Miller Inc
MS 0443
855 East Main Avenue
PO Box 302
Zeeland MI 49464 0302

1

Design Firm
Herman Miller Marketing
Communications Dept.

Art Director
Stephen Frykholm

Designer
Brian Edlefson

Photographers
Nick Merrick,
Hedrick Blessing,
Stock

Client
Herman Miller, Inc.

Software/Hardware
Adobe Photoshop 5.0,
QuarkXpress 4.0

Paper/Materials
Fox River Coronado

Printing
Foremost Graphics, Inc.

2

Design Firm
Atelier Tadeusz Piechura

Art Director
Tadeusz Piechura

Designer
Tadeusz Piechura

Client
Olli Reima

Software/Hardware
Corel 7

Printing
Offset, 2nd Edition,
New Version

2

Joyce Seegers & Paul Emmen

Pelsakker 4, 4834 AG Breda
076-5602835 ✵ mmcgers@casema.net

1

2

1
Design Firm
   Case
Designer
   Kees Wagenaars
Client
   Seegers & Emmen
Software/Hardware
   QuarkXpress
Paper/Materials
   Lightning Gold 240 gr.
Printing
   Expel

2
Design Firm
   DMX Design
Art Director
   Petrie Hahn
Designer
   Sara Crivello, Suyeon Park
Client
   Self-promotion
Software/Hardware
   Adobe Illustrator

Design Firm
   DMX Design
Art Director
   Petrie Hahn
Designer
   Sara Crivello
Client
   Iscom
Software/Hardware
   Adobe Illustrator

ISAAC SALEM
President

Iscom, Inc.
One Silicon Alley Plaza
90 William Street, Suite 1202
New York, NY 10038

p: 212.324.1100
f: 212.324.1101
isaac@iscom.net
www.iscom.net

COPYGRAPHICS

PETER ELLZEY

314 READ STREET
SANTA FE, NM 87505
505 988 1438 VOICE
505 988 3155 FAX

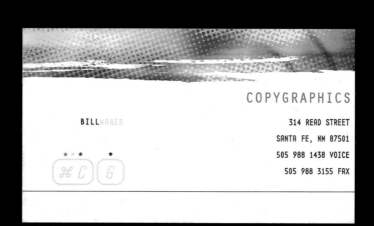

COPYGRAPHICS

BILLMAKER

314 READ STREET
SANTA FE, NM 87501
505 988 1438 VOICE
505 988 3155 FAX

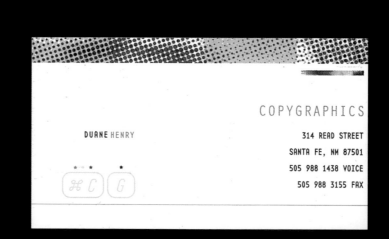

COPYGRAPHICS

DUANE HENRY

314 READ STREET
SANTA FE, NM 87501
505 988 1438 VOICE
505 988 3155 FAX

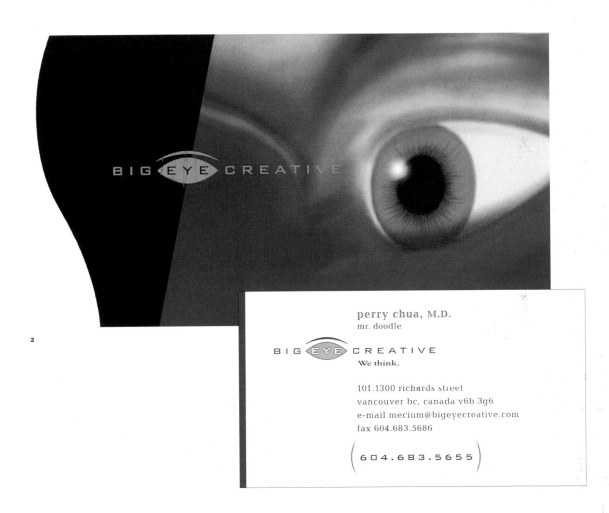

1
Design Firm
  Cisneros Design
Art Director
  Harry M. Forehand III
Designers
  Harry M. Forehand III,
  Brian Hurshman
Client
  Copygraphics
Software/Hardware
  Macintosh
Printing
  Local Color, Santa Fe

2
Design Firm
  Big Eye Creative
Art Directors
  Perry Chua, Dann Ilicic
Designer
  Perry Chua
Photographer
  Grant Waddell
  (digital imaging)
Client
  Self-promotion
Software/Hardware
  Adobe Illustrator,
  Adobe Photoshop
Paper/Materials
  Potlatch McCoy
Printing
  Clarke Printing

perry chua, M.D.
mr. doodle

BIG EYE CREATIVE
We think.

101.1300 richards street
vancouver bc, canada v6b 3g6
e-mail mecium@bigeyecreative.com
fax 604.683.5686

(604.683.5655)

TEL 415·482·9324

digital

hothouse

FAX 415·482·9314

EMAIL ron@dahothouse.com

1323 Fourth Street · San Rafael · CA · 94901

1

1
Design Firm
be
Art Director
Will Burke
Designers
Eric Read, Enrique Gaston
Client
hothouse digital
Printing
Photon Press

2
Design Firm
be
Art Director
Will Burke
Designer
Eric Read
Illustrator
Coralie Russo
Client
light rain
Software/Hardware
Adobe Illustrator, Adobe Photoshop,
Macintosh
Printing
Photon Press

digital image magic

Steve Kimball   Principal

2 Magnolia Avenue
San Anselmo Ca 94960

phone   415 453 2828
fax   415 453 0828
e-mail   steve@lightrain.com

2

Design Firm
  Studio Boot
Art Directors
  Petra Janssen, Edwin Vollebergh
Designers
  Petra Janssen, Edwin Vollebergh
Illustrator
  Studio Boot
Client
  Self-promotion
Paper/Materials
  MC on 3mm Grey Board
Printing
  Full Color and Laminate

BOOT ©

studio Boot · Brede Haven 8a
5211 T1 's-Hertogenbosch
Tel.073-6143593 · Fax 073-6133190
ISDN 073-6129865 · bootst@wxs.nl

Design Firm
IUADOME
Art Director
Sang Han
Designers
Jeeho Kim, Sung
Hyun Park
Photographer
Chang Han
Client
Self-promotion
Software/Hardware
Adobe Illustrator,
Adobe Photoshop, 3D Max
Paper/Materials
65 lb. Cougar White,
Cellophane
Printing
Mcbride Printing

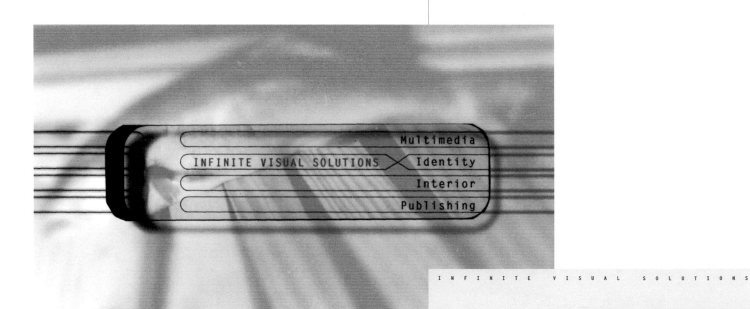

DETERMAN BROWNIE, INC.

Ron Determan
Field Service

1241 72nd Avenue NE
Minneapolis, MN 55432

PHONE: 612.571.8110 | FAX: 612.502.9862

1

DIGITAL MEDIA GROUP

Digital Media Group s.r.l.
Via Tadino 20 20124 Milano
tel 02 29.41.21.74 Fax 02 29.41.52.66
e-mail: monti@dmg it
Punto Vendita Autorizzato Apple Computer
Partita Iva 12365290159

Auro Monti

2

1
Design Firm
Design Center
Art Director
John Reger
Designer
Jon Erickson
Client
Determan Brownie, Inc.
Software/Hardware
Freehand, Macintosh
Paper/Materials
Strathmore Writing

2
Design Firm
Inox Design
Art Director
Sabrina Elena
Designer
Sabrina Elena
Client
Digital Media Group
Software/Hardware
Freehand
Paper/Materials
Zanders Chromolux
Printing
Offset, 1 & 2 Colors

Design Firm
Studio Boot
Art Directors
Petra Janssen,
Edwin Vollebergh
Designers
Petra Janssen,
Edwin Vollebergh
Illustrator
Studio Boot
Client
AGENT-X
Paper/Materials
Chromolux
Printing
Offset

PHILIPPE G. VADALEAU

SCHRÖDERSTIFTSTR. 28 / 20146 HAMBURG / TEL.: 040 · 41 81 11 / FAX: 41 82 10

Design Firm
Bettina Huchtemann Art -
Direction & Design
Designer
Bettina Huchtemann
Illustrator
Bettina Huchtemann
Client
Philippe Vadaleau
Software/Hardware
QuarkXpress, Brush
Paper/Materials
Countryside
Printing
Offset, 2 Colors

Jed Somit, Attorney (415) 839-3215

1440 Broadway, Suite 910
Oakland, California 94612
FAX (415) 272-0711

1

1
Design Firm
    Fifth Street Design
Art Director
    J. Clifton Meek
Designer
    Brenton Beck
Client
    Jed Somit
Software/Hardware
    Corel Draw
Paper/Materials
    Strathmore Writing Laid
Printing
    Kerwin Graphic Arts

3
Design Firm
    Zeroart Studio
Art Director
    Josef Lo
Designer
    Simon Tsang
Client
    Self-promotion
Software/Hardware
    Adobe Illustrator 8.0, Macintosh
Paper/Materials
    Rives Paper, Bright White 250
    gsm
Printing
    Charming Print
    Production House

2 (see also page 149, bottom)
Design Firm
    Esfera Design
Designers
    Cecilia Consolo, Luciano Cardinali
Client
    Self-promotion
Software/Hardware
    QuarkXpress, Corel Draw
Paper/Materials
    Star White Vicksburg, Tiara 216 g
Printing
    Offset

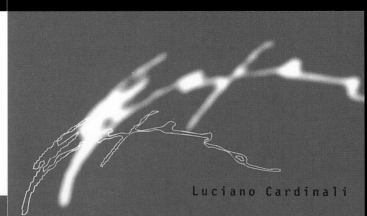

2

creativity-always-on-my-mind

* simon tsang 曾繁光 chief designer
zeroart@netvigator.com * p.o.box 71466, kowloon central post office, hong kong.
* tel / fax 26 09 40 50

93 04 36 09

3

zeroart
zeroart studio

Luciano Cardinali

ESFERA DESIGN
design & assessoria de imagem

[rua barão de santa marta 519 são paulo sp 04372-100
fone fax (0++11) **5563 1454** Cel (0++11) 9611.3023
e s f e r a d g @ u o l . c o m . b r

1

Design Firm
Erwin Zinger Graphic Design
Designer
Erwin Zinger
Client
Hans Kliphuis Public Relations & Public
Affairs
Software/Hardware
Adobe Illustrator, QuarkXpress
Paper/Materials
Countryside
Printing
2 Colors, Offset

2

Design Firm
Erwin Zinger Graphic Design
Designer
Erwin Zinger
Client
Poggibonsi
Software/Hardware
Adobe Illustrator
Paper/Materials
Confetti
Printing
Black and Silver (PMS 877)

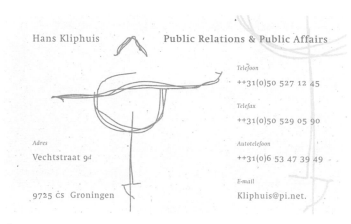

1

2

michael BARTALOS   *p* 415 863 4569 *f* 415 252 7252

mike @ bartalos.com

30 RAMONA AVENUE NO.2 **SAN FRANCISCO** CA 94103

represented in japan by **CWC**
p 03 3496 0745 *f* 03 3496 0747 *e* junko @ cwctokyo.com

1

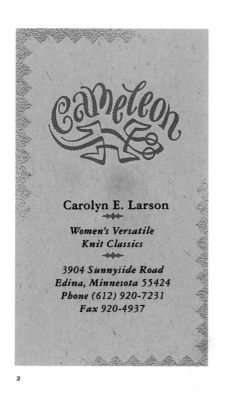

2

1
Design Firm
  Natto Maki
Art Director
  Lili Ong
Designer
  Lili Ong
Illustrator
  Michael Bartalos
Client
  Michael Bartalos
Software/Hardware
  Adobe Illustrator
Paper/Materials
  Strathmore Off-White Cover
Printing
  Letter Press By One Heart Press,
  San Francisco

2
Design Firm
  Design Center
Art Director
  John Reger
Designer
  Sherwin Schwartzrock
Client
  Cameleon
Software/Hardware
  Freehand, Macintosh
Paper/Materials
  Strathmore Writing
Printing
  Pro-Craft

Design Firm
   Cincodemayo Design
Art Director
   Mauricio H. Alanis
Designer
   Adriana Garcia
Client
   BAR-CELONA
Software/Hardware
   Freehand 8.01, Macintosh
Paper/Materials
   Magnomatt 250
Printing
   50M Offset Printing

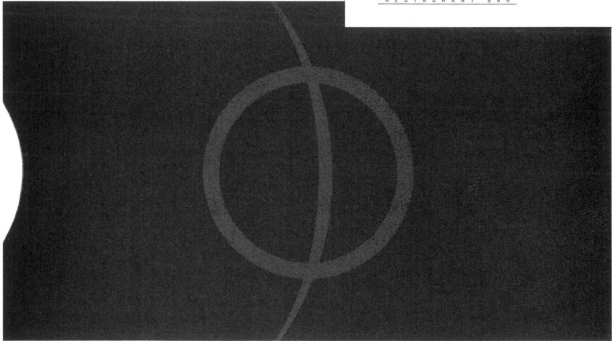

SEQUENCE
PLANNING & DESIGN

INTERIOR DESIGN

SPACE PLANNING

PROJECT MANAGEMENT

MOVE COORDINATION

1

SEQUENCE
PLANNING & DESIGN

DOTTIE BRIGGS
ASID · IFMA

883 NORTH SHORELINE BLVD., SUITE C-120

MOUNTAIN VIEW, CA 94043

TEL 650.967.3394

FAX 650.934.2950

1
Design Firm
Free-Range Chicken Ranch
Art Director
Kelli Christman
Designer
Kelli Christman
Illustrator
Sandy Gin
Client
Sequence
Software/Hardware
QuarkXpress, Adobe Illustrator
Paper/Materials
Starwhite Vicksburg 130 lb.
Cover
Printing
Offset, PMS inks

2
Design Firm
Sb Design - Brazil
Designer
Ricardo Bastos
Client
Le Bistrot Restaurant
Software/Hardware
Corel Draw, PC
Paper/Materials
Esse, Dark Tan (216glm2) Texture
Printing
Offset

Fernando Marins

Fernando Gomes, 58 · 90.510-010 · Porto Alegre · RS
Fone: (051) 346.3812

2

THE TIME

224 West 49th Street New York, NY 10019

ULRICH R. WALL
General Manager

Tel 212.320.2910
Fax 212.320.2941
E-mail uwalltime@sprynet.com

1

1
Design Firm
Mirko Ilić Corp.
Art Director
Mirko Ilić
Designer
Mirko Ilić
Client
The Time Hotel

2
Design Firm
Sibley Peteet Design
Designers
Donna Aldridge, Tom Kirsch,
David Beck
Client
AGI Klearfold
Software/Hardware
Adobe Illustrator, Macintosh
Printing
Monarch Press

3
Design Firm
Sackett Design Associates
Art Director
Mark Sackett
Designers
George White, James Sakamoto,
Wendy Wood
Photographer
Stock
Client
communities.com
Software/Hardware
QuarkXpress, Adobe Illustrator,
Adobe Photoshop
Paper/Materials
100 lb. Bright White
Vellum Cover
Printing
Forman Lithograph

www.communities.com
www.thepalace.com
www.onlive.com

CAROLYN E. VAN NESS
EXECUTIVE ADMINISTRATOR & OFFICE MANAGER
DIRECT 408.342.9506

communities.

10101 NORTH DE ANZA BLVD · SUITE 100
CUPERTINO, CALIFORNIA · 95014.2264
PHONE 408.342.9500 · FAX 408.777.9200

carolyn@communities.com

3

IMPAC ™
G R O U P

AGI
KLEARFOLD

RICHARD BLOCK
President & CEO

1776 BROADWAY
NEW YORK, NY 10019-2002
TEL 212.489.0973 Ext. 7110
FAX 212.489.0255

rblock@impacgroup.com

2

4
Design Firm
  Free-Range Chicken Ranch
Art Director
  Kelli Christman
Designer
  Kelli Christman
Client
  web•ex by ActiveTouch
Software/Hardware
  QuarkXpress, Adobe Illustrator
Paper/Materials
  Starwhite Vicksburg 130 lb.
Printing
  Offset, Special Inks

Charles J. Orlando
**DIRECTOR OF MARKETING
COMMUNICATIONS**

5225 Betsy Ross Drive
Santa Clara, California 95054
408.980.5200 x2145
fax: 408.980.5280
charles@webex.com
www.activetouch.com

**we've got to start
meeting like this**™

www.webex.com

4

Pan-Asian Café
and catering company

4753 McPherson
Saint Louis, MO 63108
Phone: 314/361-0013 Fax: 361-4041

1

1
Design Firm
    The Puckett Group
Art Director
    Candy Freund
Designer
    Candy Freund
Illustrator
    Candy Freund
Client
    Zoë Pan-Asian Café
Software/Hardware
    QuarkXpress, Adobe Photoshop
Paper/Materials
    80 lb. Strathmore Ultimate
    White Wove Cover
Printing
    Offset, 4 PMS Colors,
    Printer: Reprox

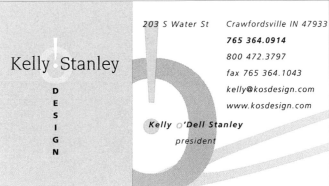

Vestígio: Consultores de Design, Lda.
Edifício Hoechst, Av. Sidónio Pais, 379, Salas 4-5
P-4100 Porto • Portugal • Email: vestigio@ip.pt
Tel. 02. 6064117 **Fax** 02. 6064117

Fátima Guimarães
Design Editorial

V:

1

203 S Water St   Crawfordsville IN 47933

Kelly · Stanley

D
E
S
I
G
N

765 364.0914
800 472.3797
fax 765 364.1043
kelly@kosdesign.com
www.kosdesign.com

Kelly O'Dell Stanley
president

2

Paul F. Brewster
Vice President, Technology

4915 Saint Elmo Avenue · Suite 403
Bethesda, MD 20814

Phone: 301 657 2487
Pager: 800 251 2083
Mobile: 301 351 1949
Fax: 301 657 2448
Email: pbrewster@global-cable.com

GlobalCable CONSULTING GROUP

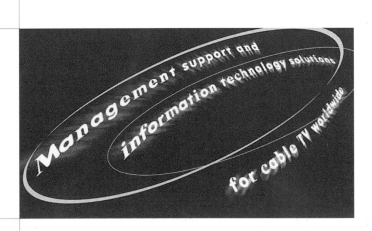

3

1
Design Firm
  Vestígio
Art Director
  Emanuel Barbosa
Designer
  Emanuel Barbosa
Client
  Self-promotion
Software/Hardware
  Freehand, Macintosh
Paper/Materials
  Favini Milho
Printing
  1 Color

2
Design Firm
  Kelly O. Stanley Design
Art Director
  Kelly O'Dell Stanley
Client
  Self-promotion
Software/Hsrdware
  Freehand, QuarkXpress,
  Macintosh
Paper/Materials
  Esse Smooth White
Prinitng
  2 Color

3
Design Firm
  Tim Kenney Design Partners
Art Director
  Tim Kenney
Designer
  Monica Banko
Client
  Global Cable Consulting
  Group
Software/Hardware
  Freehand, QuarkXpress,
  Macintosh
Paper/Materials
  Gilbert Neutech Ultra White
  Wove
Printing
  London Litho

1

Design Firm
Hornall Anderson Design Works

Art Director
Jack Anderson

Designers
Jack Anderson, David Bates

Illustrator
David Bates

Client
Self-promotion

Paper/Materials
French Durotone, Packaging
Gray Liner 80 lb. C

2

Design Firm
Second Floor

Art Director
Warren Welter

Designer
Warren Welter

Illustrator
Lori Powell

Client
5th Avenue Suites Hotel

Software
QuarkXPress, Adobe Illustrator,
Macintosh

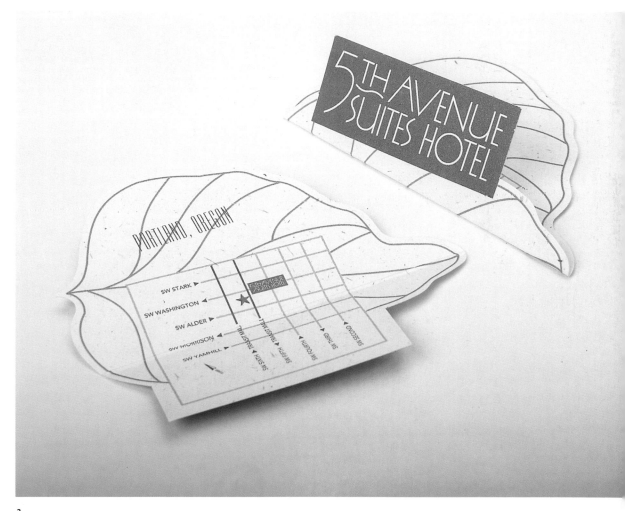

2

Estudio Hache
Diseño Gráfico y Multimedia

Vedia 1682 - 3º
1429 Buenos Aires
República Argentina

4704-0202
4446-1393

info@estudiohache.com
www.estudiohache.com

Laura Lazzeretti

Marcelo Varela

Design Firm
Estudio Hache S.A.

Designers
Laura Lazzeretti,
Marcelo Varela

Photographers
Marcelo Varela,
Laura Lazzeretti

Client
Self-promotion

Software/Hardware
Adobe Photoshop, Adobe
Illustrator, Macintosh

Paper/Materials
4 Color Printing, Water Based
Varnish on 235 g Coated Paper

Printing
Neuhaus S.A.

Lynn Ridenour
Director of
Corporate
Communications
425.519.9313
lynnr@onyx.com

310-120th Ave NE
Bellevue, WA 98005
(T) 425.451.8060
(F) 425.519.4002
www.onyx.com

Design Firm
Hornall Anderson Design Works
Art Director
John Hornall
Designers
Debra McCloskey,
Holly Finlayson,
Jana Wilson Esser
Client
Onyx Software Corporation
Software/Hardware
Freehand, Macintosh

Design Firm
  Ricardo Mealha Atelier
  Design Estrategico
Art Director
  Ricardo Mealha
Designer
  Leonel Duarte
Client
  Luis De Barros
Software/Hardware
  Freehand 8.0
Paper/Materials
  Martin Paper
Printing
  Ma Artes Graficas

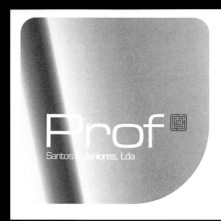

Porto

Póvoa

Braga

Lisboa

Administração / Direcção
av. Mouzinho de Albuquerque,
n.º 184 R/c
4490 Póvoa de Varzim

tel.: 351 - 52 - 298 0 80
fax: 351 - 52 - 298 0 89

Armazém rua Silveira Campos,
n.º 38, Arm. a — Aver-o-Mar,
4490 Póvoa de Varzim

tel.: 351 - 52 - 61 45 56
fax: 351 - 52 - 61 89 71

Shopping Cidade do Porto
tel.: 02 - 600 91 70

Pr. Galiza - Porto
tel.: 02 - 600 95 05

Viacatarina Shopping - Porto
tel.: 02 - 200 36 73

Arrábida Shopping - Porto
tel.: 02 - 374 54 53

Norte Shopping - Porto
tel.: 02 - 955 98 86

Póvoa de Varzim
tel.: 052 - 298 0 81

Braga Shopping
tel.: 053 - 267 0 61

Braga Parque
tel.: 053 - 257 9 31

Centro Vasco da Gama
Lisboa
tel.: 01 - 895 13 98

Design Firm
Ricardo Mealha Atelier
Design Estrategico
Art Director
Ricardo Mealha
Designer
Ana Margarida Gunha
Client
Prof
Software/Hardware
Freehand 8.0
Paper/Materials
Martin Paper
Printing
M2 Artes Graficas

Design Firm
be
Art Director
Eric Read
Designer
Eric Read
Client
inhaus industries
Software/Hardware
Adobe Illustrator,
Macintosh

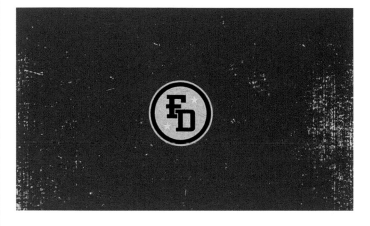

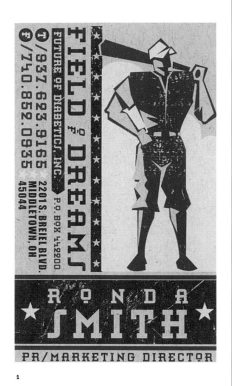

1900 E Shore Avenue
Freeland, WA 98249

p 360.321.4675
e livingbydesign@hotmail.com

2

1

Design Firm
  Visual Marketing Associates
Art Directors
  Jason Selke, Ken Botts
Designer
  Jason Selke
Illustrator
  Jason Selke
Client
  Future of Diabetics, Inc.
Software/Hardware
  Freehand 8.0, Photoshop 5.0
Paper/Materials
  Proterra
Printing
  Thomas Graphics

2

Design Firm
  Girvin
Art Director
  Gretchen Cook
Designer
  Sam Knight
Illustrator
  Gretchen Cook
Client
  Living by Design
Software/Hardware
  Freehand, Adobe Illustrator 8.0,
  Macintosh
Paper/Materials
  Strathmore Renewal
  Smooth, Calm
Printing
  2 Color Offset

Design Firm
  1 Horsepower Design
Designer
  Brian Hurshman
Client
  Self-promotion
Software/Hardware
  Macintosh

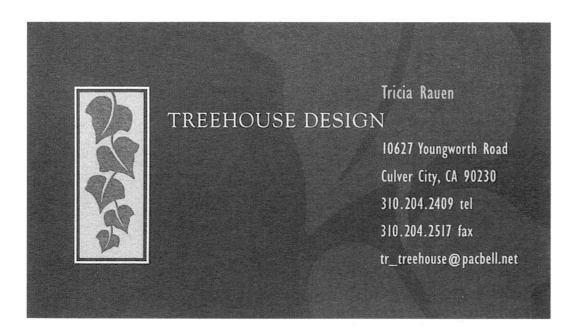

Tricia Rauen

TREEHOUSE DESIGN

10627 Youngworth Road

Culver City, CA 90230

310.204.2409 tel

310.204.2517 fax

tr_treehouse@pacbell.net

Design Firm

Treehouse Design

Art Director

Tricia Rauen

Designer

Tricia Rauen

Illustrator

Tricia Rauen

Client

Self-promotion

Software/Hardware

Adobe Illustrator

Paper/Materials

Classic Crest Duplex Cover,
(Saw Grass, Natural White)

Printing

Typecraft, Inc.

SPIN PRODUCTIONS TORONTO/ATLANTA WWW.SPINPRO.COM
620 KING ST WEST TORONTO ONTARIO CANADA M5V 1M6
TELEPHONE 416 504 8333 FACSIMILE 416 504 3876

CONNIE DERCHO
SENIOR PRODUCER
connie@spinpro.com

SPIN PRODUCTIONS

SPIN PRODUCTIONS TORONTO/ATLANTA WWW.SPINPRO.COM
620 KING ST WEST TORONTO ONTARIO CANADA M5V 1M6
TELEPHONE 416 504 8333 FACSIMILE 416 504 3876

2

1

Design Firm
Spin Productions

Art Director
Spin Productions

Designer
Spin Productions

Illustrator
Spin Productions

Photographer
Spin Productions

Client
Self-promotion

Software/Hardware
QuarkXpress, Adobe Photoshop, Macintosh

Printing
CJ Graphics

2

Design Firm
Hornall Anderson Design Works

Art Director
Jack Anderson

Designers
Jack Anderson, Kathy Saito, Alan Copeland

Client
Wells Fargo "innoVisions"

Software/Hardware
Freehand, Macintosh

Paper/Materials
Mohawk Superfine, Bright White

**TOWN
HOUSE**
PROPIEDADES
Y SERVICIOS

AGUILAR 2436
1426 BUENOS AIRES
TELEFAX: 4780-2200
e-mail: townhouse
@interlink.com.ar

Arq. Abel Trybiarz
Director

**WOHLGEMUTH
TAUBER SA**
E M P R E S A
CONSTRUCTORA

AGUILAR 2436
1426 BUENOS AIRES
TEL.: 4780-2200
e-mail: townhouse
@interlink.com.ar

Daniel Wohlgemuth
Presidente

GRUPO TOWN HOUSE

**WAISMAN
TRYBIARZ**
ARQUITECTURA
POR OBJETIVOS

**WOHLGEMUTH
TAUBER S.A.**
E M P R E S A
CONSTRUCTORA

TOWN HOUSE
PROPIEDADES
Y SERVICIOS

Arq. Gerardo Waisman

AGUILAR 2436
1426 BUENOS AIRES
TEL: 4780-2200
e-mail: townhouse
@interlink.com.ar

1

**WAISMAN
TRYBIARZ**
**ARQUITECTURA
POR OBJETIVOS**

AGUILAR 2436
1426 BUENOS AIRES
TEL.: 4780-2200
e-mail: townhouse
@interlink.com.ar

Arq. Abel Trybiarz

1

Design Firm
  Estudio Hache S.A.
Designers
  Laura Lazzeretti,
  Marcelo Varela
Client
  Grupo Town House
Software/Hardware
  Adobe Illustrator, Macintosh
Paper/Materials
  Oreplus 240g
Printing
  Bahía Graf SRL

2
Design Firm
  Studio Boot
Art Directors
  Petra Janssen,
  Edwin Vollebergh
Designers
  Petra Janssen,
  Edwin Vollebergh
Client
  Self-promotion
Paper/Materials
  MC on 3mm Grey Board
Printing
  Full Color and Laminate

2

Design Firm
Voice Design
Art Director
Clifford Cheng
Designer
Clifford Cheng
Client
Self-promotion
Software/Hardware
Adobe Photoshop,
QuarkXpress, Macintosh
Printing
Offset, 2 Color

1

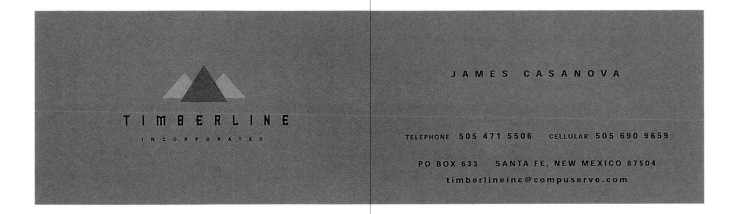

JAMES CASANOVA

TIMBERLINE
INCORPORATED

TELEPHONE 505 471 5506   CELLULAR 505 690 9659

PO BOX 633   SANTA FE, NEW MEXICO 87504

timberlineinc@compuserve.com

1

1

Design Firm
Cisneros Design
Designer
Eric Griego
Client
Timberline Inc.
Software/Hardware
Macintosh
Paper/Materials
Evergreen
Printing
Aspen Printing, Albuquerque

2

Design Firm
Geographics
Designer
Tanya Doell
Client
Coyotes Deli & Grill
Software/Hardware
Adobe Illustrator, Adobe
Photoshop, QuarkXpress
Paper/Materials
Genesis Husk
Printing
3 Spot

2

Job⊙rder™

maximizing business productivity

Victor Siegle
PRESIDENT

Management Software Inc.
17 Main Street, Suite 313
Cortland, New York 13045
e-mail victor_siegle@joborder.com
Phone 607.**756.4150**
Facsimile 607.756.5550

Design Firm
    Big Eye Creative
Art Director
    Perry Chua
Designers
    Perry Chua, Nancy Yeasting
Client
    Management Software, Inc.
Software/Hardware
    Adobe Illustrator,
    Adobe Photoshop

GROUND

ROB RINDOS

T 719.955.1100 ext:415
F 719.955.1104
Toll Free: 877.363.8449
CORPORATE OFFICE:
2845 JANITELL ROAD COLORADO SPRINGS COLORADO 80906

GROUND

ROB RINDOS

rrindos@gzdesign.com

www.gzdesign.com

T 614.764.0227
F 614.764.3796

297 TREE HAVEN NORTH POWELL OHIO 43065

1

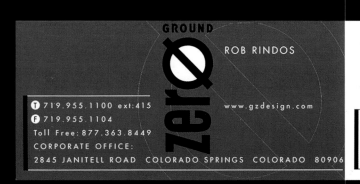

Design

Ramona Hutko   4712 South Chelsea Lane   301
                     Bethesda Maryland 20814   656 2763

2

1
Design Firm
    Hornall Anderson Design Works
Art Director
    Jack Anderson
Designers
    Kathy Saito, Julie Lock, Ed Lee,
    Heidi Favour, Virginia Le
Client
    Ground Zero
Software/Hardware
    Freehand, Macintosh

2
Design Firm
    Ramona Hutko Design
Art Director
    Ramona Hutko
Designer
    Ramona Hutko
Client
    Self-promotion
Software/Hardware
    QuarkXpress
Paper/Materials
    Mohawk Superfine Cover
Printing
    Bruce Printing

Design Firm
   Skarsgard Design
Designer
   Susan Skarsgard
Hand-lettering
   Susan Skarsgard
Client
   Ann Arbor Street Art Fair
Printing
   Offset 4 Color

Design Firm
  Visser Bay Anders Toscani
Art Director
  Thea Bakker
Designer
  Thea Bakker
Client
  Qi At Vbat
Paper/Materials
  Royal Quadrant High White
  250 gr.

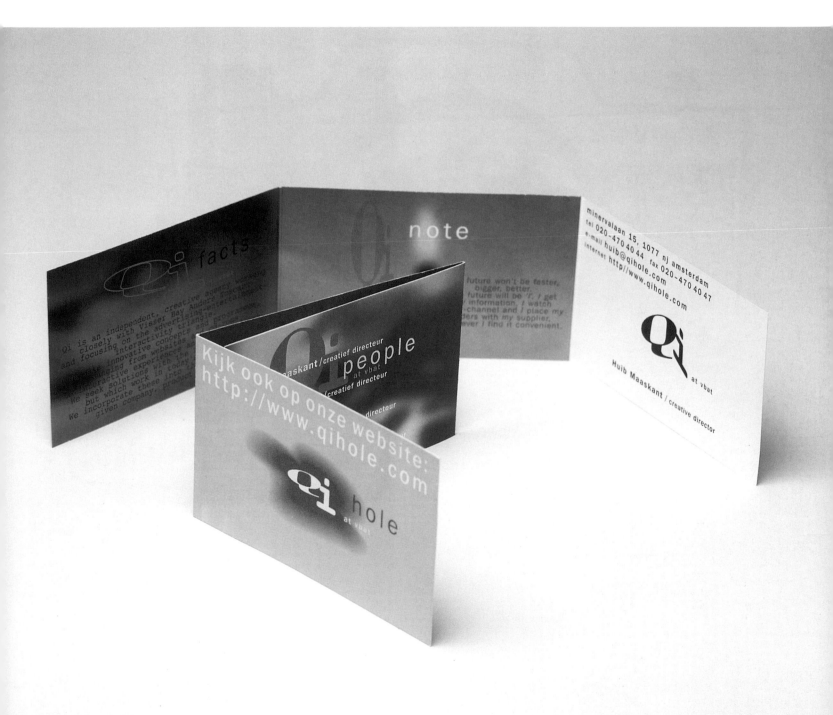

Design Firm
Sayles Graphic Design

Art Director
John Sayles

Designer
John Sayles

Illustrator
John Sayles

Client
Big Daddy Photography

Software/Hardware
Adobe Illustrator 7.0

Paper/Materials
Classic Crest 110 lb. Cover:
Natural White

Printing
Artcraft

Design Firm
  Sayles Graphic Design
Art Director
  John Sayles
Designer
  John Sayles
Illustrator
  John Sayles
Client
  Barrick Roofing
Software/Hardware
  Adobe Illustrator 7.0
Paper/Materials
  Classic Crest 100 lb. Cover,
  Bright White
Printing
  Artcraft

CECILIA R. GAUDINEER   PRESIDENT

PHONE | FAX
(515) 244-3513 | (515) 244-3557

"We're on top of things"

BARRICK ROOFING & SHEET METAL INC.

10 COLLEGE AVE.   DES MOINES IOWA 50314

FOUNDED IN 1878

IE DESIGN

[i]e design

13039 VENTURA BLVD
STUDIO CITY, CA 91604
TEL 818 907 8000
FAX 818 907 8830
EMAIL mail@iedesign.net

COREY BAIM
PRINCIPAL/BUSINESS

Design Firm
[i]e design
Designer
Marcie Carson
Photographer
Kevin Merrill
Client
Self-promotion
Software/Hardware
Adobe Photoshop,
QuarkXpress, Macintosh
Paper/Materials
Esse Paper, 4 Color Tip-in
Printing
Silver PMS and 4 Color Process

GeoForm Products, LLC
3803 E. 75th Terrace
P.O. Box 320176
Kansas City, MO
64132

Cell: 816-916-6865

Phone: 816-333-6967

Fax: 816-333-6922

Email:
GBrattrud@geoformproducts.com

GEOFORM
PRODUCTS, LLC

Gale Brattrud
President

*Manufacturer of Ashton Bay
Bath & Lighting Accessories*

1

1
Design Firm
  Love Packaging Group
Art Director
  Chris West
Designer
  Lorna West
Illustrator
  Lorna West
Client
  Geoform Products, L.L.C.
Software/Hardware
  Freehand 8.0
Paper/Materials
  White Strathmore 80 lb.
Printing
  Litho Press

2
Design Firm
  Guidance Solutions
Art Director
  Rob Bynder
Designer
  Brad Benjamin
Client
  Self-promotion

guidance solutions

4134 Del Rey Avenue
Marina del Rey, CA 90292
310.754.4000
310.754.4010 fax
www.guidance.com

info@guidance.com

www.guidance.com

2

ANDRESEN

Ben Low

General Manager

T 415.421.2900
F 415.421.5842
P 415.560.2385

ben@planetandresen.com

1500 Sansome St. | Suite 100 | San Francisco | CA 94111 |
www.planetandresen.com

[service & beyond™]

1
Design Firm
be
Art Director
Will Burke
Designer
Eric Read
Client
Andresen
Printing
Andresen

2
Design Firm
Atelier Tadeusz Piechura
Art Director
Tadeusz Piechura
Designer
Tadeusz Piechura
Client
Self-promotion
Software/Hardware
Corel 7
Printing
Offset

2

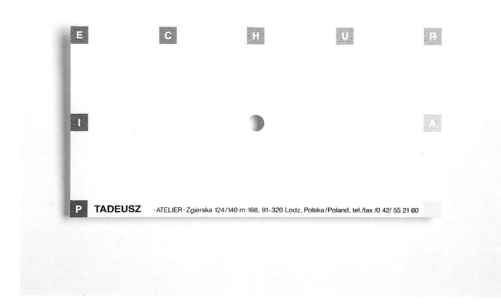

Oak Systems

Harold Shore

10201 Wayzata Boulevard
Suite 320
Minnetonka, MN 55305

Work (612) 542-8910
Fax (612) 595-8227
E-mail: hshore@OAKSYS.COM

DESIGN FIRM Design Center
ART DIRECTOR John Reger
DESIGNER Sherwin Schwartzrock
CLIENT Oak Systems
TOOLS Macintosh
PAPER/PRINTING Procraft Printing

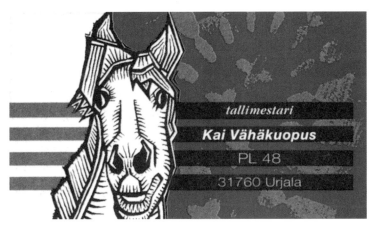

DESIGN FIRM M-DSIGN
ALL DESIGN Mika Ruusunen
CLIENT Kai Vähäkuopus
TOOLS Macintosh
PAPER/PRINTING Offset

DESIGN FIRM Design Ahead
DESIGNER Ralf Stumpf
CLIENT Ralf Stumpf
TOOLS Macromedia FreeHand, Macintosh

DESIGN FIRM LSL Industries
DESIGNER Elisabeth Spitalny
CLIENT JP Davis & Co.
TOOLS QuarkXPress
PAPER/PRINTING French Newsprint White

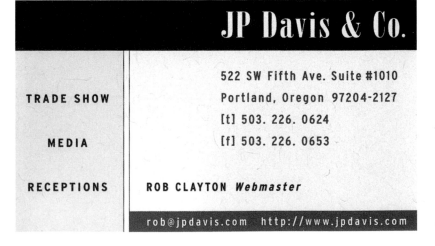

DESIGN FIRM Clark Design
ART DIRECTOR Annemarie Clark
DESIGNER Thurlow Washam
CLIENT Sauvage Marketing Group
TOOLS QuarkXPress
PAPER/PRINTING Strathmore Cover

DESIGN FIRM 9 Volt Visuals
ART DIRECTOR/DESIGN Bobby Jones
CLIENT 23 Skateboards
TOOLS Adobe Illustrator
PAPER/PRINTING Twin Concepts

DESIGN FIRM LSL Industries
DESIGNER Elisabeth Spitalny
CLIENT LSL Industries
TOOLS QuarkXPress, Adobe Photoshop
PAPER/PRINTING Encore 130 lb. gloss

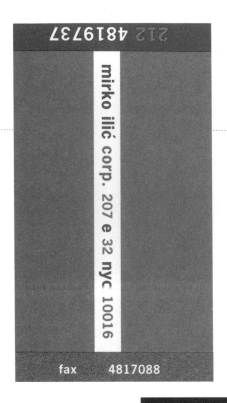

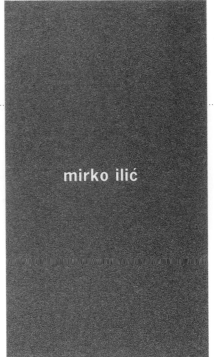

DESIGN FIRM
Mirko Ilić Corp.
ART DIRECTOR/DESIGNER
Nicky Lindeman
CLIENT
Mirko Ilić Corp.
TOOLS
QuarkXPress
PAPER/PRINTING
Cougar Smooth white 80 lb.
cover/Rob-Win Press

DESIGN FIRM
Di Luzio Diseño
ART DIRECTOR/DESIGNER
Hector Di Luzio
PAPER/PRINTING
Screen-printed

DESIGN FIRM Design Infinitum
ALL DESIGN James A. Smith
CLIENT French Quarter
TOOLS QuarkXPress, Adobe Illustrator

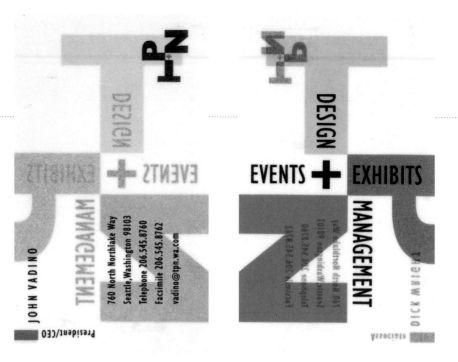

DESIGN FIRM Widmeyer Design
ART DIRECTORS Dale Hart, Tony Secolo
DESIGNER Tony Secolo
ILLUSTRATOR Misha Melikov
CLIENT The Production Network
TOOLS Power Macintosh,
Macromedia FreeHand
PAPER/PRINTING UV Ultra/Offset

DESIGN FIRM Amplifier Creative
DESIGNER/ILLUSTRATOR Jeff Fuson
CLIENT Amplifier Creative
TOOLS Adobe Photoshop
PAPER/PRINTING Four-color process

DESIGN FIRM Multimedia Asia
ART DIRECTOR G. Lee
ILLUSTRATOR J. E. Jesus
CLIENT Multimedia Asia
TOOLS PageMaker
PAPER/PRINTING Milkweed
Genesis 80 lb./Four-color process

Multimedia Asia Inc.
www.mmasia.com

USA	: PO Box 18416
	San Jose, CA
	95158
Tel/Fax	: (408) 264 7799
Asia	: PO Box 1345
	Ortigas Center
	Metro Manila
	PHILIPPINES 1653
Tel	: (63-2) 7160670
Fax	: (63-2) 7135182
Email	: glee@mmasia.com

Georgina Lee

DESIGN FIRM MA&A—Mário Aurélio & Associados
ART DIRECTOR Mário Aurélio
DESIGNERS Mário Aurélio, Rosa Maia
CLIENT Decopaço

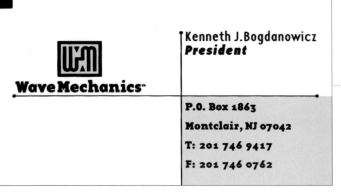

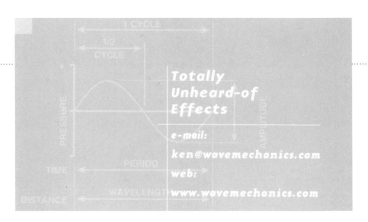

DESIGN FIRM Susan Guerra Design
ART DIRECTOR/DESIGNER Susan Guerra
CLIENT Wave Mechanics
TOOLS Adobe Illustrator
PAPER/PRINTING Classic Crest/Two color

DESIGN FIRM Sayles Graphic Design
ART DIRECTOR John Sayles
DESIGNERS John Sayles, Jennifer Elliott
CLIENT Consolidated Correctional Food Service
PAPER/PRINTING Graphika parchment gray riblaid/Offset

DESIGN FIRM Fire House, Inc.
ART DIRECTOR/DESIGNER Gregory R. Farmer
CLIENT Creatures of Habit
TOOLS QuarkXPress, Adobe Photoshop, Macintosh
PAPER/PRINTING Moore Laugen Printing Co.

DESIGN FIRM
Hieroglyphics Art & Design
DESIGNER/ILLUSTRATOR
Christine Osborn Tirotta
PHOTOGRAPHER
John Tirotta
CLIENT
Tirotta Photo Productions
PAPER/PRINTING
Starwhite Vicksburg UV Ultra II

DESIGN FIRM Jeff Fisher Logomotives
ALL DESIGN Jeff Fisher
CLIENT Barrett Rudich, Photographer
TOOLS Macromedia FreeHand
PAPER/PRINTING Fine Arts Graphics

DESIGN FIRM pw design graphics

ART DIRECTOR/DESIGNER Preston Wood

CLIENT pw design graphics

TOOLS Adobe Illustrator

PAPER/PRINTING Domtar Naturals Brick, Neenah Classic Columns Green

4557 46TH AVENUE N.E.
SEATTLE, WASHINGTON 98105

VOICE: 206.527.8286
FAX: 206.524.6641

CARY PILLO LASSEN
ILLUSTRATOR

4557 46TH AVENUE N.E.
SEATTLE, WASHINGTON 98105

VOICE: 206.527.8286
FAX: 206.524.6641

CARY PILLO LASSEN
ILLUSTRATOR

4557 46TH AVENUE N.E.
SEATTLE, WASHINGTON 98105

VOICE: 206.527.8286
FAX: 206.524.6641

CARY PILLO LASSEN
ILLUSTRATOR

4557 46TH AVENUE N.E.
SEATTLE, WASHINGTON 98105

VOICE: 206.527.8286
FAX: 206.524.6641

CARY PILLO LASSEN
ILLUSTRATOR

DESIGN FIRM
Belyea Design Alliance
ART DIRECTOR
Patricia Belyea
DESIGNER
Tim Ruszel
ILLUSTRATOR
Cary Pillo Lassen
CLIENT
Cary Pillo Lassen

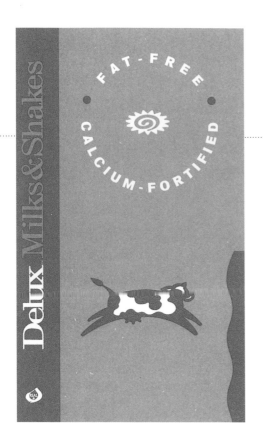

F. KENNITH NIXON

President

MENDENHALL LABORATORIES, LLC

1042 MINERAL WELLS AVE.

PARIS, TN 38242

TEL 901-642-9321

1-800-642-9321

FAX 901 644 2398

DESIGN FIRM
Greteman Group
ART DIRECTORS/DESIGNERS
Sonia Greteman, James Strange
CLIENT
Delux
TOOLS
Macromedia FreeHand
PAPER/PRINTING
Cougar white/Two-color offset

DESIGN FIRM On The Edge
ART DIRECTOR/ILLUSTRATOR Jeff Gasper
DESIGNER Gina Mims
CLIENT Five Seven Five
TOOLS Adobe Illustrator, QuarkXPress
PAPER/PRINTING Karma Natural

HAIKU/Hi-ku/n,:
An unrhymed poem or verse of three lines containing usually (but not necessarily) five, seven, and five syllables respectively.

Haiku was born in 17th century Japan. It was adopted by New York and San Francisco beat poets in the 50's with the publication of Kerouac's "Dharma Bums".

One writes a haiku to recreate an intimate moment and communicate the feelings it inspired to another.

DESIGN FIRM Bluestone Design
ART DIRECTOR Ian Gunningham
ILLUSTRATOR Symon Sweet
TOOLS Macintosh
PAPER/PRINTING Silkscreen on PVC, opaque varnish

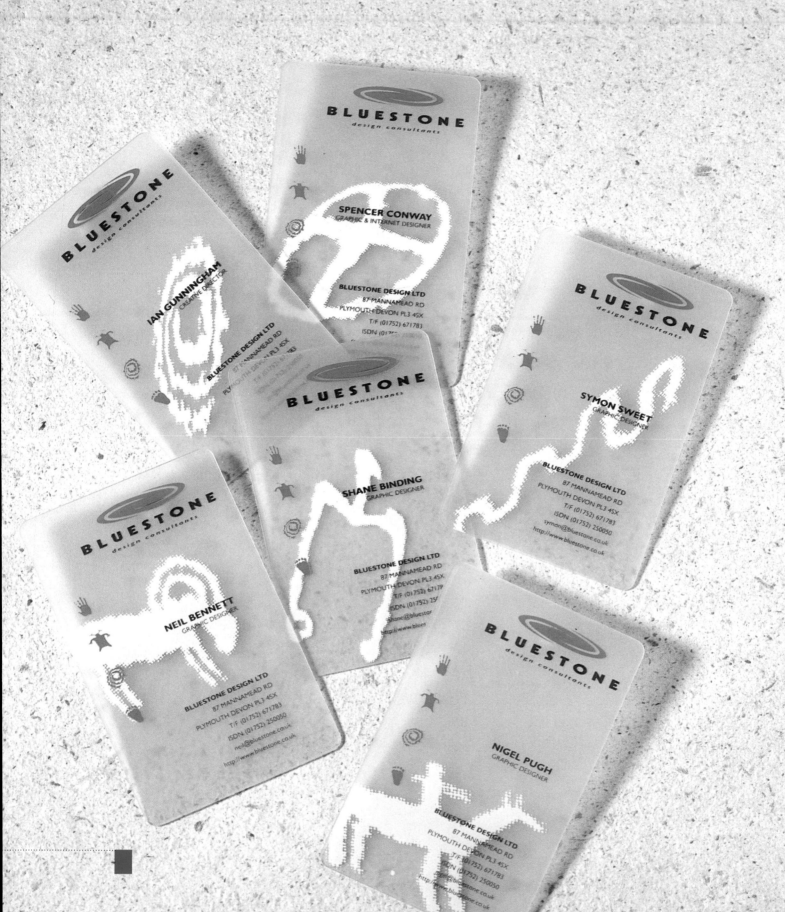

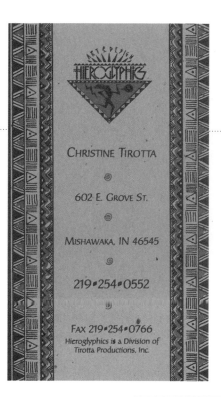

DESIGN FIRM
Hieroglyphics Art & Design
DESIGNER/ILLUSTRATOR
Christine Osborn Tirotta
CLIENT
Hieroglyphics Art & Design
PAPER/PRINTING
Fox River Confetti

DESIGN FIRM Elena Design
ALL DESIGN Elena Baca
CLIENT InterCity Services
TOOLS Adobe Illustrator,
QuarkXPress

InterCity Services

Cody Wilson

email

cewilson@icmall.com

tel

817.329.5275

fax

817.329.1189

mobile

817.946.5376

http://www.icmall.com/

1133 AIRLINE DRIVE B201 GRAPEVINE TEXAS 76051

DESIGN FIRM (ojo)^2
ALL DESIGN Ignacio Martinez-Villalba
CLIENT (ojo)^2
TOOLS Macintosh
PAPER/PRINTING Opaline/Offset

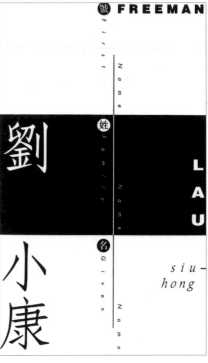

DESIGN FIRM
Kan & Lau Design Consultants
ART DIRECTOR/DESIGNER
Freeman Lau Siu Hong
CLIENT
Freeman Lau Siu Hong
PAPER/PRINTING
Conqueror Diamond White
250 gsm/Offset

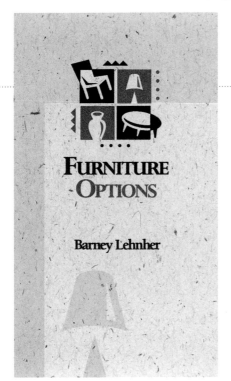

DESIGN FIRM
Greteman Group
ART DIRECTORS/DESIGNERS
Sonia Greteman, James Strange
ILLUSTRATORS
James Strange, Sonia Greteman
CLIENT
Furniture Options
PAPER/PRINTING
Speckletone/Offset

DESIGN FIRM Stephen Peringer Illustration
DESIGNER/ILLUSTRATOR Stephen Peringer
CLIENT Paul Mader/DreamWorks
TOOLS Adobe Photoshop, pen, ink
PAPER/PRINTING LaValle Printing

DESIGN FIRM LSL Industries

DESIGNER Franz M. Lee

CLIENT LSL Industries

TOOLS QuarkXPress, Adobe Photoshop

PAPER/PRINTING Encore 130 lb. gloss

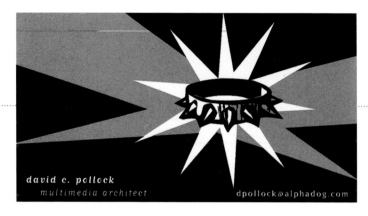

DESIGN FIRM Tanagram

ART DIRECTOR Lance Rutter

DESIGNER David Kaplan

CLIENT Alpha Dog

TOOLS Macromedia FreeHand,
Adobe Streamline

PAPER/PRINTING Strathmore Elements

DESIGN FIRM Mirko Ilić Corp.

ART DIRECTOR/DESIGNER Nicky Lindeman

CLIENT La Paella Restorante

TOOLS Adobe Illustrator

PAPER/PRINTING Cougar 80 lb. white smooth
cover/Rob-Win Press

DESIGN FIRM Sayles Graphic Design
ALL DESIGN John Sayles
CLIENT Timbuktuu Coffee Bar
PAPER/PRINTING Cross Pointe Genesis copper/Offset

DESIGN FIRM Sayles Graphic Design
ALL DESIGN John Sayles
CLIENT Des Moines Plumbing
PAPER/PRINTING Neenah Classic Crest gray/Offset

DESIGN FIRM Duck Soup Graphics
ART DIRECTOR/DESIGNER William Doucette
CLIENT Lemmerick Marketing
TOOLS Macromedia FreeHand, QuarkXPress
PAPER/PRINTING Classic Columns/
Two match colors

DESIGN FIRM Hornall Anderson Design Works, Inc.
ART DIRECTOR Jack Anderson
DESIGNERS Jack Anderson, Julie Keenan, Mary Chin Hutchinson
ILLUSTRATOR George Tanagi
CLIENT Rod Ralston Photography
TOOLS Macromedia FreeHand

DESIGN FIRM Gini Chin Graphics
ART DIRECTOR/DESIGNER Gini Chin
CLIENT 24.7 Marketing Bloc, Inc.
TOOLS Adobe Photoshop, QuarkXPress
PAPER/PRINTING Classic Crest

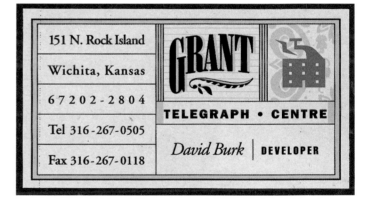

DESIGN FIRM Greteman Group
ART DIRECTORS/DESIGNERS Sonia Greteman, James Strange
CLIENT Grant Telegraph Centre
TOOLS Macromedia FreeHand
PAPER/PRINTING Genesis, Sticker/Three-color offset

DESIGN FIRM
Insight Design Communications
ART DIRECTORS/DESIGNERS
Sherrie Holdeman, Tracy Holdeman
CLIENT
Insight Design Communications
TOOLS
Power Macintosh 7500,
Macromedia FreeHand, Adobe Photoshop
PAPER/PRINTING
Dull Enamel Coat 65 lb. cover

christian tours

telephone 800 505 tour facsimile 601 685 9066

post office box 447 blue mountain, ms 38610

barry goolsby
cruise consultant

DESIGN FIRM David Carter Design
ART DIRECTOR Lori B. Wilson
DESIGNER/ILLUSTRATOR Tracy Huck
CLIENT Christian Tours

DESIGN FIRM Melissa Passehl Design
ART DIRECTOR Melissa Passehl
DESIGNERS Melissa Passehl,
Charlotte Lambrechts
CLIENT Leadership Connection

Opening the way to change

LEADERSHIP
CONNECTION

Barbara Moore
Individuals•Teams•Organizations

1225 Brace Avenue
San Jose•CA•95125
Email•Lead@Leaders4U•com
Phone•408•286•7399
Fax•408•286•4715

335
High   415
Street   321
Palo Alto 2246
CA 94301

DESIGN FIRM Sandy Gin Design
DESIGNER/ILLUSTRATOR Sandy Gin
CLIENT Sandy Gin Design
TOOLS Macromedia FreeHand
PAPER/PRINTING Simpson Evergreen
80 lb. cover/One-color offset

Amphora

distinctive
gifts for
distinguished
people.

Post Office Box 781234
Wichita, KS 67278-1234
316.634.6887

DESIGN FIRM Greteman Group
ART DIRECTOR/ILLUSTRATOR Sonia Greteman
DESIGNERS Sonia Greteman, Craig Tomison
CLIENT Amphora
TOOLS Macromedia FreeHand
PAPER/PRINTING Genesis Script/Two-color offset

DESIGN FIRM
Siebert Design Associates
ART DIRECTOR Lori Siebert
DESIGNERS Lori Siebert,
Lisa Ballard
CLIENT Scott Hull Associates
PAPER/PRINTING Starwhite
Vicksburg/Arnold Printing

DESIGN FIRM Insight Design Communications
ART DIRECTORS/DESIGNERS
Sherrie Holdeman, Tracy Holdeman
CLIENT Kendall McMinimy Photography
TOOLS Power Macintosh 7500,
Macromedia FreeHand
PAPER/PRINTING French Speckletone Straw

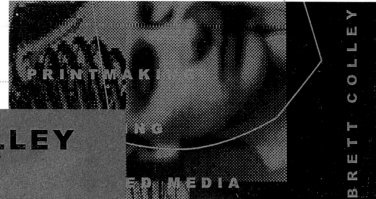

BRETT COLLEY

PRINTMAKING

PAINTING

MIXED MEDIA

Home Phone:
603/536-4143
email:
BCOLLEY@plymouth.edu

DESIGN FIRM Michelle Bowers
TOOLS Adobe Photoshop, Macromedia FreeHand

DESIGN FIRM
Icehouse Design
ART DIRECTOR
Pattie Belle Hastings
DESIGNER Bjorn Akselsen
CLIENT Graebel Fine Art
TOOLS Power Macintosh 8100

BJORN AKSELSEN

ICEHOUSE DESIGN

2009 PALIFOX DR NE

ATLANTA

G A 30307

P 404 373 5220

F 404 378 9880

HIGH OCTANE DESIGN
HIGH OCTANE DESIGN
www.commonlink.com\users\zanesroot\default.html
OCTANE DESIGN
OCTANE DESIGN

Angeline Beckley
DESIGNER

GASOLINE
GRAPHIC DESIGN

5701 College Avenue
DES MOINES, IOWA 50310
PH./FAX (515) 255-7095
GASGRAPHICS@COMMONLINK.COM

DESIGN FIRM Gasoline Graphic Design
ART DIRECTORS/DESIGNERS Zane Vredenburg, Angeline Beckley
TOOLS Adobe Illustrator, Adobe Streamline,
QuarkXPress, Adobe Photoshop
PAPER/PRINTING Neenah/Alpaca Christian Printers

WaterWorks

The Tavern

Summer House

The Oyster Bar

La Bodega

Eating Up The Coast, Inc.

Phil Cocco
Director of Operations

333 Victory Road, Marina Bay, Quincy, MA 02171
617-786-9600 • Fax 617-786-0700

DESIGN FIRM Flaherty Art & Design
ALL DESIGN Marie Flaherty
CLIENT Eating Up The Coast
TOOLS Adobe Illustrator

DESIGN FIRM Sagmeister, Inc.
ART DIRECTOR Stefan Sagmeister
DESIGNERS Veronica Oh, Stefan Sagmeister
PHOTOGRAPHER Michael Grimm
CLIENT Toto
PAPER/PRINTING Strathmore Writing 25% cotton

(F)343.5116 (T)206.343.7170 **DALE HART**

(F)343.5116 (T)206.343.7170 **KEN WIDMEYER**

(F)343.5116 (T)206.343.7170 **KEN WIDMEYER**

(F)343.5116 (T)206.343.7170 **ANTHONY SECOLO**

911 WESTERN #305 SEATTLE WA 98104 **WIDMEYERDESIGN**

DESIGN FIRM Widmeyer Design
ALL DESIGN Ken Widmeyer, Dale Hart, Tony Secolo
CLIENT Widmeyer Design
TOOLS Power Macintosh, Adobe Photoshop, Macromedia FreeHand
PAPER/PRINTING Stonehenge 100% cotton/Offset

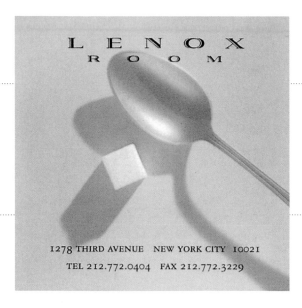

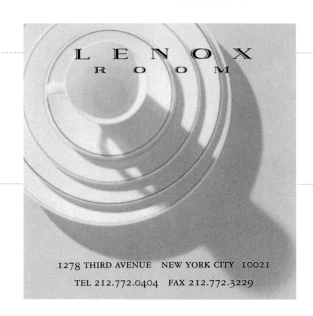

TIP WELL AND PROSPER

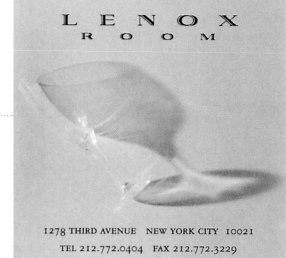

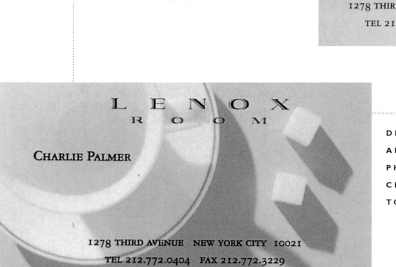

DESIGN FIRM Aerial
ART DIRECTOR/DESIGNER Tracy Moon
PHOTOGRAPHER R. J. Muna
CLIENT Lenox Room Restaurant
TOOLS Adobe Photoshop, QuarkXPress

DESIGN FIRM Flaherty Art & Design

ALL DESIGN Marie Flaherty

CLIENT Grafton Street

TOOLS Adobe Illustrator

DESIGN FIRM Sagmeister, Inc.

ALL DESIGN Stefan Sagmeister

CLIENT Frank's Disaster Art

PAPER/PRINTING Strathmore Writing 25% cotton

DESIGN FIRM Sandy Gin Design

DESIGNER/ILLUSTRATOR Sandy Gin

CLIENT Sandy Gin Design

TOOLS Macromedia FreeHand

PAPER/PRINTING Simpson Starwhite Vicksburg
110 lb. cover/Two-color offset

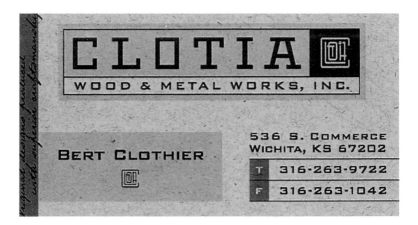

DESIGN FIRM Insight Design Communications

ART DIRECTORS/DESIGNERS Sherrie Holdeman, Tracy Holdeman

CLIENT Clotia

TOOLS Power Macintosh 7500, Macromedia FreeHand, Adobe Photoshop

PAPER/PRINTING French Speckletone Oatmeal 80 lb. cover

DESIGN FIRM Stowe Design
ART DIRECTOR/DESIGNER Jodie Stowe
CLIENT Whizdom
PAPER/PRINTING Aztec Printing

DESIGN FIRM
pw design graphics
ART DIRECTOR/DESIGNER
Preston Wood
CLIENT
Fathomworks Industries, Inc.
TOOLS
Adobe Illustrator
PAPER/PRINTING
Domtar Naturals Wicker Brick

DESIGN FIRM Sayles Graphic Design
ALL DESIGN John Sayles
CLIENT Lazarus Corporation
PAPER/PRINTING Curtis Tuscan Terra,
Pacific blue/Offset

DESIGN FIRM Katie Van Luchene & Associates
ART DIRECTOR Katie Van Luchene
DESIGNERS Katie Van Luchene, Jan Tracy
ILLUSTRATOR Jan Tracy
CLIENT Katie Van Luchene
TOOLS Macromedia FreeHand, QuarkXPress
PAPER/PRINTING Zellerbach 90 lb. Riblaid/
Black and spot color

GRIEF COUNSELING +

MASSAGE THERAPY

TEL 206.545.4266

ROOM NUMBER 340
GOOD SHEPHERD CTR.

4649 SUNNYSIDE AVE N.
SEATTLE, WA 98103

LANIE RILEY
M.S.W. - L.M.P.

LANIE RILEY
M.S.W. + L.M.P.

DESIGN FIRM Rick Eiber Design (RED)
ART DIRECTOR/DESIGNER Rick Eiber
CLIENT Lanie Riley
TOOLS Debossing Die
PAPER/PRINTING Two colors over one, watercolor crayon

Tarot Consultation

THE HIGH PRIESTESS

By Appointment Jeanie Maceri 408.462.4872

DESIGN FIRM Charney Design
ALL DESIGN Carol Inez Charney
CLIENT Jeanie Maceri
TOOLS QuarkXPress, Adobe Photoshop
PAPER/PRINTING Vintage/Offset

DESIGN FIRM Jill Morrison Design
ALL DESIGN Jill Morrison
CLIENT A Show of Hands
TOOLS Adobe Photoshop, Macromedia
FreeHand, QuarkXPress
PAPER/PRINTING Two color

A
SHOW
OF
HANDS

FULL SERVICE SALON

AMANI
owner/nail artist

408.371.8877

2160 S. Bascom Ave. Campbell, California
95008

DESIGN FIRM Prestige Design
ALL DESIGN Sarah Harris
CLIENT Creative Surfaces
TOOLS Adobe Illustrator, Adobe
Photoshop, QuarkXPress
PAPER/PRINTING Speckletone
Oatmeal/One PMS

APPLICATORS OF CONCRETE STAIN
SPECIALIZING IN UNIQUE DESIGNS

SARAH HARRIS
ARTIST

602 JOHNS DRIVE
EULESS, TX 76039
METRO 817.540.1560
FAX 817.540.1680
VM/PAGER 817.858.1510

CREATIVE SURFACES

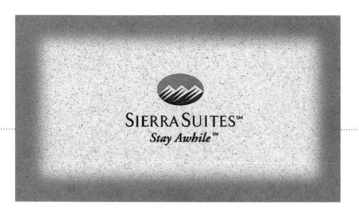

DESIGN FIRM Greteman Group
ART DIRECTOR Sonia Greteman
DESIGNERS Sonia Greteman, James Strange
CLIENT Sierra Suites
TOOLS Macromedia FreeHand
PAPER/PRINTING Passport/Two-color offset

Sierra Suites Hotel
2010 Powers Ferry Road
Atlanta, Georgia 30339
Tel 770-933-8010
Fax 770-933-8181
For Reservations
Tel 800-474-3772

Maura Dube
Assistant Manager

MAUREEN
bradshaw

Hard Drive Design Inc.
260 King Street East
Suite 204 B
Toronto Ontario
Canada M5A 4L5
T 416 363 9902
F 416 363 1705
e hddesign@istar.ca

DESIGN FIRM Hard Drive Design
ART DIRECTOR Maureen Bradshaw
DESIGNERS Eymard Angulo, Maureen Bradshaw
CLIENT Hard Drive Design
TOOLS QuarkXPress
PAPER/PRINTING Domtar Naturals
Jute 80 lb. cover

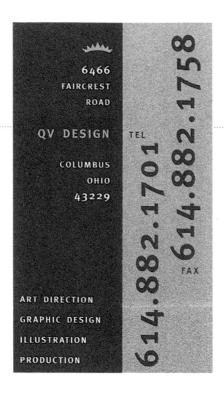

DESIGN FIRM
Angry Porcupine Design
DESIGNER/ILLUSTRATOR
Cheryl Roder-Quill
CLIENT
QV Design
TOOLS
Macintosh, QuarkXPress
PAPER/PRINTING
Strathmore Script/Two color

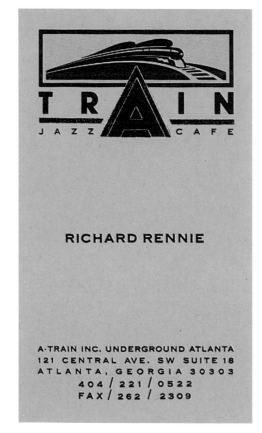

DESIGN FIRM Bartels & Company, Inc.
ART DIRECTOR David Bartels
DESIGNER/ILLUSTRATOR Brian Barclay
CLIENT A-Train Jazz Cafe
PAPER/PRINTING DeVere Printing

DESIGN FIRM Design Ahead
DESIGNER Ralf Stumpf
CLIENT Detlef Odenhausen
TOOLS Macromedia FreeHand, Macintosh

306 NORTH ROCK ROAD   WICHITA, KS 67206   TEL 316 881 0077   FAX 316 652 0240

SHAWNA

YOUR NEXT APPOINTMENT

This time is reserved exclusively for you. 24 hours notice is appreciated if you are unable to keep your appointment.

DESIGN FIRM Greteman Group
ART DIRECTOR/DESIGNER Sonia Greteman
CLIENT Eric Fisher Salon
TOOLS Macromedia FreeHand
PAPER/PRINTING Genesis/Two-color offset

DESIGN FIRM Design Ahead
DESIGNER Ralf Stumpf
CLIENT Fiction Factory
TOOLS Macromedia FreeHand, Macintosh

VOLKER STUMPF   MULTIMEDIA DESIGNER

Fon & Fax (49) 0208-42 87 41 · Hermannstraße 32 · 45479 Mülheim-Ruhr

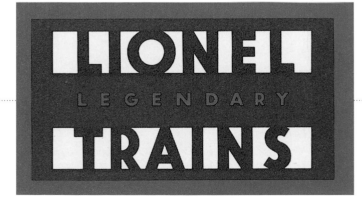

DESIGN FIRM Michael Stanard Design, Inc.
ART DIRECTOR Michael Stanard
DESIGNERS Marc C. Fuhrman, Kristy Vandekerckhove
CLIENT Lionel Trains
PAPER/PRINTING Strathmore Bright White/Engraved, offset

GARY L. MOREAU
PRESIDENT,
CHIEF EXECUTIVE OFFICER

THE LIONEL CORPORATION

50625 RICHARD W. BOULEVARD
CHESTERFIELD, MICHIGAN
48051-2493

TELEPHONE 810.949.4100
FACSIMILE 810.949.8721

Printed with vegetable based inks on 100% recycled paper

DESIGN FIRM Icehouse Design
ART DIRECTOR Pattie Belle Hastings
DESIGNER Bjorn Akselsen
ILLUSTRATOR Turner Broadcasting System inhouse
CLIENT TBS
TOOLS Power Macintosh 8100
PAPER/PRINTING Benefit Natural Flax

DESIGN FIRM Cahoots
ART DIRECTOR Carol Lasky
DESIGNER Erin Donnellan
ILLUSTRATORS Bill Mayers, Mark Allen
CLIENT Cahoots
TOOLS Adobe Illustrator, QuarkXPress
PAPER/PRINTING Strathmore Elements/The Ink Spot

Where Design and Marketing Fly

DESIGN FIRM Fordesign
ALL DESIGN Frank Ford
TOOLS Adobe Illustrator, Macromedia Fontographer, Macromedia FreeHand, Adobe Photoshop
PAPER/PRINTING Various papers/Aluminum printing plate

DESIGN FIRM Sayles Graphic Design

ALL DESIGN John Sayles

CLIENT Cutler Travel Marketing

PAPER/PRINTING Curtis Brightwater riblaid slate/Offset

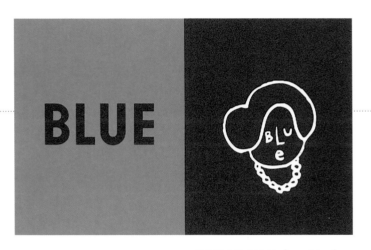

DESIGN FIRM Sagmeister, Inc.

ART DIRECTOR Stefan Sagmeister

DESIGNERS Stefan Sagmeister, Eric Zim

ILLUSTRATOR Stefan Sagmeister

CLIENT Blue Fashion Retail

PAPER/PRINTING Strathmore Writing 25% cotton

You spoke to:

Name

BLUE Clothing in Feldkirch:

Marktgasse 13, A-6800 Feldkirch, Austria

Please call us at: 05522 73 722-0

When abroad, dial: 43 5522 73 722-0

YES! We do speak German.

DESIGN FIRM Black Letter Design, Inc.

ART DIRECTOR/DESIGNER Ken Bessie

ILLUSTRATOR Rick Sealock

CLIENT Mad Dog Equities Group

TOOLS Adobe Illustrator, QuarkXPress

PAPER/PRINTING Expression Iceberg/Offset

DESIGN FIRM Gillis & Smiler
ART DIRECTORS/DESIGNERS Cheryl Gillis, Ellen Smiler
CLIENT Gillis & Smiler
TOOLS Adobe Illustrator
PAPER/PRINTING Neenah Classic Crest 3/1

DESIGN FIRM Icehouse Design
ART DIRECTOR Pattie Belle Hastings
DESIGNER Bjourn Akselsen
CLIENT Graebel Fine Art
TOOLS Power Macintosh 8100

HILDA G. LATORRE
Director of Marketing

Customized distribution for
the fragile and priceless

5105 Avalon Ridge Parkway

Norcross, Georgia 30071

Phone 404 263 6311

Toll Free 800 383 6311

Fax 404 242 1891

DESIGN FIRM Design Ahead
DESIGNER Ralf Stumpf
CLIENT Digital Audio Design
TOOLS Macromedia FreeHand, Macintosh

Re-Inventing
the Laws
of Quality

CORPORATE
COMMUNICATION & PRINT
PROJECT MANAGEMENT

$$PP = MG^{2}$$

PRINTELLIGENT
PEOPLE

Garry Furzer

SUITE ONE, 20
COMMERCIAL RD
MELBOURNE 3004
PH: 03) 9866 4966
FAX: 03) 9866 4164
MOBILE 018 352 827

DESIGN FIRM Storm Design & Advertising Consultancy
ART DIRECTORS/DESIGNERS Dean Butler, David Ansett
ILLUSTRATOR Dean Butler
CLIENT Printelligent People
TOOLS Adobe Photoshop
PAPER/PRINTING Three PMS colors, Saxton Smoothe, special varnish/Embossed

DESIGN FIRM Design Ahead
DESIGNER Theo Decker
CLIENT Frank Buchheister
TOOLS Macromedia FreeHand, Macintosh

DESIGN FIRM Kiku Obata & Company
ART DIRECTOR Pam Bliss
DESIGNER John Schetel
CLIENT Plaza Frontenac
PAPER/PRINTING Reprox

DESIGN FIRM Gackle Anderson Henningsen, Inc.
DESIGNER Jason Bramer
CLIENT Gackle Anderson Henningsen, Inc.
TOOLS QuarkXPress, Adobe Illustrator

655 Fort Street
Victoria BC
v8w 1g6

PH 250.382.8838
FX 250.382.8878

Michael
Burr, CCIM
PRESIDENT

burr
PROPERTIES
LTD

DESIGN FIRM Suburbia Studios
ART DIRECTOR Russ Williams
DESIGNER/ILLUSTRATOR Jeremie White
CLIENT Burr Properties Ltd.
TOOLS Adobe Illustrator, QuarkXPress
PAPER/PRINTING Classic Columns/Two
color one side, one color one side

A P E X
352 - 8888
PERSONAL TRAINERS

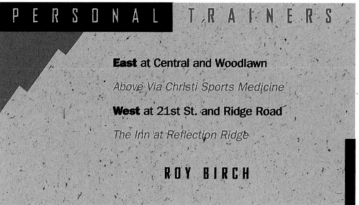

PERSONAL TRAINERS

East at Central and Woodlawn
Above Via Christi Sports Medicine
West at 21st St. and Ridge Road
The Inn at Reflection Ridge

ROY BIRCH

DESIGN FIRM Greteman Group
ART DIRECTOR Sonia Greteman
DESIGNERS Sonia Greteman, James Strange
CLIENT Apex
TOOLS Macromedia FreeHand
PAPER/PRINTING Genesis/Two-color offset

DESIGN FIRM Bruce Yelaska Design
ART DIRECTOR/DESIGNER Bruce Yelaska
CLIENT La Rotonda sul Mare
TOOLS Adobe Illustrator
PAPER/PRINTING Strathmore Writing/Offset

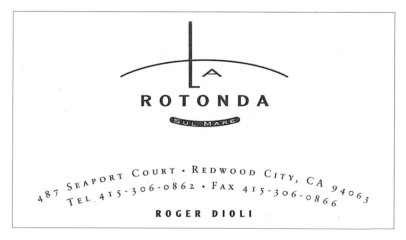

LA
ROTONDA
SUL MARE

487 SEAPORT COURT · REDWOOD CITY, CA 94063
TEL 415-306-0862 · FAX 415-306-0866
ROGER DIOLI

DESIGN FIRM
Mason Charles Design
ART DIRECTOR/DESIGNER
Jeffrey Speiser
CLIENT
Mason Charles Design
TOOLS
QuarkXPress,
Adobe Illustrator
PAPER/PRINTING
Neenah Classic Columns Duplex
cover flat/Foil

DESIGN FIRM
Foco Media Digital Media Design &
Production GmbH. & Cie.
ART DIRECTOR/DESIGNER
Steffen Janus
CLIENT
Foco Media Digital Media Design &
Production GmbH. & Cie.
TOOLS
Adobe Photoshop, QuarkXPress
PAPER/PRINTING
Luxosatin 300gsm; Two-color offset

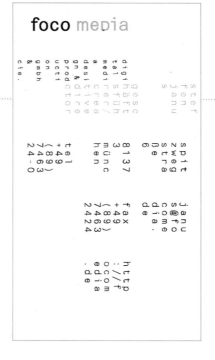

DESIGN FIRM Tanagram
DESIGNER/ILLUSTRATOR Anthony Ma
CLIENT Lankmar Corp.
TOOLS Macromedia FreeHand

DESIGN FIRM
Val Gene Associates
DESIGNER Lacy Leverett
PRODUCTION Morrow Design
CLIENT Restaurant Concepts & Design
PAPER/PRINTING Baker's Printing

R. Fairchild

66 I got it at a yard sale. 99

66 I'd like 10 of those. 99

66 Where did
you get that –
it's *wuuunderful.* 99

66 I didn't buy it...
hell, I made it! 99

66 Nail it. Nail it. Nail it. 99

66 Don't ask me where
we're going,
you'll irritate me –
no maps,
no interstates,
no itinerary.
Just Drive. 99

**Restaurant
Concepts & Design**
Renovation,
Creation,
Decoration

66 *I'm back.* 99

Richard Fairchild
Consulting,
Construction,
Design and
Professional Junking

✗ We are here:
Tel: 405/843/9474   Fax: 405/842/5063
Mob: 641/5321   Pag: 800/636/8914
5208 Classen Blvd. Oklahoma City, OK 73118

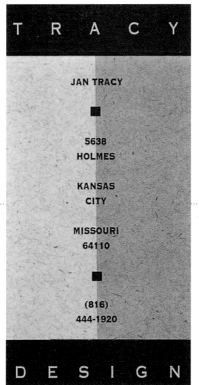

T R A C Y

JAN TRACY

■

**5638
HOLMES**

**KANSAS
CITY**

**MISSOURI
64110**

■

**(816)
444-1920**

D E S I G N

DESIGN FIRM Tracy Design
ART DIRECTOR Jan Tracy
DESIGNERS Jan Tracy, Jason Lilly
CLIENT Tracy Design
PAPER/PRINTING Black on Duplex "Environment"

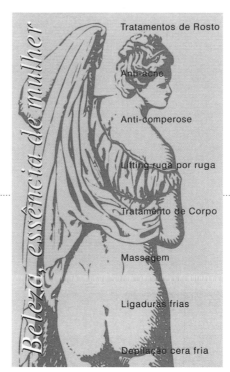

DESIGN FIRM
MA&A—Mário Aurélio & Associados
ART DIRECTOR Mário Aurélio
DESIGNERS Mário Aurélio, Rosa Maia
CLIENT Celeste Nunes/Gabinete
de Etética

DESIGN FIRM Barbara Brown Marketing & Design
CREATIVE DIRECTOR/DESIGNER Barbara Brown
ILLUSTRATOR Darthe Silver (digital design)
CLIENT Regional Management Inc.

DESIGN FIRM Elena Design
ART DIRECTOR/DESIGNER Elena Baca
CLIENT Wendy Thomas
TOOLS QuarkXPress, Adobe Photoshop
PAPER/PRINTING French Speckeltone

DESIGN FIRM Shields Design
ART DIRECTOR/DESIGNER Charles Shields
CLIENT Phil Rudy Photography
TOOLS Adobe Illustrator, Adobe Photoshop
PAPER/PRINTING Strathmore Elements
Soft White Dots/Offset

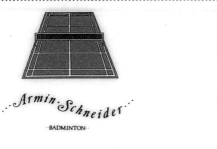

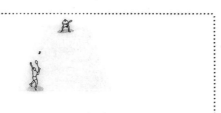

DESIGN FIRM Sagmeister, Inc.
ALL DESIGN Stefan Sagmeister
CLIENT Armin Schneider
PAPER/PRINTING Strathmore Writing 25% cotton

DESIGN FIRM
Borchew Design Group, Inc.
ART DIRECTOR/DESIGNER
Anne Bahan
CLIENT
Earl Schneider, DDS
TOOLS
QuarkXPress, Adobe Photoshop
PAPER/PRINTING
Neenah Classic Columns

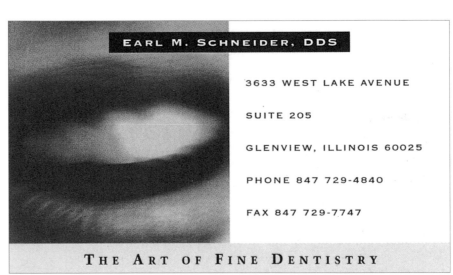

DESIGN FIRM Gardiner & Nobody, Inc.
ART DIRECTOR/DESIGNER Diana Gardiner
CLIENT Gardiner & Nobody, Inc.
TOOLS QuarkXPress, Adobe Illustrator
PAPER/PRINTING Strathmore Writing

5709 HICKMAN ROAD
DES MOINES, IOWA 50310
|||||||| 515-277-1709 ||||||||

YOUR APPOINTMENT IS:

DESIGN FIRM Sayles Graphic Design
ALL DESIGN John Sayles
CLIENT Martin Crowder Hair Salon
PAPER/PRINTING Springhill tag coated one side/Offset

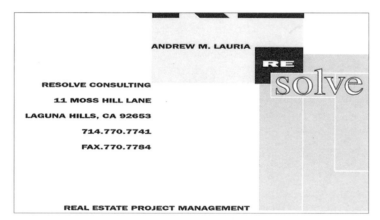

DESIGN FIRM Vrontikis Design Office
ART DIRECTOR Petrula Vrontikis
DESIGNER Kim Sage
CLIENT Resolve Consulting
PAPER/PRINTING Neenah Classic Crest

DESIGN FIRM Vrontikis Design Office
ART DIRECTOR Petrula Vrontikis
DESIGNER Samuel Lising
CLIENT Greenhold and Company
PAPER/PRINTING Duratone/rubber stamp
and laser printing

DESIGN FIRM Design Ahead
DESIGNER Ralf Stumpf
CLIENT Fritzen & Partner
TOOLS Macromedia FreeHand, Macintosh

DESIGN FIRM MA&A—Mário Aurélio & Associados
ART DIRECTOR Mário Aurélio
DESIGNERS Mário Aurélio, Rosa Maia
CLIENT Rui Soares Esteves/Fotografia

DESIGN FIRM Mires Design
ART DIRECTOR John Ball
DESIGNERS John Ball, Miguel Perez
CLIENT Verde Communications

6170 Cornerstone Court East, Suite 380 San Diego, CA 92121
ph: 619 622 1411 fx: 619 622 1214 e-mail: csimunec@verdestyle.com
http://www.verdestyle.com

Cindy Simunec
Vice President, Sales and Marketing

DESIGN FIRM Mires Design
ART DIRECTOR John Ball
DESIGNERS John Ball, Miguel Perez
CLIENT Mires Design
PAPER/PRINTING Gilbert Correspond
heavy watercolor board

MIRES DESIGN INC

2345 KETTNER BLVD SAN DIEGO CA 92101

PHONE: 619 234 6631 FAX: 619 234 1807

E MAIL: MIRES@MIRESDESIGN.COM

SCOTT MIRES

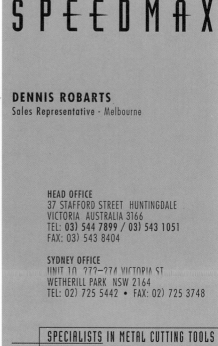

DESIGN FIRM
Mammoliti Chan Design
ART DIRECTOR/DESIGNER
Tony Mammoliti
CLIENT Speeedmax
TOOLS Adobe Illustrator, QuarkXPress
PAPER/PRINTING Four-color plus
two PMS reverse

DESIGN FIRM Greteman Group
ART DIRECTOR Sonia Greteman
DESIGNERS Sonia Greteman, James Strange
CLIENT Greteman Group
TOOLS Macromedia FreeHand
PAPER/PRINTING Conquest/Two-color offset

DESIGN FIRM Nancy Yeasting Design & Illustration
ALL DESIGN Nancy Yeasting
CLIENT Zoey Ryan
TOOLS Brush, QuarkXPress
PAPER/PRINTING Genesis husk/One color

DESIGN FIRM
The Design Company
ART DIRECTOR
Marcia Romanuck
DESIGNER/ILLUSTRATOR
Alison Scheel
CLIENT
Snelling Real Estate
PAPER/PRINTING
Champion Carnival 80 lb. Ivory

DESIGN FIRM Cahoots
ART DIRECTOR Carol Lasky
DESIGNERS Kerri Bennett, Laura Herrmann
ILLUSTRATOR Richard Goldberg
CLIENT Sandra Kimball Photography
TOOLS Macromedia FreeHand, QuarkXPress
PAPER/PRINTING Curtis Brightwater

DESIGN FIRM Sagmeister, Inc.
ART DIRECTOR/DESIGNER
Stefan Sagmeister
ILLUSTRATOR Veronica Oh
CLIENT Aguilar
PAPER/PRINTING Strathmore
Writing 25% cotton

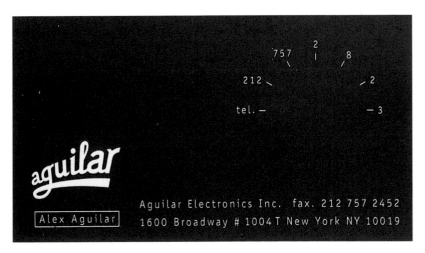

29140 Buckingham Ave. Suite 5

Livonia, MI 48154

313 261-2001

Fax: 313 261-3282

email: epicnode@aol.com

12330 Conway Road

St. Louis, MO 63141

314 205-2266

Fax: 314 205-2540

National Outreach

Corbett Heimburger

National Outreach Director

Evangelical Presbyterian Church

DESIGN FIRM Jacque Consulting & Design
DESIGNER/ILLUSTRATOR Janelle Sayegh
CLIENT Evangelical Presbyterian Church
TOOLS Adobe FreeHand
PAPER/PRINTING Neenah Classic Crest

DESIGN FIRM 9 Volt Visuals
ART DIRECTOR/DESIGNER Bobby June
CLIENT 9 Volt Visuals
TOOLS Adobe Photoshop, Adobe Illustrator
PAPER/PRINTING Twin Concepts

DESIGN FIRM Elena Design
ART DIRECTOR/DESIGNER Elena Baca
CLIENT Wendy Thomas
TOOLS Adobe Photoshop, QuarkXPress
PAPER/PRINTING French Speckeltone

DESIGN FIRM Duck Soup Graphics
ART DIRECTOR/DESIGNER William Doucette
CLIENT Sunbaked Software
TOOLS Macromedia FreeHand, QuarkXPress
PAPER/PRINTING Circa select/
Two match colors, blowtorch

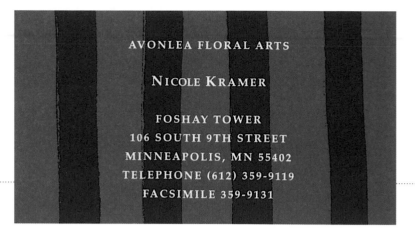

AVONLEA FLORAL ARTS

NICOLE KRAMER

FOSHAY TOWER
106 SOUTH 9TH STREET
MINNEAPOLIS, MN 55402
TELEPHONE (612) 359-9119
FACSIMILE 359-9131

DESIGN FIRM Design Center
ART DIRECTOR John Reger
DESIGNER Sherwin Schwartzrock
CLIENT AvonLea
TOOLS Macintosh
PAPER/PRINTING Procraft Printing

DESIGN FIRM Mother Graphic Design
ALL DESIGN Kristin Thieme
CLIENT Art House

ALI YELDHAM

ART HOUSE

64 Elizabeth Street Paddington 2021
New South Wales Australia
Tel 61 2 328 7587 Fax 61 2 328 7901

JIMMY DAAN DWINGER
Keizersgracht 798
1017 ED Amsterdam
Telefoon 020 - 624 64 59
Gelieve op aanvraag te tonen

NED. SPEC. DRUKK. DELI

081471

Jimmy Daan Dwinger Telefoon 020 - 624 64 59

081471

0704

DESIGN FIRM Moos Design
ALL DESIGN Moos Kuppers
CLIENT Dennis Dwinger
TOOLS Macintosh, numbering by printer

ZARA GINA DWINGER
Keizersgracht 798
1017 ED Amsterdam
Telefoon 020 - 624 64 59
Gelieve op aanvraag te tonen

NED. SPEC. DRUK

Zara Gina Dwinger Telefoon 020 - 624 64 59

070468

Craig Webster

PO Box 344
Deer Harbor, WA 98243
Fax (360) 376-6091
Tel (360) 376-3037
VHF Channel 78

DESIGN FIRM Widmeyer Design
ART DIRECTORS Ken Widmeyer, Dale Hart
DESIGNER/ILLUSTRATOR Dale Hart
CLIENT Deer Harbor Marina
TOOLS Power Macintosh, Macromedia FreeHand, Adobe Photoshop
PAPER/PRINTING Proterra Flecks/Offset

DESIGN FIRM Blue Suede Studios
ALL DESIGN Justin Baker
CLIENT Waisman Photography
PAPER/PRINTING Genesis/Hemlock Express

DESIGN FIRM Tharp Did It
ART DIRECTOR Rick Tharp
DESIGNERS Rick Tharp, Jana Heer
ILLUSTRATOR Georgia Deaver
CLIENT Yorkville Cellars
TOOLS Ink, traditional typography
PAPER/PRINTING Simpson Paper Company/Simon Printing

DESIGN FIRM Corridor Design
ART DIRECTOR/DESIGNER Ejaz Saifullah
CLIENT Corridor Design
TOOLS Adobe Illustrator, QuarkXPress
PAPER/PRINTING French construction, pure white/Rooney Printing Co.

CORRIDOR DESIGN

EJAZ SAIFULLAH   **ART DIRECTOR**

STRANDWARE BUILDING
1529 CONTINENTAL DR
EAU CLAIRE   WI 54701

PHO   715 | 832 | 6666
FAX   715 | 832 | 4550
EML   ejaz@corridor-design.com
URL   www.corridor-design.com

DESIGN FIRM Imagine That, Inc.

ART DIRECTOR/DESIGNER Sue Manian

CLIENT Sue Manian Graphic Design

TOOLS Adobe Illustrator

PAPER/PRINTING Classic Crest/Clark's Litho

DESIGN FIRM Ameer Design

ART DIRECTOR/DESIGNER Janet Ameer

CLIENT Ameer Design

A

AMEER DESIGN 16 KEYES ROAD LONDON NW2 3XA

TELEPHONE AND FAX 0181 450 0464 **JANET AMEER**

apple graphics
& advertising, inc.

ALLISON SCHNEIDER

2314 merrick road

merrick, ny 11566

tel.: 516. 868. 1919

fax: 516. 868. 1982

apple graphics & advertising, inc.

DESIGN FIRM Apple Graphics & Advertising of Merrick, Inc.

DESIGNER Allison Blair Schneider

ILLUSTRATOR Michael Perez

CLIENT Apple Graphics

TOOLS Macromedia FreeHand, QuarkXPress,
Power Macintosh 7500

PAPER/PRINTING Fox River Circa Select Moss/Foil, offset

BRUTON|STROUBE

38 NORTH VANDEVENTER

SAINT LOUIS, MO 63108

314

FAX 533.806

5999EES

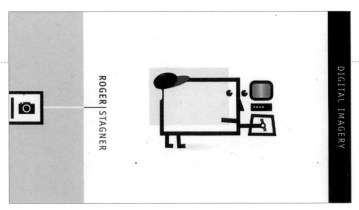

ROGER|STAGNER

DIGITAL IMAGERY

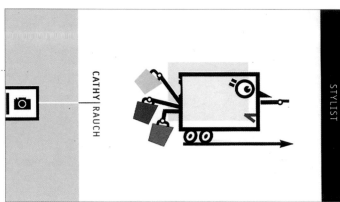

CATHY|RAUCH

STYLIST

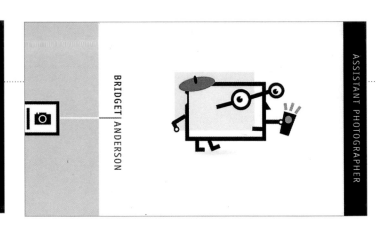

BRIDGET|ANDERSON

ASSISTANT PHOTOGRAPHER

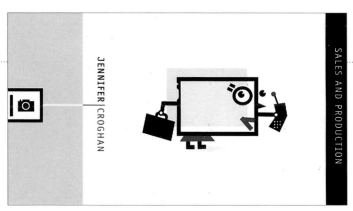

JENNIFER|CROGHAN

SALES AND PRODUCTION

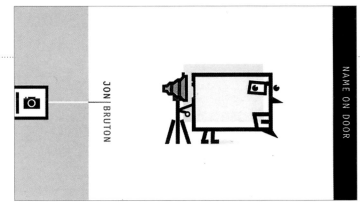

JON|BRUTON

NAME ON DOOR

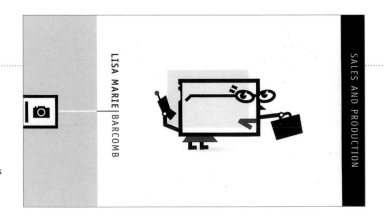

LISA MARIE|BARCOMB

SALES AND PRODUCTION

DESIGN FIRM Phoenix Creative
ART DIRECTOR/DESIGNER Eric Thoelke
ILLUSTRATORS Eric Thoelke, Kathy Wilkinson
CLIENT Bruton/Stroube Studios
TOOLS QuarkXPress
PAPER/PRINTING Strathmore/Six PMS, two sides

Jason Vaughn
806.762.3726 Studio
806.762.3885 Fax
800.846.6263 Toll free
dwstudio@dwstudio.com
www.dwstudio.com

Concept Development ▪ Printing
Advertising ▪ Graphic Design ▪ Marketing

AN AFFILIATE OF MY DESTINY INC.
2201 University, Lubbock, Texas 79410

RESTAURANT DESIGN
INTERIOR DESIGN
CONCEPT DEVELOPMENT
GRAPHIC DESIGN
MARKETING / ADVERTISING
TELEVISION / RADIO
COPYRIGHTING
BILLBOARD ADVERTISING
APPAREL DESIGN
FUND RAISING
PROMOTIONAL PRODUCTS
CHRISTIAN APPAREL
LOGO CREATION
TRADEMARKING
ANIMATION
WEB PAGE DESIGN
TRADITIONAL PAINTING
MURAL DESIGN
FULL COLOR PRINTING
SCREEN PRINTING
LARGE FORMAT PRINTING
DIGITAL PRINTING
PHOTO COPY
CD • JCARD DESIGN
PHONE BOOK AD DESIGN
SIGN PAINTING
BUMPER STICKERS
SCANNING
PHOTOGRAPHY
PHOTO RETOUCHING
COMPUTER TRAINING
MINOR COMPUTER REPAIR
AND SO MUCH MORE!

1.800.846.6263
2201 UNIVERSITY, LUBBOCK, TEXAS 79410

DESIGN FIRM Designworks Studio, Ltd.
ALL DESIGN Jason Vaughn
CLIENT Designworks Studio, Ltd.
TOOLS Adobe Photoshop, Adobe Illustrator,
Adobe Dimensions
PAPER/PRINTING 10 pt. gloss/Four color

KEES-KIEREN
W E I N G U T

Ernst-Josef Kees   Verkauf & Kellerei

Hauptstraße 22   Tel 0 65 31-34 28
54470 Graach   Fax 0 65 31-15 93

HESED BIOMED

Larry J. Smith, Ph.D.

7824 Jackson Street
Omaha, Nebraska 68114
TEL | 402-398-0230
FAX | 402-398-0455
E-mail | hesedbio@ne.uswest.net

DESIGN FIRM
Nagorny Design
ALL DESIGN
Andrey Nagorny
CLIENT
Hesed Biomed
TOOLS
Macromedia FreeHand
PAPER/PRINTING
Neenah Classic Laid/Two-color

DESIGN FIRM Geffert Design
DESIGNER/ILLUSTRATOR Gerald Geffert
CLIENT Kees-Kieren/Weingut

Richard Kehl

DESIGN FIRM Rick Eiber Design (RED)
ART DIRECTOR/DESIGNER Rick Eiber
CLIENT Sam A. Angeloff
TOOLS Macintosh
PAPER/PRINTING Cougar/Four-color process over black

DESIGN FIRM Lynn Wood Design
ART DIRECTOR/DESIGNER Lynn Wood
CLIENT Floyd Johnson
TOOLS QuarkXPress, Adobe Illustrator
PAPER/PRINTING Benefit

DESIGN FIRM 9 Volt Visuals
ART DIRECTOR/DESIGNER Bobby June
CLIENT 23 Skateboards
TOOLS Adobe Illustrator
PAPER/PRINTING Twin Concepts

DESIGN FIRM David Carter Design
ART DIRECTORS Sharon LeJeune, Randall Hill
DESIGNER Sharon LeJeune
ILLUSTRATOR Tracy Huck
CLIENT Dani, Kent Rathbun

Mazy Asky
assistant restaurant manager

• • •

telephone 214.922.1260   pager 214.848.0005
facsimile 214.922.1381   www.dani1717.com
dallas museum of art • seventeen seventeen restaurant
1717 n. harwood street   dallas, texas 75201

SEVENTEEN SEVENTEEN
RESTAURANT

world class cuisine

DESIGN FIRM Judy Kahn
DESIGNER Judy Kahn
CLIENT Judy Kahn
TOOLS Adobe Illustrator
PAPER/PRINTING Champion Benefit
Vertical 80 lb. cover/Cactus

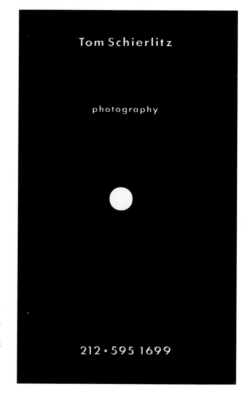

DESIGN FIRM Sagmeister, Inc.
ALL DESIGN Stefan Sagmeister
CLIENT Tom Schierlitz
PAPER/PRINTING Strathmore Writing 25% cotton

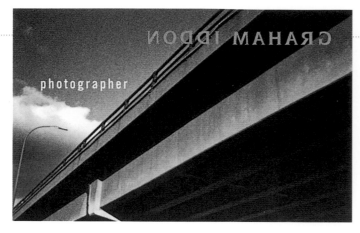

DESIGN FIRM Teikna

ART DIRECTOR/DESIGNER Claudia Neri

PHOTOGRAPHER Graham Iddon

CLIENT Graham Iddon

TOOLS QuarkXPress

PAPER/PRINTING Strathmore Elements/Two color

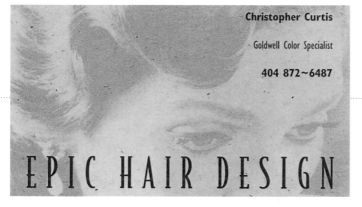

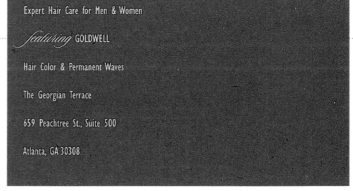

DESIGN FIRM The Design Company

ART DIRECTOR Marcia Romanuck

CLIENT Epic Hair Design

PAPER/PRINTING Fraser Genesis Dawn 80 lb. cover

DESIGN FIRM Communication Arts Company

ART DIRECTOR/DESIGNER Mary Kitchens

ILLUSTRATOR Cathy Kitchens

CLIENT Creations by Cathy

TOOLS Calligraphy, pen, ink, Macintosh

PAPER/PRINTING Offset lithography

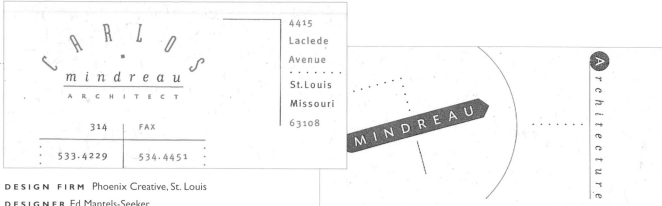

DESIGN FIRM Phoenix Creative, St. Louis
DESIGNER Ed Mantels-Seeker
CLIENT Carlos Mindreau, Architect
TOOLS Adobe Illustrator
PAPER/PRINTING Two-color litho

Duane Wood

WDG COMMUNICATIONS

3011 Johnson Avenue NW • Cedar Rapids, Iowa 52405
Telephone 319.396.1401 • Facsimile 319.396.1647

DESIGN FIRM WDG Communications
ALL DESIGN Duane Wood
CLIENT WDG Communications
TOOLS Pencil, paper, Adobe Illustrator, QuarkXPress
PAPER/PRINTING Neenah Classic Crest
Sawgrass 80 lb. cover/Cedar Graphics

stubblefield

PROPERTIES, INC.

Fee Stubblefield

JOHN'S LANDING WATER TOWER
5331 SW MACADAM AVE • SUITE 260 • PORTLAND, OR 97201
TELE: 503-827-3366 • FAX: 503-827-3466

DESIGN FIRM Oakley Design Studios
ART DIRECTOR/DESIGNER Tim Oakley
CLIENT Stubblefield Properties
TOOLS QuarkXPress
PAPER/PRINTING Proterra flecks/Two color

Hand thrown earthwares in the fine Berea Crafts tradition.

**Tater Knob
Pottery & Farm
Jeff Enge
Sarah Culbreth**

260 Wolf Gap Road
Berea, Kentucky 40403
(606) 986 2167

DESIGN FIRM
Kirby Stephens Design, Inc.
ART DIRECTOR Kirby Stephens
DESIGNER/ILLUSTRATOR William V. Cox
CLIENT Tater Knob Pottery & Farm
TOOLS Pencil, Macintosh PPC, Camera, Adobe
Photoshop, Macromedia FreeHand
PAPER/PRINTING Environment Recycled

OBJECT ENTERPRISES INCORPORATED

Jesse Tayler

OBJECT ENTERPRISES INCORPORATED
2608 2nd Avenue Suite 119
Seattle, WA 98121-1276 USA

Tel 206.217.0891
Fax 206.217.0394
Cel 206.954.3284

Jesse.Tayler@OEinc.com
www.oeinc.com

DESIGN FIRM Widmeyer Design
ART DIRECTORS Ken Widmeyer, Christopher Downs
DESIGNER Christopher Downs
ILLUSTRATOR Misha Melikov
CLIENT Object Enterprises, Inc.
TOOLS Power Macintosh, Adobe Photoshop, QuarkXPress
PAPER/PRINTING Mead Signature Satin/Four-color offset

DESIGN FIRM Melissa Passehl Design
ART DIRECTOR Melissa Passehl
DESIGNERS Melissa Passehl, Jill Steinfeld
CLIENT Alka Joshi Marketing

**ALKA JOSHI
MARKETING**

....

Building Brands

Through Creative

Marketing

128 Middlefield Road, Palo Alto, CA 94301
Vox 415.326.7130 **Fax** 415.326.7044

Centris, LLC

10900 NE 4th Street

Suite 2300

Bellevue, Washington 98004

Tel 206.635.7700

Fax 206.635.7799

Email sharip@centris.net

DESIGN FIRM Widmeyer Design
ART DIRECTORS Ken Widmeyer, Dale Hart
DESIGNER Dale Hart
CLIENT Centris
TOOLS Power Macintosh, Macromedia FreeHand
PAPER/PRINTING Environment/Three-color offset

DESIGN FIRM Susan Guerra
ART DIRECTOR/DESIGNER Susan Guerra
CLIENT Robert Guerra
TOOLS Adobe Photoshop, Adobe Illustrator
PAPER/PRINTING One-color offset

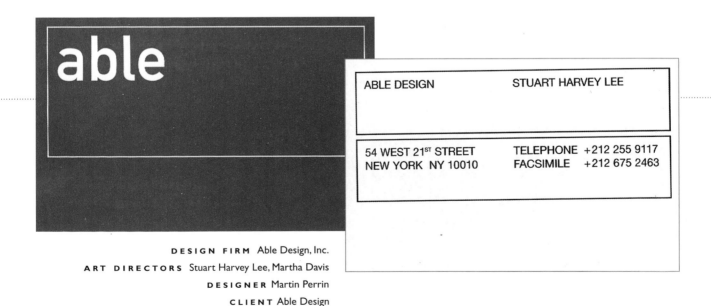

DESIGN FIRM Able Design, Inc.
ART DIRECTORS Stuart Harvey Lee, Martha Davis
DESIGNER Martin Perrin
CLIENT Able Design
TOOLS Power Macintosh, QuarkXPress
PAPER/PRINTING Ikonofix 80 lb./Two-color printing, matte varnish

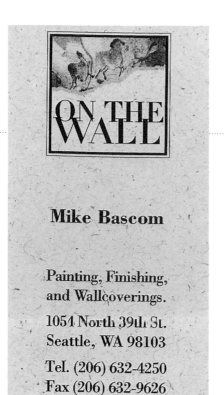
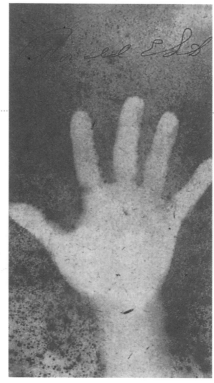

DESIGN FIRM
Rick Eiber Design (RED)
ART DIRECTOR/DESIGNER
Rick Eiber
ILLUSTRATORS
Cave Dweler, Gary Vock
CLIENT
On The Wall
PAPER/PRINTING
Speckletone/Two color

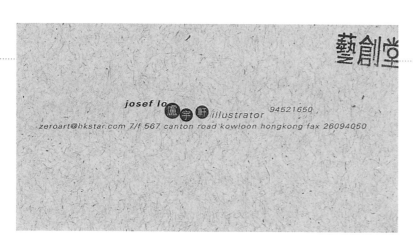

DESIGN FIRM Zeroart Studio
ART DIRECTORS/DESIGNERS Lo Yu Hin, Josef
TOOLS Apple computer, Adobe Illustrator
PAPER/PRINTING 216 gsm recycled paper/Two spot colors
plus black, ink stamp

DESIGN FIRM Blackfish Creative
ALL DESIGN Drew Force
CLIENT Jerrod Philipps Illustration
TOOLS QuarkXPress, Adobe Photoshop

DESIGN FIRM
Heart Graphic Design/Bull's Eye Marketing
ART DIRECTOR Clark Most
DESIGNERS Clark Most, Joan Most
CLIENT Bull's Eye Marketing
TOOLS Macromedia FreeHand

DESIGN FIRM Elena Design
ALL DESIGN Elena Baca
CLIENT Bac-Ground
TOOLS Adobe Illustrator, Adobe Photoshop
PAPER/PRINTING Simpson Quest

DESIGN FIRM Melissa Passehl Design
ART DIRECTOR Melissa Passehl
DESIGNERS Melissa Passehl,
Charlotte Lambrechts
CLIENT Melissa Passehl Design

MELISSA PASSEHL DESIGN CHARLOTTE LAMBRECHTS. DESIGNER

1275 LINCOLN AVE. #7. SAN JOSE. CA 95125. F 408.294.4104. T 408.294.4422.

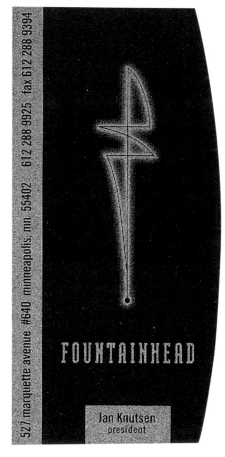

COMMERCIAL FURNITURE INTERIORS

Regina Daly
Sales Consultant

1135 Spruce Drive Mountainside, NJ 07092
Phone 908 518 1670 Fax 908 654 8436

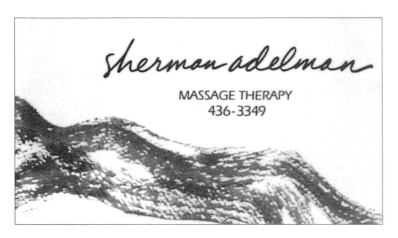

sherman adelman

MASSAGE THERAPY
436-3349

DESIGN FIRM Nancy Stutman Calligraphics
ALL DESIGN Nancy Stutman
CLIENT Sherman Adelman

TERPSICHORE

school of dance

Diane Danhieux
director

1011 Arthur Street
Iowa City, Iowa 52240

319.341.7833

DESIGN FIRM Design Ranch
ART DIRECTOR Gary Gnade
DESIGNERS Danette Angerer, Gary Gnade
CLIENT Terpsichore School of Dance
PAPER/PRINTING Wausau Royal
Fiber/Goodfellow Printing

12028 maidstone ave.

norwalk, ca. 90650

tel/fax
[562] 864.1181

éng Tang design

DESIGN FIRM éng Tang Design
ART DIRECTOR/DESIGNER éng Tang
CLIENT éng Tang
TOOLS Adobe Illustrator

GREEN CITY

Alexander Gröger

718 599 4867

65 South 8th St. #4
Brooklyn, NY 11211

DESIGN FIRM Sagmeister, Inc.
ART DIRECTOR Stefan Sagmeister
DESIGNERS Stefan Sagmeister, Veronica Oh
ILLUSTRATOR Veronica Oh
CLIENT Green City
PAPER/PRINTING Strathmore Writing
25% cotton

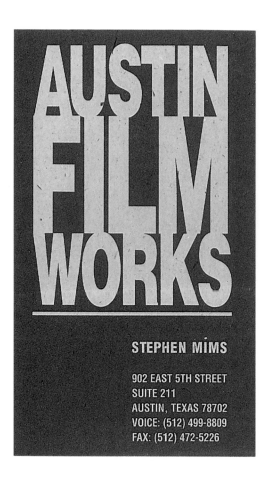

DESIGN FIRM
Kanokwalee Design

ART DIRECTOR/DESIGNER
Kanokwalee Lee

CLIENT
Austin Film Works

TOOLS
QuarkXPress

PAPER/PRINTING
Protera fleck

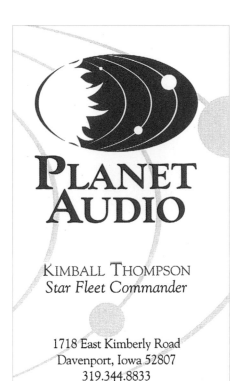

DESIGN FIRM
Gackle Anderson Henningsen, Inc

DESIGNER
Wendy Anderson

CLIENT
Planet Audio

TOOLS
QuarkXPress, Adobe Illustrator

PAPER/PRINTING
Neenah Classic Laid
Solar White/Two PMS

DESIGN FIRM Cordoba Graphics
ALL DESIGN éng Tang
CLIENT Pacific Coast
TOOLS Adobe Illustrator
PAPER PRINTING Flomar

DEBRA ROBERTS

15345 VIA SIMPATICO

AND ASSOCIATES

RANCHO SANTA FE

INCORPORATED

CALIFORNIA 92091

DEBRA J. ROBERTS, CFA

TEL 619-759-2649

PRESIDENT AND CEO

FAX 619-759-2653

DESIGN FIRM Mires Design
ART DIRECTOR Scott Mires
DESIGNERS Deborah Horn, Scott Mires
CLIENT Debra Roberts and Associates

RON MONTORO
VICE PRESIDENT

4678 ALVARADO CANYON ROAD
POST OFFICE BOX 601224
SAN DIEGO, CALIFORNIA 92120
TELEPHONE 619-281-7759
FACSIMILE 619-283-5467

DESIGN FIRM
Mires Design
ART DIRECTOR/DESIGNER
José Serrano
ILLUSTRATOR
Tracy Sabin
CLIENT
Chaos Lures

INTERGRAPHICS, S.A. DE C.V.
Cerrada de Pino No. 26
Col. Candelaria Coyoacán
C.P. 04380 , México, D.F.
Tel.: 619 4580 Tel./Fax: 619 2499

DESIGN FIRM Zappata Designers
ART DIRECTOR Ibo Angulo
DESIGNERS Ibo, Ana, Claudio
CLIENT Intergraphics Printing
TOOLS Macromedia FreeHand
PAPER/PRINTING Cambric/Silkscreen

DESIGN FIRM Vrontikis Design Office
ART DIRECTOR Petrula Vrontikis
DESIGNER/ILLUSTRATOR Kim Sage
CLIENT Hasegawa Enterprises
PAPER/PRINTING Potlatch Korma/Four-color, Login Printing

WEST
END
PLACE

CINDY MCGOURTY
Marketing Director

150 STANIFORD STREET
BOSTON, MA 02114
PHONE [617] 720-4646
FAX [617] 725-1888

DESIGN FIRM Phillips Design Group
ART DIRECTOR Steve Phillips
DESIGNER Alison Goudreault
CLIENT West End Place
TOOLS Adobe Illustrator
PAPER/PRINTING Strathmore
Natural White/Peacock Press

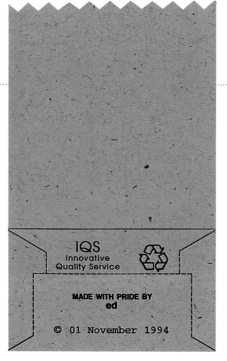

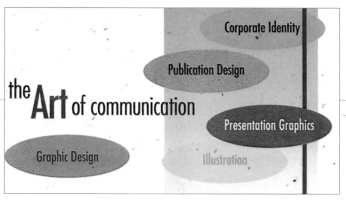

GARRETT SOLOMON

▲ CHANNEL ISLANDS PROPERTIES

500 ESPLANADE DRIVE · SUITE 400
OXNARD CALIFORNIA 93030
PHONE 805·278·6600 FAX 805·278·6606

PHOTOGRAPHY | 415/731-2524

JUSTIN CURTIS

1222 8th Avenue, San Francisco, CA 94122

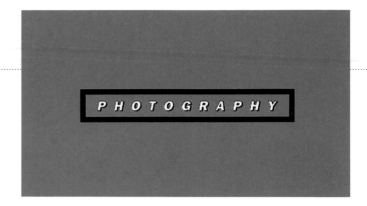

DESIGN FIRM Charney Design
ART DIRECTOR/DESIGNER Carol Inez Charney
CLIENT Justin Curtis Photography
TOOLS QuarkXPress
PAPER/PRINTING Vintage/Offset

DeCurtis McMillan

Hair & Beauty

1497 YONGE STREET TORONTO, M4T 1Z2

TELEPHONE (416) 323 1739

DESIGN FIRM Teikna
ART DIRECTOR/DESIGNER Claudia Neri
CLIENT DeCurtis McMillan Hair Salon
TOOLS QuarkXPress
PAPER/PRINTING Roll and evolution/One color

To look and feel good

To take better care of each

other and our Planet

HAMILTON HOP ASSET MANAGEMENT GROUP

DESIGN FIRM Highwood Communications
ART DIRECTOR/DESIGNER Darcy Parke
CLIENT Hamilton Hop Asset Management Group
TOOLS Adobe Photoshop, QuarkXPress
PAPER/PRINTING Classic Crest cover

R. Darol Hamilton, CLU, Ch.F.C.,CFP
Principal
Estate • Succession • Retirement

1100, 734 - 7 Avenue S.W.
Calgary, Alberta T2P 3P8
Tel 403.262.2080
Fax 403.262.2074
www.hamilton-hop.com

still | moving | pictures

still | moving | pictures

still | moving | pictures

R J MUNA

PICTURES

GISELA HERMELING

225 INDUSTRIAL STREET
SAN FRANCISCO, CALIFORNIA
ZIP 94124-8975

415.468.8225 TEL
415.468.8295 FAX
pictures@rjmuna.com NET

DESIGN FIRM Aerial

ART DIRECTOR/DESIGNER
Tracy Moon

PHOTOGRAPHER R. J. Muna

CLIENT R. J. Muna Pictures

TOOLS Adobe Photoshop,
Adobe Illustrator, QuarkXPress

PAPER/PRINTING Strathmore
Natural White/Leewood Press

WENDY P. BASIL
EXEC. VICE PRESIDENT

HALSTED
COMMUNICATIONS
INC.

FONE
800.600.7111
X222
FAX
800.600.7112
E-MAIL
HALSTED@IX.NETCOM.COM

DESIGN FIRM Vrontikis Design Office
ART DIRECTOR Petrula Vrontikis
DESIGNER/ILLUSTRATOR Kim Sage
CLIENT Halsted Communications
PAPER/PRINTING Starwhite
Vicksburg Vellum/Two-color offset, Login Printing

DESIGN FIRM Aerial
ART DIRECTOR/DESIGNER Tracy Moon
PHOTOGRAPHER R. J. Muna
CLIENT Aerial
TOOLS Adobe Photoshop, Live Picture, QuarkXPress

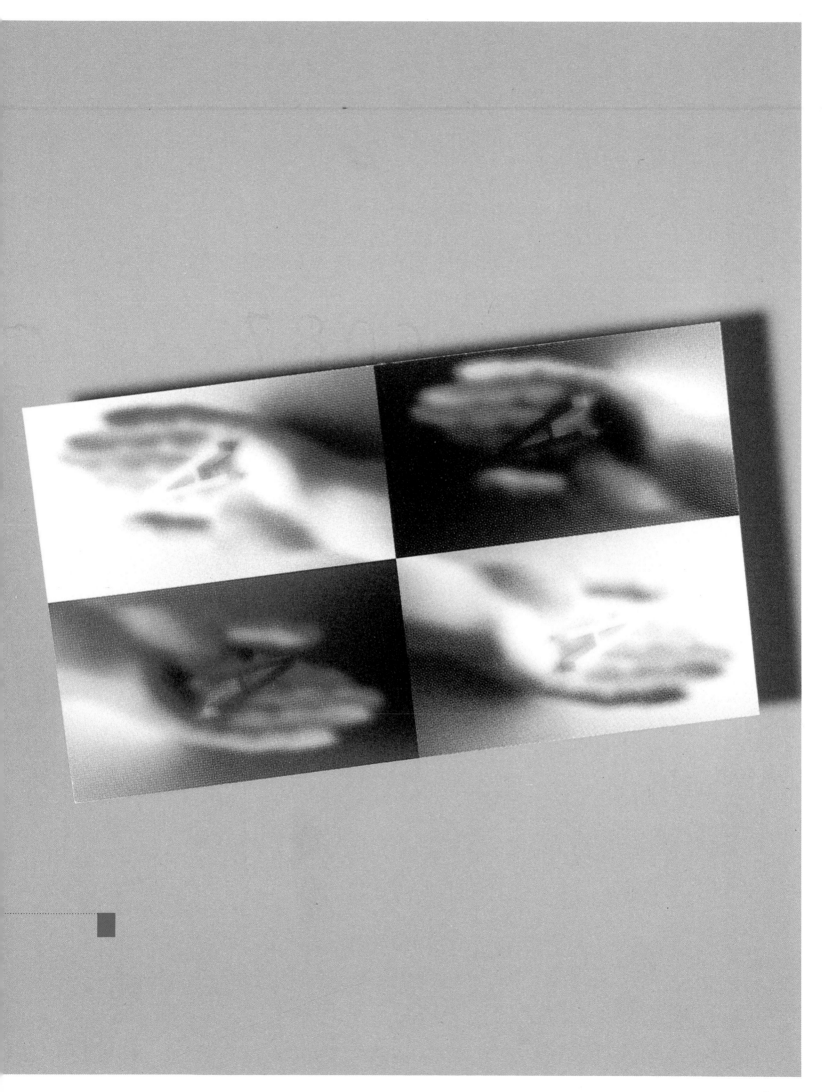

DESIGN FIRM Phoenix Creative

DESIGNER Ed Mantels-Seeker

CLIENT Simply Cruises

TOOLS QuarkXPress, Adobe Illustrator

PAPER/PRINTING Two-color litho with one color change

DESIGN FIRM MA&A—Mário Aurélio & Asscociados

ART DIRECTOR Mário Aurélio

DESIGNERS Mário Aurélio, Rosa Maia

CLIENT Prémaman

DESIGN FIRM Tower of Babel

DESIGNER Eric Stevens

CLIENT SP Masonry

TOOLS Macromedia FreeHand

PAPER/PRINTING Confetti Rust/Groves Printing

DESIGN FIRM The Running Iron Studio

ALL DESIGN Rachelle Kolby

CLIENT The Running Iron Studio

TOOLS Pen and ink

PAPER/PRINTING Astroparche Ancient
Gold 65 lb./Offset printing

DESIGN FIRM MA&A—Mário Aurélio Associados

ART DIRECTOR Mario Aurélio

DESIGNERS Mario Aurélio, Rosa Maia

CLIENT DecoPaço

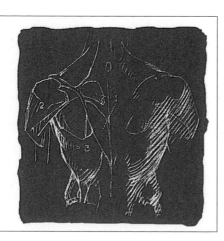

DESIGN FIRM Charney Design

ART DIRECTOR/DESIGNER Carol Inez Charney

CLIENT Darla Parr, D.C.

TOOLS QuarkXPress, Adobe Photoshop

PAPER/PRINTING Starwhite Vicksburg/Offset

DESIGN FIRM Corridor Design
ALL DESIGN Ejaz Saifullah
CLIENT Stout's Lodge
TOOLS Adobe Photoshop,
Adobe Illustrator, QuarkXPress
PAPER/PRINTING French Speckletone,
Oatmeal/Rooney Printing Co.

DESIGN FIRM
Stowe Design
ART DIRECTOR/DESIGNER
Jodie Stowe
CLIENT
Symmetry Productions
PAPER/PRINTING
Aztec Printing

DESIGN FIRM Hornall Anderson
Design Works, Inc.
ART DIRECTOR John Hornall
DESIGNERS John Hornall,
Debra Hampton, Mary Chin Hutchinson
ILLUSTRATOR Jerry Nelson
CLIENT Columbia Crest Winery
TOOLS QuarkXPress
PAPER/PRINTING Neenah Environment
Recycled, Desert Storm, Wove, Woodstock Wove

DESIGN FIRM Dogstar
ART DIRECTOR/DESIGNER Jennifer Martin
ILLUSTRATOR Rodney Davidson
CLIENT Roaring Tiger Films
TOOLS Adobe Photoshop, Macromedia FreeHand, QuarkXPress

D'Angelo

Construction Ltd.

Franco D'Angelo

34628 Ascott Avenue
Abbotsford, B.C. V2S 4V9
Telephone (604) 556-3727
Facsimile (604) 556-3728

DESIGN FIRM Blue Suede Studios
ALL DESIGN Justin Baker
CLIENT D'Angelo Construction
PAPER/PRINTING Classic Laid/Ultratech Printers

DESIGN FIRM The Home Studio
ART DIRECTOR/DESIGNER C. Benjamin Dacus
CLIENT Douglas C. Shibut
TOOLS QuarkXPress, Adobe Photoshop, Adobe Illustrator
PAPER/PRINTING Classic Crest/Offset

DESIGN FIRM Sagmeister, Inc.
ART DIRECTOR Stefan Sagmeister
DESIGNERS Stefan Sagmeister, Eric Zim
ILLUSTRATOR Eric Zim
CLIENT Dennis Hayes
PAPER/PRINTING Strathmore Writing 25% cotton

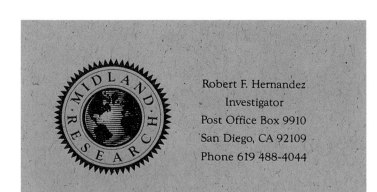

DESIGN FIRM Mires Design
ART DIRECTOR/DESIGNER José Serrano
ILLUSTRATOR Tracy Sabin
CLIENT Midland Research
PAPER/PRINTING Speckletone

Joel Morgenstern

444 Columbus Avenue
San Francisco, CA 94133

Tel: 415.433.9111
Fax: 415.362.6292

Email: HotelBoheme@
MCIMail.com

DESIGN FIRM Aerial
ART DIRECTOR/DESIGNER Tracy Moon
ILLUSTRATOR John Mattos (logotype)
PHOTOGRAPHERS Jerry Stoll, R. J. Muna
CLIENT Hotel Bohème
TOOLS Adobe Photoshop, QuarkXPress

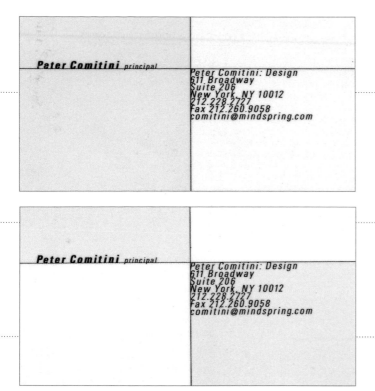

DESIGN FIRM Peter Comitini Design

ART DIRECTOR/DESIGNER Peter Comitini

TOOLS Adobe Illustrator, QuarkXPress, Power PC

PAPER/PRINTING Neenah UV Ultra

DESIGN FIRM Jim Terrinoni Line of Design

ART DIRECTOR Jim Terrioni

TOOLS Freehand artwork, Adobe Photoshop, QuarkXPress, Adobe Illustrator

PAPER/PRINTING 80 lb. cover

DESIGN FIRM Witherspoon Advertising

ALL DESIGN Rishi Seth

TOOLS Adobe Illustrator

CLIENT RaceFest Fort Worth

PAPER/PRINTING Starwhite Vicksburg Tiara High-Tech Finish Cover Plus

RaceFest Fort Worth, Inc.
777 Taylor Street, Suite 1080
Fort Worth, Texas 76102
817.335.RACE (7223)
FAX 817.335.2626
RaceFest@downiepro.com

Gary Cumbie
Steering Committee
Chairman

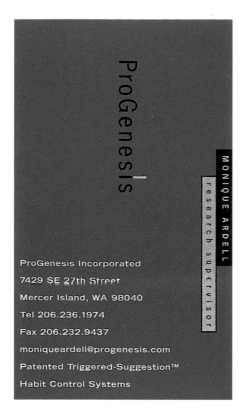

DESIGN FIRM
Widmeyer Design

ART DIRECTORS
Ken Widmeyer, Dale Hart

DESIGNER
Dale Hart

CLIENT
Progenesis

TOOLS
Power Macintosh,
Macromedia FreeHand

PAPER/PRINTING
Environment/Offset

DESIGN FIRM
Clearpoint Communications

ART DIRECTOR/DESIGNER
Lynn Decouto

CLIENT
Perron Family Chiropractic

PAPER/PRINTING
Reacraft Press

DESIGN FIRM Insight Design Communications
ALL DESIGN Sherrie Holdeman, Tracy Holdeman
CLIENT Jitters
TOOLS Power Macintosh 7500, Macromedia
FreeHand, Adobe Photoshop
PAPER/PRINTING French Speckletone Oatmeal
70 lb. text, Classic Crest Solar White 80 lb. cover

DESIGN FIRM Alison Goudreault, Inc.
ALL DESIGN Alison Goudreault
CLIENT Bloomer's Upholstery
TOOLS Adobe Illustrator
PAPER/PRINTING Strathmore Ultimate
White/Copy Cop

COONARA PRIVATE HOSPITAL

LORETO DAVEY CEO

6TH FLOOR
ALFRED HOSPITAL
COMMERCIAL ROAD
PRAHAN VICTORIA 3181
PHONE (03) 9520 9200
FAX (03) 9521 2775

A meeting place for quality health care

DESIGN FIRM
Watts Graphic Design
ART DIRECTORS/ DESIGNERS
Helen Watts, Peter Watts
CLIENT
Coonara Private Hospital
TOOLS
Macintosh
PAPER/PRINTING
Two color

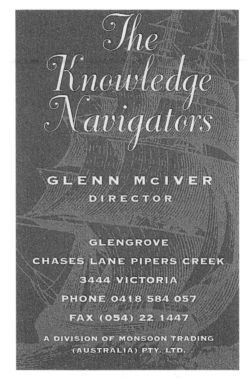

The Knowledge Navigators

GLENN McIVER
DIRECTOR

GLENGROVE
CHASES LANE PIPERS CREEK
3444 VICTORIA
PHONE 0418 584 057
FAX (054) 22 1447

A DIVISION OF MONSOON TRADING
(AUSTRALIA) PTY. LTD.

DESIGN FIRM Watts Graphic Design
ART DIRECTORS/DESIGNERS Helen Watts,
Peter Watts
CLIENT The Knowledge Navigators
TOOLS Macintosh
PAPER/PRINTING Teton/one color

Virtual Garden

Shirley Read-Jahn
communications manager

221 Main Street
Suite 480
San Francisco, CA 94105
P 415.908.4967
F 415.908.2010
E readjahns@tpv.com

http://vg.com

DESIGN FIRM Tharp Did It
ART DIRECTOR Rick Tharp
DESIGNERS Rick Tharp, Nicole Coleman
ILLUSTRATOR Rick Olson
CLIENT Time Warner
TOOLS Ink, Macintosh

t 310 204 1995   f 310 204 4879

4445 overland avenue
culver city california 90230
evensoninc@aol.com

Stan Evenson
principal

edg

evenson design group

DESIGN FIRM Evenson Design Group
ART DIRECTOR Stan Evenson
DESIGNER Amy Hershman
PAPER/PRINTING Anderson Printing

Leslie Vasquez

...nnex

...prises
...ue, Santa Cruz CA 95062
...4-6456 Fax 408/477-0289

DESIGN FIRM Charney Design
ALL DESIGN Carol Inez Charney
CLIENT Annex Enterprises
TOOLS QuarkXPress, Adobe Photoshop
PAPER/PRINTING Vintage/Offset

telemóvel 0931 57 97 69
tel/fax +351.2.454 20 63
rua das valas de cima 49, jovim
4420 gondomar
portugal

DESIGN FIRM
MA&A—Mário Aurélio & Associados
ART DIRECTOR Mário Aurélio
DESIGNERS Mário Aurélio, Rosa Maia
CLIENT Lumiforma/Iluminage, LDA

DESIGN FIRM Sivustudio
ART DIRECTOR Jaana Aartomaa
CLIENT Pirjo Lindstrom
TOOLS Macromedia FreeHand, Macintosh
PAPER/PRINTING Offset

Pirjo Lindström

Lastenkodinkatu 2-10 R 6
00180 Helsinki
Puh. (09) 694 9969
(Tel. +358 9 694 9969)

ALIYA S. KHAN

graphic design & consulting

864.627.9065
aliya@viperlink.com
812 Gloucester Ferry Road
Greenville, SC 29607

DESIGN FIRM One, Graphic Design & Consulting
ART DIRECTOR/DESIGNER Aliya S. Khan
CLIENT One, Graphic Design & Consulting
TOOLS CorelDraw, PC
PAPER/PRINTING Neenah Paper
Classic Crest New Sawgrass

THOMAS M. WICINSKI
Executive Chef

THE BROILER
Restaurant & Bar
13255 SAN PABLO AVE.
SAN PABLO, CA 94806

TELEPHONE
800.811.8862
510.215.7888

DESIGN FIRM Tharp Did It
ART DIRECTOR Rick Tharp
DESIGNERS
Rick Tharp, Amy Bednarek, Susan Craft
CLIENT Ladbrokes/London
TOOLS Macintosh
PAPER/PRINTING
Simpson Starwhite Vicksburg/Simon Printing

DESIGN FIRM Tower of Babel
DESIGNER Eric Stevens
CLIENT Tower of Babel
TOOLS Macromedia FreeHand
PAPER/PRINTING Groves Printing

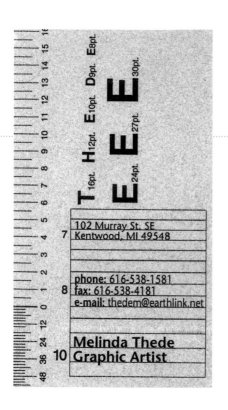

DESIGN FIRM
Melinda Thede
DESIGNER
Melinda Thede
CLIENT
Melinda Thede
TOOLS
Adobe Illustrator
PAPER/PRINTING
Transparency film/handmade

Carlos Barros
gerente

Bizance · Pedro Miguel & Irmãos, Lda

R. Quinta de Santa Maria, 119

Maximinos

4700 Braga

Telefone:(053)691 486

Fax:(053)691 486

DESIGN FIRM MA&A—Mário Aurélio & Associados
ART DIRECTOR Mário Aurélio
DESIGNERS Mário Aurélio, Rosa Maia
CLIENT Bizance Interiors

DESIGN FIRM
Lucy Walker Graphic Design
ART DIRECTOR/DESIGNER Lucy Walker
CLIENT Williams MacKay Advertising
TOOLS Adobe Illustrator
PAPER/PRINTING Coated artboard

DESIGN FIRM Charney Design
ALL DESIGN Carol Inez Charney
CLIENT Heinz Communications
TOOLS Adobe Illustrator
PAPER/PRINTING Environment
Duplex/Offset

HEINZ COMMUNICATIONS
ZIGI Z. HEINZ

VIDEO PRODUCTION

6950 HIGHWAY 9
FELTON, CA 95018
PHONE 408/335-3456
FAX 408/335-0722
PAGER 408/989-7777

FUSION MEDIA

Mark
Freedman

President
619 490 5182

7 Morena Boulevard, Suite 302
n Diego, California 92117
il:mark@fusionmedia.com
p://www.fusionmedia.com
telephone 619 490 5182
fax 619 490 5185

DESIGN FIRM Mires Design
ART DIRECTOR John Ball
DESIGNERS John Ball, Deborah Horn
CLIENT Fusion Media
PAPER/PRINTING Starwhite

Franciscan Health Community

Sally Staggert, PHN
Director of Community Services

1925
Norfolk Avenue
St. Paul, MN
55116-2699
(612) 699-3952
Fax 698-7322

Services for
Seniors and their
Families

DESIGN FIRM Design Center
ART DIRECTOR John Reger
DESIGNER Sherwin Schwartzrock
CLIENT Franciscan Health Company
TOOLS Macintosh
PAPER/PRINTING Procraft Printing

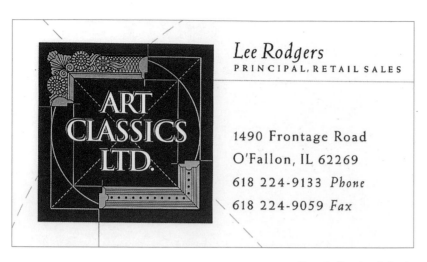

DESIGN FIRM Phoenix Creative, St Louis
ART DIRECTOR/DESIGNER
Ed Mantels-Seeker
ILLUSTRATORS Ed Mantels-Seeker, Ann Guillot
TOOLS Macromedia FreeHand
PAPER/PRINTING Four-color offset

DESIGN FIRM On The Edge
ART DIRECTOR Jeff Gasper
DESIGNER Gina Mims
CLIENT Sorrento Grille
TOOLS Adobe Illustrator,
QuarkXPress, Adobe Photoshop
PAPER/PRINTING Quest brown

DESIGN FIRM Jim Lange Design
ALL DESIGN Jim Lange
CLIENT Lee Langill
TOOLS Pen and ink

DESIGN FIRM M-DSIGN
ALL DESIGN Mika Ruusunen
CLIENT M-DSIGN
TOOLS Macintosh
PAPER/PRINTING Offset

Ida Linnet

REKLAMEAFDELINGEN

LØVENS KEMISKE FABRIK

Industriparken 55

2750 Ballerup

Telefon 44 94 58 88

Direkte 44 92 36 66 ⇢ 2563

Privat 44 68 05 40

Fax 44 92 35 95

DESIGN FIRM
Department 058
ART DIRECTOR/DESIGNER
Vibeke Nødskov
CLIENT
Løvens Kemiske Fabrik
TOOLS
Adobe Illustrator, QuarkXPress
PAPER/PRINTING
Green cardboard/One color

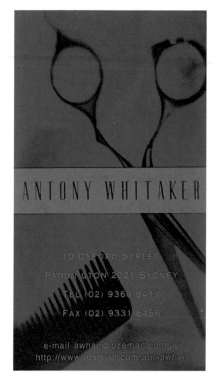

DESIGN FIRM Mother Graphic Design
ART DIRECTOR/DESIGNER Kristin Thieme
PHOTOGRAPHER Petrina Tinslay
CLIENT Antony Whitaker Hairdressing

Kimberly Bykerk, ASID

ASSOCIATE

THE RETAIL GROUP

2025 FIRST AVENUE, SUITE 470

SEATTLE, WASHINGTON 98121

FACSIMILE 206.441.8710

TELEPHONE 206.441.8330

DESIGN FIRM Widmeyer Design
ART DIRECTORS Ken Widmeyer, Dale Hart
DESIGNER/ILLUSTRATOR Dale Hart
CLIENT The Retail Group
TOOLS Power Macintosh, Adobe Photoshop,
Macromedia FreeHand
PAPER/PRINTING Environment/Offset

ART DIRECTOR/ILLUSTRATOR Ralf Huss
TOOLS Macintosh, Adobe Photoshop, QuarkXPress

lima design

215 hanover street

boston, massachusetts 02113

617-FOR-BEAN [367-2326]

617-367-1255 [FAX]

LIMADE@aol.com

mary a. kiene
owner

DESIGN FIRM Lima Design
DESIGNERS L. McKenna, M. Kiene
TOOLS QuarkXPress, Macromedia FreeHand
PAPER/PRINTING Potlatch Paper

TV | RADIO | PRINT | WEB

Kurt Shore
A Helluva Nice Guy

4100 Main Street, Suite 210
Philadelphia, PA 19127-1623
215.483.4555 fax 215.483.4554
http://www.d4tv.com

DESIGN FIRM D4 Creative Group
ALL DESIGN Wicky Lee
CLIENT D4 Creative Group
TOOLS Adobe Photoshop, Adobe Illustrator, QuarkXPress
PAPER/PRINTING Strathmore Writing/Five
colors over one color

LORI BOOTH (404) 577-9591

DESIGN FIRM Bumbershoot, CSC
ILLUSTRATOR Chris Thorne
CLIENT Lori Booth, Architectural Photography
TOOLS Pen and Ink, Adobe Photoshop
PAPER/PRINTING Watercolor paper/Ink jet

NAME
BARRY LAWSON
CHIEF FINANCIAL OFFICER

ADDRESS
5497 170TH PLACE SE
BELLEVUE, WA 98006

PHONE
VOICE 206.649.0346
FAX 206.649.0122

TICKETING

TOURS & CRUISES

PASSPORT & CURRENCY SERVICES

TRAVEL BOOKS, GUIDES & VIDEOS

LUGGAGE & ACCESSORIES

BON VOYAGE BASKETS

ON-LINE INFORMATION

GIFT CERTIFICATES

DESIGN FIRM Rick Eiber Design (RED)
ALL DESIGN Rick Eiber
CLIENT Today's Traveler
PAPER/PRINTING Three-colors,
over two-colors offset

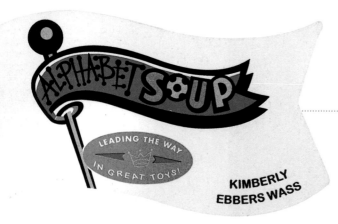

KIMBERLY
EBBERS WASS

5012 E.P. TRUE PARKWAY • WEST DES MOINES, IA 50265
(515) 221-0821 • FAX (515) 221-9890

833 42ND STREET • DES MOINES, IA 50312
(515) 255-8998 • FAX (515) 255-9040

233 MAIN STREET • AMES, IA 50010
(515) 232-1580 • FAX (515) 232-1580

DESIGN FIRM Sayles Graphic Design
ALL DESIGN John Sayles
CLIENT Alphabet Soup
PAPER/PRINTING Neenah Environment
white wove, double cover/Offset

Planet Comics

Smith Haven Mall, Space E-15

Middle Country Road

Lake Grove, New York 11755

516-724-4096

John A. Gagliardi, CEO

DESIGN FIRM Kiku Obata & Company
ART DIRECTOR/DESIGNER Rich Nelson
CLIENT Planet Comics

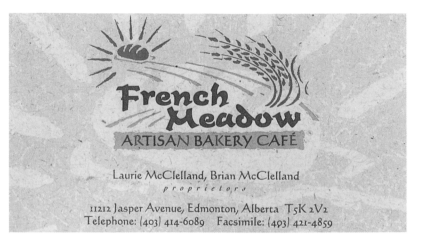

DESIGN FIRM Duck Soup Graphics

ART DIRECTOR/DESIGNER William Doucette

CLIENT French Meadow Bakery

TOOLS Macromedia FreeHand, QuarkXPress

PAPER/PRINTING Classic Laid/Three match colors

CREECHCREATIVE

6319 FAIRHURST AVENUE
CINCINNATI, OHIO
45213
513/351-3818
FACSIMILE: 513/631-6938

TIMOTHY J. CREECH

DESIGN FIRM Creech Creative

ALL DESIGN Tim Creech

CLIENT Creech Creative

TOOLS Adobe Photoshop, Adobe Illustrator

DESIGN FIRM

Storm Design & Advertising Consultancy

ART DIRECTORS/DESIGNERS

Dean Butler, David Ansett

CLIENT

Dusk Film and Video Production

TOOLS

Adobe Photoshop, QuarkXPress

PAPER/PRINTING

One color, duotone, packing brown wrap

An Eat Well Production

DESIGN FIRM Flaherty Art & Design
ALL DESIGN Marie Flaherty
CLIENT Fireking Baking Company of Eat Well, Inc.
TOOLS Adobe Illustrator

Patty Kane
owner

15 North Street • Hingham • MA • 02043
617-740-9400 • Fax 617-740-0440

An Eat Well Production

Todd Burgard Design
342 Walnut Street
Columbia, PA 17512
717·684·5896
gideon@redrose.net

Burgard Design
342 Walnut Street
Columbia, PA 17512
717·684·5896
gideon@redrose.net

DESIGN FIRM Burgard Design
ART DIRECTOR/DESIGNER Todd Burgard
CLIENT Burgard Design
TOOLS Hand-perfed using antique wheel punch
PAPER/PRINTING Neenah classic laid mahogany, camel hair duplex/
Letterpress with linotype typesetting, two color over one

DESIGN FIRM Solo Grafica
ART DIRECTOR/DESIGNER Yelena Suleyman
CLIENT Extrema Software International
TOOLS Macintosh
PAPER/PRINTING Neenah, Two color

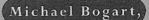

Michael Bogart,

dr Michael Bogart, M.D., F.R.C.P. (C)

366 ADELAIDE STREET EAST SUITE 345 TORONTO

ONTARIO M5A 3X9 TELEPHONE (416) 361 6182

DESIGN FIRM Teikna
ART DIRECTOR/DESIGNER Claudia Neri
CLIENT Michael Bogart
TOOLS QuarkXPress
PAPER/PRINTING Graphika/Two color

chris st. cyr
graphic design
ph. no. 617.625.7265
fax no. 617.625.9388
chrissc@usal.com
4 electric ave. #2
somerville,
ma 02144

chris st. cyr
graphic design
ph. no. 617.625.7265
fax no. 617.625.9388
chrissc@usal.com
4 electric ave. #2
somerville,
ma 02144

chris st. cyr
graphic design
ph. no. 617.625.7265
fax no. 617.625.9388
chrissc@usal.com
4 electric ave. #2
somerville,
ma 02144

DESIGN FIRM Chris St. Cyr Graphic Design
ART DIRECTOR/DESIGNER Chris St. Cyr
CLIENT Chris St. Cyr Graphic Design
TOOLS QuarkXPress, Adobe Illustrator,
rubber stamp

DESIGN FIRM Widmeyer Design
ART DIRECTORS Ken Widmeyer, Dale Hart
DESIGNER/ILLUSTRATOR Dale Hart
CLIENT Rolling Cones
TOOLS Power Macintosh, Adobe Photoshop,
Macromedia FreeHand
PAPER/PRINTING Mead paper/Offset

FEATURING BEN&JERRY'S PEACE POPS

RollingCones

Andy Davidson
117 EAST LOUISA STREET
SUITE NUMBER 315
SEATTLE, WA 98102
Phone 206.527.8388

NANCY YEASTING
DESIGN & ILLUSTRATION

3490 MONMOUTH AVENUE
VANCOUVER, B.C.
CANADA V5R 5R9

(604) 435-4965

DESIGN FIRM Nancy Yeasting
Design & Illustration
ALL DESIGN Nancy Yeasting
CLIENT Nancy Yeasting Design
& Illustration
TOOLS Hand drawn on marker pad,
QuarkXPress
PAPER/PRINTING Genesis
Milkweed/Two-color thermography

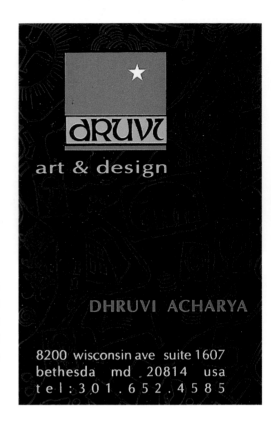

DESIGN FIRM Dhruvi Art & Design
ALL DESIGN Dhruvi Acharya
CLIENT Druvi Art & Design
PAPER/PRINTING 80/100 lbs. card
stock/Screen

DESIGN FIRM One, Graphic Design & Consulting
ART DIRECTOR/DESIGNER Aliya S. Khan
CLIENT Sabila Zakir Husnain
TOOLS CorelDraw, PC
PAPER/PRINTING Genesis Tallow

DESIGN FIRM Bartels & Company, Inc.
ART DIRECTOR David Bartels
DESIGNER/ILLUSTRATOR Aaron Segall
CLIENT Companion Baking Company
PAPER/PRINTING Mid West Printing

DESIGN FIRM
Fire House, Inc.
ART DIRECTOR/DESIGNER
Gregory R. Farmer
CLIENT
Twist Salon, Daphne Raider
TOOLS
QuarkXPress, Macromedia
FreeHand, Macintosh
PAPER/PRINTING
Schulze Printing

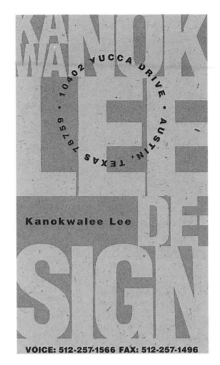

DESIGN FIRM Kanokwalee Design
ART DIRECTOR/DESIGNER Kanokwalee Pusitanun
CLIENT Kanokwalee Design
TOOLS Adobe Illustrator, QuarkXPress
PAPER/PRINTING Speckletone/Kraft

DESIGN FIRM Transparent Office
ART DIRECTOR/DESIGNER Vibeke Nødskov
CLIENT Ventana Europe
TOOLS Adobe Illustrator, QuarkXPress
PAPER/PRINTING Copper Cromalux/Two color

DESIGN FIRM Mother Graphic Design
ART DIRECTOR/DESIGNER Kristin Thieme
ILLUSTRATOR Melinda Dudley
CLIENT RA Records

DESIGN FIRM
Duck Soup Graphics
ART DIRECTOR/DESIGNER
William Doucette
CLIENT
Videotron
TOOLS
Adobe Illustrator, QuarkXPress
PAPER/PRINTING
Strathmore Elements/One match color,
foil embossed

DESIGN FIRM
Raven Madd Design
ART DIRECTOR/DESIGNER
Mark Curtis
CLIENT
Bowerman School

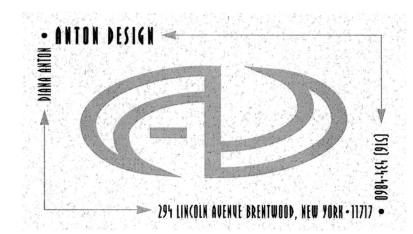

DESIGN FIRM Anton Design
ALL DESIGN Diana Anton
CLIENT Anton Design
TOOLS QuarkXPress, Adobe Illustrator

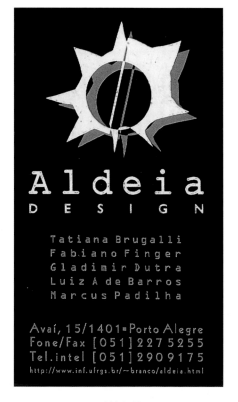

DESIGN FIRM Aldeia Design
ART DIRECTORS Marcus Padilha, Tatiana Brugalli
DESIGNERS Luis Barros, Fabiano Finger
ILLUSTRATOR Gladimir Dutra
CLIENT Aldeia Design
TOOLS CorelDraw
PAPER/PRINTING Couche 180 gsm/Silkscreen

DESIGN FIRM Charney Design
ART DIRECTOR/DESIGNER Carol
Inez Charney
PHOTOGRAPHER Carol Charney
CLIENT Jose McKanobb
TOOLS QuarkXPress, Adobe Photoshop
PAPER/PRINTING Vintage Velvet
Creme/Offset

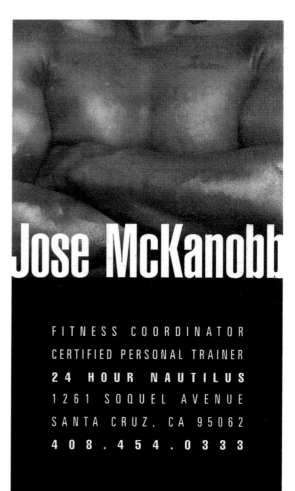

Bischoff & Thiede

Fassaden & Bausanierung
Dualweg 10
28239 Bremen
Telefon/Telefax
(0421 64 49 018

DESIGN FIRM
Büro B.
DESIGNER/ILLUSTRATOR
Daniel Bastian
CLIENT
Bischoff & Thiede
TOOLS
QuarkXPress, Adobe Photoshop
PAPER/PRINTING
Karten Karton/Offset

Fransbal
sociedade de representações de produtos e derivados metálicos, lda.

Francisco J. R. Barbosa
Direcção Comercial

Rua Gonçalo Cristóvão, 347 · sala 310 · 4000 Porto Portugal
Tel:(02)208 88 01 · Fax:(02)208 88 01

DESIGN FIRM MA&A—Mário Aurélio & Associados
ART DIRECTOR Mário Aurélio
DESIGNERS Mário Aurélio, Rosa Maia
CLIENT Fransbal

Acessórios para a indústria
e matéria-primas
Sociedade de representações
para metalo-mecânica
de produtos e derivados metálicos
Manutenção industrial
Acessórios para a indústria
e matéria-primas
para metalo-mecânica
Sociedade de representações
de produtos e derivados metálicos Manutenção industrial

David M. Chandler
President

(319) 377-9245
(319) 377-9541 Fax
chandler @ iwork.net
http://www.iwork.net

5250 North Park Place NE
Suite 111
Cedar Rapids, IA 52402

DESIGN FIRM Marketing and Communications
Strategies, Inc.
ART DIRECTOR/DESIGNER Lloyd Keels
CLIENT Internet at Work
TOOLS Adobe Illustrator, QuarkXPress, Power
Macintosh 8100
PAPER/PRINTING Two color

form fünf

Verbale und visuelle Kommunikation

Daniel Henry Bastian

Alexanderstraße 9B
28203 Bremen

Telefon
0421 782 26
Fax
0421 70 06 17
Isdn
0421 70 30 74

DESIGN FIRM Form 5
DESIGNERS Daniel Bastian,
Ulysses Voecker, Martin Veicht
CLIENT Form 5
TOOLS QuarkXPress, Macromedia
Fontographer, Adobe Photoshop, Stamp
PAPER/PRINTING Karten Karton

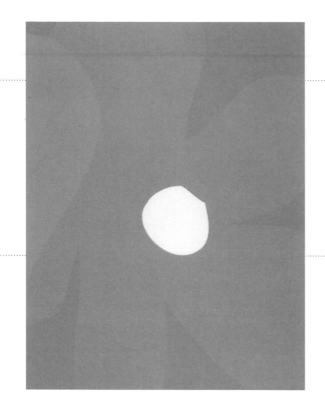

DESIGN FIRM The Design Company
ART DIRECTOR/ILLUSTRATOR Marcia Romanuck
CLIENT E. Claire Therapy
PAPER/PRINTING Champion Carnival Wove

Emilio Mazzonna
Executive Vice President

1045 Tristar Drive
Mississauga
Untario L5T 1W5

Fax 905 795-5550
Telephone 905 795-5555
Toll Free 1 800 468-CYAN

DESIGN FIRM Eskind Waddell
ART DIRECTOR Malcolm Waddell
DESIGNERS Maggi Cash, Nicola Lyon
Florence Ngan, Gary Mansbridge
CLIENT Imaginex, Inc.
TOOLS Adobe Photoshop,
Adobe Illustrator, QuarkXPress

Belluno Ristorante

340 Lexington Avenue • New York, NY 10016
Between 39th & 40th Streets
(212) 953-3282

DESIGN FIRM Rick Eiber Design (RED)
ART DIRECTOR/DESIGNER Rick Eiber
CLIENT Mindshare Media
PAPER/PRINTING Engraved, offset yellow

DESIGN FIRM Angry Porcupine Design
DESIGNER/ILLUSTRATOR Cheryl Roder-Quill
CLIENT Cheryl Roder-Quill
TOOLS Macintosh, QuarkXPress

cheryl roder.quill

industrial
strength
design

4662 hidden
pond drive
allison park
pa 15101

fax [412]
492 9975

[412]
tel 492 9973

cheryl roder.quill

industrial
strength
design

492 9973

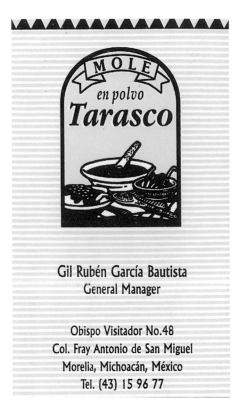

DESIGN FIRM Animus Comunicaçáo
ART DIRECTOR Rique Nitzsche
DESIGNER Victal Caesar
CLIENT Neisa Nitzsche Teixeira
TOOLS Macromedia FreeHand,
Adobe Photoshop
PAPER/PRINTING
Opaline 180 gsm/Five color

DESIGN FIRM Büro B.
DESIGNER Daniel Bastian
CLIENT Caro Fotoagentur
TOOLS QuarkXPress
PAPER/PRINTING Karten
Karton/Offset

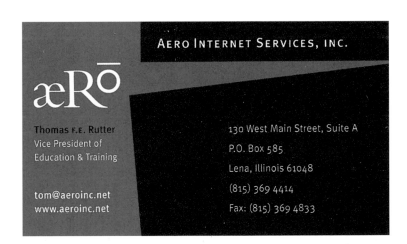

DESIGN FIRM Tanagram
DESIGNER Lance Rutter
CLIENT Aero Internet Services
TOOLS Macromedia FreeHand

DESIGN FIRM Held Diedrich
ART DIRECTOR Dick Held
DESIGNER Sander Leech
CLIENT Grand Slam
TOOLS Adobe Illustrator, QuarkXPress
PAPER/PRINTING Neenah, Classic Crest,
Solar White/Offset

DESIGN FIRM Steve Trapero Design
ART DIRECTOR/DESIGNER Steve Trapero
CLIENT Franz & Company, Inc.
TOOLS QuarkXPress, Adobe Illustrator
PAPER/PRINTING Graphica Lineal/Two-color offset

DESIGN FIRM Bartels & Company, Inc.
ART DIRECTOR David Bartels
DESIGNER/ILLUSTRATOR Aaron Segall
CLIENT McElwain Fine Arts
PAPER/PRINTING Mid West Printing

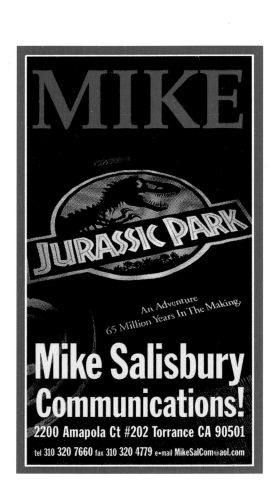

DESIGN FIRM Mike Salisbury Communications
ART DIRECTOR Mike Salisbury
DESIGNER Mary Evelyn McGough
CLIENT Mike Salisbury

DESIGN FIRM Bartels & Company, Inc.
ART DIRECTOR David Bartels
DESIGNER/ILLUSTRATOR Bob Thomas
CLIENT Bartels & Company, Inc.
PAPER/PRINTING Chromecoat/Devere Printing

HIROKO TANAKA
One Irving Place U-12b
New York, NY 10003
Tel 212·995·8489 Fax 212·254·8233

DESIGN FIRM Mirko Ilić Corp.
ART DIRECTOR/DESIGNER Nicky Lindeman
CLIENT Mirko Ilić Corp.
TOOLS QuarkXPress
PAPER/PRINTING Cougar Smooth white
80 lb. cover/Rob-Win Press

DESIGN FIRM
Carl Chiocca Creative Designs
ALL DESIGN
Carl Chiocca
TOOLS
Adobe Photoshop, QuarkXPress
PAPER/PRINTING
Lustro Gloss 80 lb. cover/
Two color offset

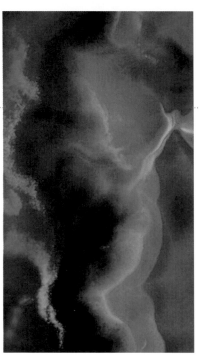

CARL CHIOCCA
CREATIVE DESIGNS
& PRINT PRODUCTION

10 renwick street   pittsburgh pa 15210

PHONE 412 431·2095   FACSIMILE 412 431·7750

GRAPHIC IDEAS
949781824

mika ruusunen

DESIGN FIRM M-DSIGN
ALL DESIGN Mika Ruusunen
CLIENT M-DSIGN
TOOLS Macintosh
PAPER/PRINTING Offset

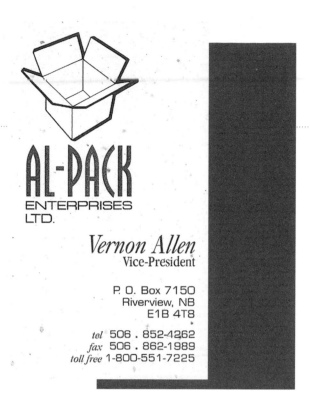

DESIGN FIRM Judy Wheaton
ART DIRECTOR/DESIGNER Judy Wheaton
ILLUSTRATOR Creative Collection
CLIENT Al-Pack
TOOLS Adobe Photoshop, Adobe PageMaker
PAPER/PRINTING Classic Laid/TK Printing

DESIGN FIRM On The Edge
ART DIRECTOR Jeff Gasper
DESIGNER Jon Nedry
ILLUSTRATOR Robert Wilhelm
CLIENT Chimayo Grill
TOOLS Adobe Illustrator, QuarkXPress, Adobe Photoshop
PAPER/PRINTING Luna White coated/Four color

ALL DESIGN James Marsh
CLIENT James Marsh
TOOLS Acrylic
PAPER/PRINTING Four color

DESIGN FIRM Charney Design
ART DIRECTOR/DESIGNER
Carol Inez Charney
ILLUSTRATOR Kim Ferrell
CLIENT Village Bakehouse
TOOLS Adobe Illustrator,
Adobe Photoshop
PAPER/PRINTING
Environment/Offset

DESIGN FIRM Kerrickters
ALL DESIGN Christine Kerrick
CLIENT Christine Kerrick
TOOLS Graphite, Adobe Illustrator

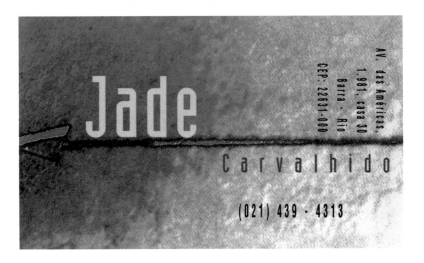

DESIGN FIRM Animus Comunicaçáo
ART DIRECTOR Rique Nitzsche
DESIGNER Victal Caesar
CLIENT Jade Carvalhido
TOOLS Macromedia FreeHand, Adobe Photoshop
PAPER/PRINTING Opaline 180 gsm/Four color

DESIGN FIRM Val Gene Associates
ART DIRECTOR/DESIGNER Lacy Leverett
ILLUSTRATOR Christopher Jennings
CLIENT Dockside
PAPER/PRINTING Baker's Printing

Gary H. Gnade
Pardner

701 East Davenport Street
Iowa City, Iowa
52245.2812
319.354.2623
FAX 319.354.6077

DESIGN FIRM
Design Ranch
ART DIRECTOR/DESIGNER
Gary Gnade
CLIENT
Design Ranch

Lacy Leverett
Advertising Director

Val Gene Associates
5208 Classen Blvd.
Oklahoma City, Oklahoma
73118
TEL 405-843-9474
FAX 405-842-5063

DESIGN FIRM Val Gene Associates
ALL DESIGN Lacy Leverett
PRODUCTION Shirley Morrow
CLIENT Val Gene Associates
PAPER/PRINTING Baker's Printing

Graphic *Designer* Graphiste
MGDC

52 Wheaton
Moncton
NB
Canada
E1E 2K2
(506)
389-8602

Graphic *Designer* Graphiste
MGDC

52 Wheaton
Moncton
NB
Canada
E1E 2K2
(506)
389-8602

DESIGN FIRM Judy Wheaton
ART DIRECTOR/DESIGNER Judy Wheaton
CLIENT Judy Wheaton
TOOLS Adobe PageMaker
PAPER/PRINTING Kromekote/TK Printing

STRATEGIC CHURCH PLANTING

7913 N.E. 58TH AVENUE
VANCOUVER, WA 98665

TEL 360.694.4985
FAX 360.694.0219

MATT HANNAN
DIRECTOR OF CHURCH PLANTING
COLUMBIA BAPTIST CONFERENCE

DESIGN FIRM Rick Eiber Design (RED)
ART DIRECTOR Rick Eiber
CLIENT Columbia Baptist Conference
PAPER/PRINTING Brightwater/Two colors over two colors

GOLF TV

DESIGN FIRM
BBS In House Design
ALL DESIGN
Joyce Woollcot
CLIENT
BBS/Golf TV
TOOLS
Adobe Illustrator
PAPER/PRINTING
Strathmore Elements Dots

SUZANNE STEEVES
SENIOR VICE-PRESIDENT
AND GENERAL MANAGER

• • • • • • • •

P.O. BOX 9, STATION "O",
TORONTO, ONTARIO, CANADA M4A 2M9
TEL: (416) 299-2070
FAX: (416) 299-2076

SUSAN BIERZYCHUDEK
SENIOR ACCOUNTS DIRECTOR

AXION   image solutions for brand success

415 258 6807 **T**
415 457 8227 **F**
susanb@axionsf.com **e**

DESIGN FIRM Axion Design, Inc.
ART DIRECTOR/DESIGNER Kenn Lewis
CLIENT Axion Design
TOOLS Adobe Illustrator
PAPER/PRINTING Environment Ivory 80 lb./Offset, embossed

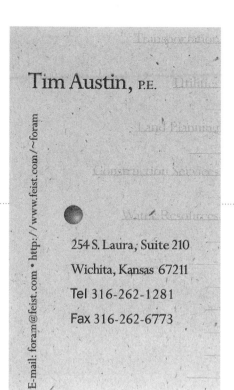

Tim Austin, P.E.

254 S. Laura, Suite 210

Wichita, Kansas 67211

Tel 316-262-1281

Fax 316-262-6773

E-mail: foram@feist.com • http://www.feist.com/~foram

DESIGN FIRM Greteman Group
ART DIRECTORS/DESIGNERS Sonia Greteman, James Strange
CLIENT Austin Miller Engineering Services
TOOLS Macromedia FreeHand
PAPER/PRINTING Genesis/Two-color offset

DESIGN FIRM Sivustudio
ART DIRECTOR Jaana Aartomaa
CLIENT Kim Haukatsalo
TOOLS Macromedia FreeHand, Macintosh
PAPER/PRINTING Flannel/Offset

KIM HAUKATSALO

Vironkatu 9 A 45
FIN-00170 Helsinki

tel +358 9 135 5568
gsm +358 400 414 510

D2 DESIGN

Dominique Duval
Designer graphique

6300 Avenue du Parc
Bureau 502
Montréal (Québec)
H2V 4H8

Téléphone
Télécopieur
(514) 495 1270

DESIGN FIRM D2 Design
ALL DESIGN Dominique Duval
CLIENT D2 Design
TOOLS Adobe Illustrator, Adobe Photoshop, Macintosh
PAPER/PRINTING Two-color offset

Maternal
Concepts™

Mark D. Emerson
President

2910 Stevens Creek Blvd.
Suite 109-1845
San Jose, CA 95128-2015
voice mail 408-599-0816
ph 408-972-9103 fx 408-226-9324

DESIGN FIRM
JWK Design Group, Inc.
ALL DESIGN Jennifer Kompolt
CLIENT Maternal Concepts Ltd.
TOOLS Adobe Illustrator
PAPER/PRINTING Simpson
Evergreen Script Aspen

DR. THOMAS S. SUZUKI
& ASSOCIATES

THOMAS SUZUKI, O.D.

DESIGN FIRM Design Source
ALL DESIGN Cari Johnson
CLIENT Dr. Thomas Suzuki
TOOLS Adobe Illustrator
PAPER/PRINTING Karma
Natural/Two-color offset

53 ASPEN WAY
WATSONVILLE, CA 95076
PHONE 408 724-1097
FAX 408 724-6364

11272 MERRITT ST., SUITE D
CASTROVILLE, CA 95012
408 633-0550

DESIGN FIRM Stefan Dziallas Design
DESIGNER/ILLUSTRATOR Stefan Dziallas
CLIENT Stefan Dziallas
TOOLS Adobe Photoshop, QuarkXPress, Macintosh
PAPER/PRINTING 300gsm Matt/Schneidersöhne

DESIGN FIRM Apple Graphics &
Advertising of Merrick, Inc.
DESIGNER Allison Blair Schneider
CLIENT The Aroma Boutique
TOOLS Macromedia FreeHand,
Power Macintosh 7500
PAPER/PRINTING Fox River Circa Select
Moss/One-color themography

DESIGN FIRM
Held Diedrich
ART DIRECTOR
Doug Diedrich
DESIGNER/ILLUSTRATOR
Megan Snow
CLIENT
Spring Hollow
TOOLS
QuarkXPress, Adobe Illustrator
PAPER/PRINTING
Neenah, Classic Laid,
Natural White/Offset

DESIGN FIRM Olive Tree
ART DIRECTOR/DESIGNER Alan Olive
ILLUSTRATOR Kent Smith
TOOLS CorelDraw
PAPER/PRINTING Edwards Dunlop
Recycled Evergreen

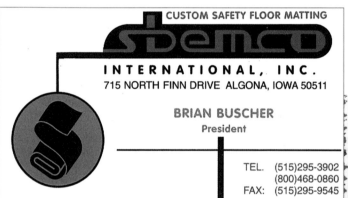

DESIGN FIRM Sayles Graphic Design
ALL DESIGN John Sayles
CLIENT Sbemco International
PAPER/PRINTING Curtis Retreeve white/Offset

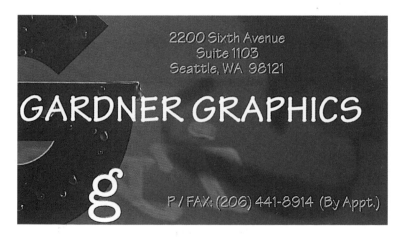

DESIGN FIRM Gardner Graphics
ALL DESIGN Dianne Gardner
CLIENT Dianne Gardner
TOOLS Adobe Photoshop
PAPER/PRINTING Coated

KRISTY ANN KUTCH

Colored Pencil Artwork/Instruction
11555 West Earl Road
Michigan City, IN 46360

219 · 874 · 4688

Berry Bounty, 16" x 18"

DESIGN FIRM Kristy A. Kutch
ILLUSTRATOR Kristy A. Kutch
TOOLS Colored pencil painting
PAPER/PRINTING Perfect Picture

PROGRESSIVE CENTER
FOR INDEPENDENT LIVING INC.

MEG NORTH
EXECUTIVE DIRECTOR

831 PARKWAY AVENUE, B-2
EWING, NJ 08618
PHONE: (609) 530-0006
FAX: (609) 530-1166
TTY: (609) 530-1234

DESIGN FIRM Howard Levy Design
ART DIRECTOR/DESIGNER Howard Levy
CLIENT Progressive Center for Independent Living, Inc.
TOOLS QuarkXPress, Adobe Illustrator
PAPER/PRINTING Two-color offset

Complete Street Rod Chassis and Suspension
3045 Jefferson St. • San Diego, CA 92110 • 619 293 0834

GARYS ROD & CUSTOM

Gary Timm

DESIGN FIRM Mires Design
ART DIRECTOR/DESIGNER John Ball
ILLUSTRATOR Tracy Sabin
CLIENT Gary's Hot Rods

DESIGN FIRM Keiler Design Group
ART DIRECTOR Jeff Lin
DESIGNERS Jeff Lin
ILLUSTRATOR Jim Coon
CLIENT Matt Rohde
TOOLS Adobe Photoshop

matt Rohde

keyboardist/pianist

5540 Roswell Road
unit E201
sandy springs,
GA 30342

404.303.7735

DESIGN FIRM Bartels & Company, Inc.
ART DIRECTOR David Bartels
DESIGNER/ILLUSTRATOR
John Postlewait
CLIENT Cheapy Smokes
PAPER/PRINTING Mid West Printing

DESIGN FIRM MA&A—Mário Aurélio & Associados
ART DIRECTOR Mário Aurélio
DESIGNERS Mário Aurélio, Rosa Maia
CLIENT F.S.B.

DESIGN FIRM
Abrams & LaBrecque Design
ALL DESIGN Ed Abrams, Elisée LaBrecque
CLIENT Mostue & Assoc. Architects, Inc.
TOOLS QuarkXPress
PAPER/PRINTING Strathmore Pure
Cotton/Benjamin Franklin Smith

The Good Life

Pam Widener

DESIGN FIRM The Eikon Marketing Team
ALL DESIGN Dannah Gresh
CLIENT K-DAY 97.5
TOOLS Macromedia FreeHand
PAPER/PRINTING Beckett Laid white

THE TRUE BLUE COMPANY

BRIAN LIPNER

PRESIDENT

939 WEST HURON, No. 108

CHICAGO, ILLINOIS 60622

PHONE 312.563.9944

FAX 312.563.0125

E-MAIL BLIPNER@AOL

DESIGN FIRM Michael Stanard Design, Inc.
ART DIRECTOR Michael Stanard
DESIGNER Kristy Vandekerckhove
CLIENT Brian Lipner/The True Blue Co.
PAPER/PRINTING Strathmore Renewal/Offset

DESIGN FIRM Carl D. J. Ison
ART DIRECTOR/DESIGNER Carl D. J. Ison
CLIENT Carl D. J. Ison
TOOLS QuarkXPress, Adobe Illustrator, Adobe Photoshop
PAPER/PRINTING One color on two sides, various metal
and alloy 3D tip ons: eyelet, nut/bolt, and lead discs

Mary Bold

Interior Designer

5016 South 110 Street

Omaha, NE 68137

402·592·6905

DESIGN FIRM New Idea Design, Inc.

DESIGNER/ILLUSTRATOR Ron Boldt

CLIENT Castle or Cottage Interiors

TOOLS Pen and ink, Macintosh, Macromedia FreeHand

PAPER/PRINTING Strathmore, metallic inks/The Print Shop

DESIGN FIRM Jon Nedry

ALL DESIGN Jon Nedry

CLIENT Classic Cigar Company

TOOLS Adobe Illustrator, QuarkXPress

PAPER/PRINTING Neenah Environment,
Cover Duplex, Desert Storm/Alpaca

DESIGN FIRM Jane Dill Calligraphy & Design

ART DIRECTORS/DESIGNER Jane Dill

CLIENT Jane Dill

TOOLS Brush, type

PAPER/PRINTING Benefit Champion/blind
emboss, foil stamp

The Pleasanton SPA

3059-K HOPYARD ROAD, PLEASANTON, CA 94588
PHONE 510 • 846 • 0544

DESIGN FIRM Designing Concepts
DESIGNERS Renee Sheppard, Mariah Parker
CLIENT The Pleasanton Spa
TOOLS QuarkXPress, Adobe Photoshop, Adobe Illustrator
PAPER/PRINTING Wigt's

GOLDEN·RATIO SPORTS

Steven M. Webb
Division Manager

P.O. Box 297
Emigrant, MT 59027
phone: 800.406.0495
fax: 406.333.4769
grw@goldenratio.com

DESIGN FIRM Roger Gefvert Designs
ALL DESIGN Roger Gefvert
CLIENT Golden Ratio Sports
TOOLS Macintosh, Adobe Illustrator, Adobe Photoshop, QuarkXPress
PAPER/PRINTING Neenah Classic Columns

Michael N. Macris
President

American Polymer Corp.® 9176 South 300 West Suite Number Four Sandy, Utah 84070	**Tel** 801.255.9505 **Fax** 801.255.7123 **Pager** 800.509.7813

DESIGN FIRM Rick Eiber Design (RED)
ART DIRECTOR/DESIGNER Rick Eiber
CLIENT American Polymer Corp.
PAPER/PRINTING Columns/Three color over two color

Rita Allman
Office Manager

EXECUTIVE DIVERSITY SERVICES, INC.

675 South Lane Street, Suite 305
Seattle, WA 98104-2942
(206) 224-9293 • Fax (206) 224-9303

DESIGN FIRM Walsh and Associates, Inc.
ART DIRECTOR/DESIGNER Miriam Lisco
CLIENT Executive Diversity Services
TOOLS Adobe Illustrator, Adobe PageMaker
PAPER/PRINTING Classic Crest Natural White/A & A Printing

THE
PAUL MARTIN
design
COMPANY

THE
PAUL MARTIN
design
COMPANY

32 Dragon Street
Petersfield
Hampshire GU31 4JJ

telephone
01730 265814
facsimile
01730 263014
ISDN
01730 261392

PAUL MARTIN MA(RCA) FCSD
Creative Director

DESIGN FIRM The Paul Martin Design Co.
ART DIRECTOR Paul Martin
DESIGNER Paul Adams
CLIENT The Paul Martin Design Co.
PAPER/PRINTING Huntsman Velvet
300 gsm/St. Richard's Press

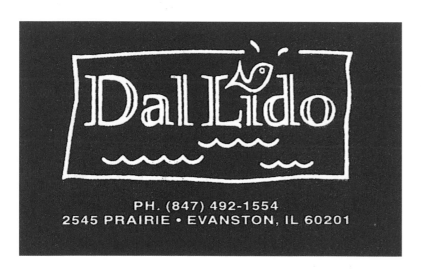

DESIGN FIRM Bullet Communications, Inc.
ALL DESIGN Tim Scott
CLIENT Dal Lido Restaurant
TOOLS QuarkXPress, Adobe Illustrator
PAPER/PRINTING Carolina 8 pt. cover/Offset

kersten hanke
diplom-designer

viktoriastraße 46
52066 aachen

fon-fax 02 41 - 50 42 50

DESIGN FIRM Hanke Kommunikation
ART DIRECTOR Kersten Hanke
CLIENT Hanke Kommunikation
TOOLS Macintosh, Adobe Photoshop,
Macromedia FreeHand

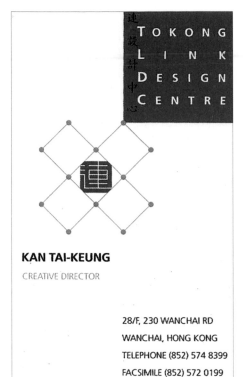

KAN TAI-KEUNG

CREATIVE DIRECTOR

28/F, 230 WANCHAI RD
WANCHAI, HONG KONG
TELEPHONE (852) 574 8399
FACSIMILE (852) 572 0199

DESIGN FIRM
Kan & Lau Design Consultants
ART DIRECTOR/DESIGNER
Kan Tai-keung
CLIENT
Tokong Link Design Centre Ltd.
PAPER/PRINTING
Gilbert White Cockle 216 gsm/Offset

DESIGN FIRM Stephen Peringer Illustration
DESIGNER/ILLUSTRATOR
Stephen Peringer
CLIENT Cool Hand Luke's Cafe

DESIGN FIRM Burgard Design
ALL DESIGN Todd Burgard
CLIENT Burgard Cycle
TOOLS Adobe Illustrator, Dimensions
PAPER/PRINTING Becket Expression Iceberg/
Two colors over one color

CHEX INTERNATIONAL SALES LIMITED

PATRICK CHAN

OFFICE 50 SILVER STAR BLVD., UNIT 207
SCARBOROUGH, ONTARIO M1V 3L3, CANADA
TEL/FAX (416) 292 4857
SHOP UNIT 56, SCARBOROUGH TOWN CENTRE
300 BOROUGH DRIVE, SCARBOROUGH
ONTARIO M1P 4P5, CANADA
TEL (416) 296 9914

DESIGN FIRM Kan & Lau Design Consultants
ART DIRECTORS Kan Tai-keung, Freeman Lau Siu Hong
DESIGNER Freeman Lau Siu Hong
CLIENT Chex International Sales Ltd.
PAPER/PRINTING Conqueror Brilliant White Wove
220 gsm/Three-color offset

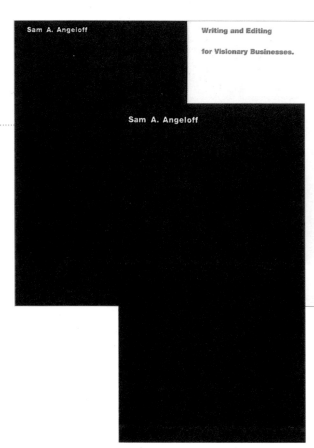

Sam A. Angeloff

Sam A. Angeloff

Writing and Editing
for Visionary Businesses.

The writer's job is to tell a story
that is compelling, factual and
easily understood.

Clear and Direct

Original and Persistent

Accurate and Inventive

Adept and Cost-Effective

DESIGN FIRM Paper Power
ART DIRECTOR/DESIGNER Lyn Hourahine
CLIENT Paper Power
TOOLS Macintosh
PAPER/PRINTING Zeta matt Post Hammer
260 gsm/One color, diecut, offset litho

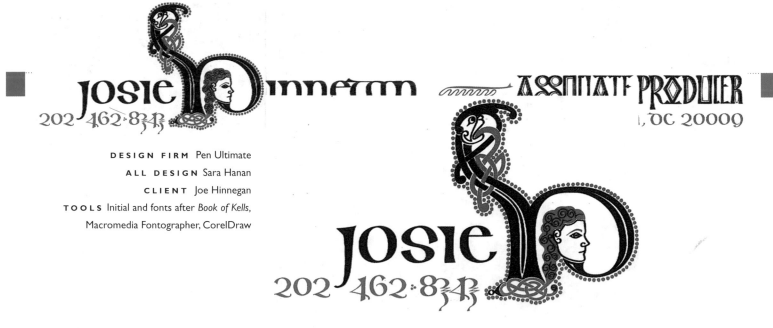

DESIGN FIRM Pen Ultimate
ALL DESIGN Sara Hanan
CLIENT Joe Hinnegan
TOOLS Initial and fonts after *Book of Kells,*
Macromedia Fontographer, CorelDraw

DESIGN FIRM Paper Power
ART DIRECTOR/DESIGNER Lyn Hourahine
DESIGNER Sherwin Schwartzrock
CLIENT Paper Power
TOOLS Macintosh
PAPER/PRINTING Zeta matt Post Hammer
260 gsm/One color, diecut, offset litho

PAPER POWER

53 WARWICK ROAD, EALING, LONDON W5 5PZ
TEL 0181 579 6631 FAX 0181 840 1990

Lyn Hourahine FCSD

CHARTERED PAPER PRODUCT DESIGNERS
CREATIVE PAPER ENGINEERING DESIGN

1

*terri gibbs
photography*

1512
Edison
Suite
100
Dallas
Texas
75207
214
748
6866

2

CENTRE
CHIROPRATIQUE

BLAINVILLE

Pour vôtre mieux-être

Dr. Michel Delorme, D.C.
Chiropraticien

10 boul. de la Seigneurie
Bureau 202
Blainville Québec
J7C 3V5
Tél.: 971.0824

3

Little&AssociatesArchitects

THOMAS L. BALKE, AIA
Senior Associate

5815 WESTPARK DRIVE
CHARLOTTE, NC 28217

DIRECT LINE: 704.561.3414
FACSIMILE: 704.522.7889
RECEPTIONIST: 704.525.6350

4

The
Jones Collection

MANUFACTURERS' REP

Jacqueline L. Jones

TEL (510) 339-1478
FAX (510) 339-7241

5744 GRISBORNE AVE
OAKLAND, CA 94611

5

METROWEST

LANDSCAPE

COMPANY

P.O. Box 874,

Natick,

Massachusetts

01760

"Complete

Landscape

Services"

METROWEST

Eric Meltzer

508.788.0552

617.444.1305

6

SHELLI McCONNELL

Food Writer - Consultant

811 North B Street
Indianola, Iowa 50125

5 1 5 - 9 6 1 - 9 2 1 3

1 Design Firm
Sibley/Peteet Design, Inc.
Designer
Derek Welch
Client
Terri Gibbs
Photography

2 Design Firm
D2 Design
Designer
Dominique Duval
Client
Centre Chiropratique Blainville
Chiropractors

3 Design Firm
Mervil Paylor Design
Designer
Mervil M. Paylor
Client
Little & Associates Architects
Commercial architecture

4 Design Firm
Visible Ink
Designer
Sharon Howard Constant
Client
The Jones Collection
Manufacturers' representative

5 Design Firm
Sullivan Perkins
Designer
Art Garcia
Client
Metrowest Landscape Company
Landscaping

6 Design Firm
Visual Advantage
Designer
Ann Hiemstra
Client
Shelli McConnell
Food writer and consultant

1

SANDI Wasserstein

SOFTWARE + HARDWARE Consulting and Training

SANDIS DESIGNS
20 Locksly Lane
San Rafael, California 94901
Voice [415] 454.0731

2

276 JERSEY STREET
SAN FRANCISCO ·
CALIFORNIA 94114

GATES
GROUP

PH 415 206 1237
FX 415 206 0711

MARKETING PUBLIC RELATIONS

LAURA GATES

3

31 HODGES ALLEY

SAN FRANCISCO

CALIFORNIA 94133

Monroy & Cover Design

GRAPHIC DESIGNER

GAIL COVER

TEL / FAX 415-986-3171

4

GINA GALLIGAN   & ASSOCIATES

MELISSA GATCHEL-NORTH   2523 MCKINNEY SUITE A

CREATIVE DIRECTOR   DALLAS, TEXAS 75201

TELEPHONE (214)871-7971

FACSIMILE (214)871-7974

5

▶ Jack Lagrassa

TREELINE MANAGEMENT CORP.

371 Merrick Road   Tel : 516. 678 2525
Rockville Centre   Fax: 516. 678 9859
NY 11570

6

NIMAN

SCHELL

818 Brannan st
Number 202 ·
San Francisco
California 94103
PH 415 552 0181
FX 415 552 0851

Pedro Gonzalez Production Manager

1 Design Firm
Sunny Shender Design
Designer
Sunny Shender
Client
Sandis Designs
Fine jewelry and beadwork retailBC

2 Design Firm
Design Group Cook
Designer
Ken Cook
Client
The Gates Group
Public relations

3 Design Firm
Monroy & Cover Design
Designer
Gail Cover
Client
Amanda Pirot
Marketing and project management

4 Design Firm
David Carter Design
Art Director
Lori B. Wilson
Designer
Ricky Brown
Illustrator
Ricky Brown
Client
Gina Galligan & Associates
Marketing and public relations

5 Design Firm
Chee Wang Ng
Designer
Chee Wang Ng
Client
Treeline Management Corporation
Property management

6 Design Firm
Design Group Cook
Designer
Ken Cook
Client
Niman Schell Ranch
Cattle-raising ranch

1

accentrix

FURNITURE

ANTIQUES

ACCESSORIES

1470

FRONTAGE

ROAD

O'FALLON,

ILLINOIS

62269

618.624.7292

FAX 618.624.8093

2

D E S I G N
MANAGEMENT
G R O U P

Kevin Bird

Suite 101
495 Wellington St. W.
Toronto ON M5V 1E9

Tel: (416) 977-4093

1-800-865-4364

Fax: (416) 977-0647

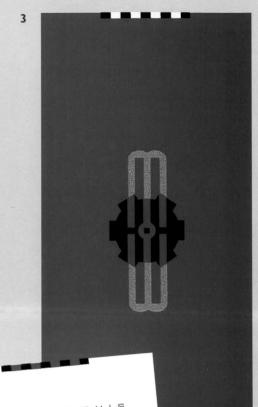

3

1 Design Firm
Phoenix Creative
Designer
Eric Thoelke
Client
Accentrix
*High-end furniture and
antique retail*

2 Design Firm
Design Management Group
Art Director
Kevin Bird
Designer
Kevin Bird
Client
Self-promotion
*Communications counseling, design,
and writing*

3 Design Firm
Greteman Group
Designers
Sonia Greteman, James Strange
Client
Motorworks by Autocraf
Auto repair

4 Design Firm
THARP DID IT
Art Director
Rick Tharp
Designers
Laurie Okamura, Colleen Sullivan, Rick Tharp
Illustrator
Georgia Deaver
Client
Integrated Media Group
Multi-media educational materials

ELAINE ARONIS

MARKETING DIRECTOR

M O T O R
W O R K S
BY AUTOCRAFT

1 1 1 6 E A S T D O U G L A S

W I C H I T A , K S 6 7 2 1 4

T E L 3 1 6 2 6 7 - 8 8 8 8

F A X 3 1 6 2 6 5 - 0 7 6 6

S P E C I A L I Z I N G I N

HONDA MAZDA NISSAN TOYOTA

4

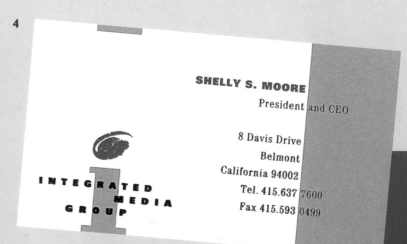

SHELLY S. MOORE
President and CEO

8 Davis Drive
Belmont
California 94002
Tel. 415.637 7600
Fax 415.593 0499

INTEGRATED
MEDIA
GROUP

Romeo to get into **VROOM!** Nobody gets it about technology. People knowing more. People finding
out. People getting the message. People fixing the details. People acting in unison. People freeing
creativity. People having the time **WHIRRR** Metatypographicon **TAPTAPPETYTAP** Your wrist is
exhausted from all that pointing and clicking. Time for some stretching exercises: Converse. Reach.
Grab. Lift. Tilt. Drink. Repeat **GLUB** Female hand reaches into view and with weary authority presses
PLAY FWEEP? 'Be it declared for ever that I Bronwyn, wife of Idris of Hampstead, in return for the
Miracle of my husband's life...' **CLANGG...** A player does a little victory jig to the congratulations of his
friends. Apparently he has just saved their fantasy lives **KA-CHING!** The bad news is: money is ugly.
Anchored in the past, hidebound by tradition, the money we scratch to get turns out to be insipid,
colorless, prosaic **WHOOSH!** Having obtained a mysterious Object in the Southern Outpost, the
players travel to Kalaman to have the Object deciphered by the Dream Merchant in Kalaman's
famous open-air bazaar **WHIFF** Pansies, those infallible border brighteners, have a remarkable past.
Apothecarists clandestinely plucked them for love potions; Victorians extolled their virtues in art.
Turkish perfumers harvested them by the ton **PLUCK** The joys of attempting and accomplishing are
powerful currency **THUNK!** Head. Heart. Hands. / The tao of gardens / informs our work. / Nurture.
Shape. Cultiva[
[cabinet door
riented **AHA!**
eighbors, a p[
Remember, if y[

1 Design Firm
Melissa Passehl Design
Designer
Melissa Passehl
Client
Ken Eklund Communications
Copywriting

2 Design Firm
The Bradford Lawton Design Group
Art Directors
Brad Lawton, Jennifer Griffith-Garcia
Designer
Brad Lawton
Illustrators
Brad Lawton, Jody Laney
Client
Redfeather Design
Snowshoe design and manufacturing

3 Design Firm
Cato, Berro García & Di Luzio S.A.
Designer
Gonzalo Berro García
Client
Jose Luis Rodriguez
Photography

4 Design Firm
Choplogic
Designer
Walter McCord
Client
Prospects for Fitness
Health club

5 Design Firm
España Design
Designer
Cecilia España
Client
Self-promotion
Graphic design

1

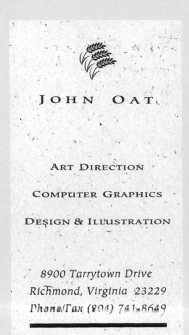

JOHN OAT

ART DIRECTION

COMPUTER GRAPHICS

DESIGN & ILLUSTRATION

8900 Tarrytown Drive
Richmond, Virginia 23229
Phone/Fax (804) 741-8649

2

Phillip Esparza

photographer

3711 Parry Avenue

Suite 103

Dallas Texas 75226

214.823.9782

214.823.9784 fax

p.e.

3

WESTMINSTER
CHRISTIAN
FELLOWSHIP

REV. HARRY METZGER

16670 Easton Avenue

Prairie View, Illinois 60069

708.367.1034

4

TRACS

Technical
Research
and
Consulting
Service

Ron Kukas

1128 W. Evergreen
Visalia, CA 93277

Phone or Fax:

209-627-6971

Mobile:

209-730-2244

5

ANTIQUES
RUSSELL P. ROUSHON
296 TAUGWONK ROAD
STONINGTON, CT 06378
SHOP 203.535.4483
RESIDENCE 203.535.9170

6

FREELANCE CAMERAMAN
STEVE BREASHEARS
2822 KINNEY DRIVE
WALNUT CREEK, CA 94595
510 / 937-2174

1 **Design Firm**
John Oat Communication Arts
Designer
John Oat
Client
Self-promotion
Graphic design

2 **Design Firm**
Gibbs Baronet
Art Directors
Steve Gibbs, Willie Baronet
Designers
Kellye Kimball, Steve Gibbs
Illustrator
Kellye Kimball
Client
Phillip Esparza
Photography

3 **Design Firm**
Associates Design
Designer
Beth Finn
Client
Westminster Christian Fellowship

4 **Design Firm**
Covi Corporation
Agency Gillham & Associates
Designer
Mona Howell
Illustrator
Mona Howell
Client
Tracs
Soil and pesticide consulting

5 **Design Firm**
PhD
Designer
Terri Haas
Client
Antiques

6 **Design Firm**
B3 Design
Designer
Barbara B. Breashears
Client
Steve Breashears
Freelance cameraman

1

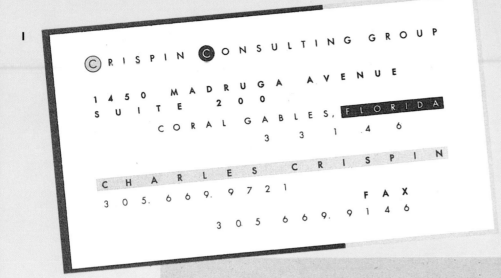

©RISPIN ©ONSULTING GROUP
1450 MADRUGA AVENUE
SUITE 200
CORAL GABLES, FLORIDA
33146
CHARLES CRISPIN
305.669.9721
FAX
305 669.9146

C

2

SCOTT GATZKE PHOTOGRAPHY

153 26TH AVE S.E.
SUITE 101
MPLS, MN 55414
TEL: 612·378·0517
FAX: 612·378·9456

3

HUNTER FREEMAN STUDIO

123 South Park

San Francisco

California 94107

Represented by

Bobbi Wendt

HUNTER FREEMAN

Pho 415 495 1900

Fax 415 495 2594

4

CONSERVATION

PARTNERS

1138 Humboldt Street

Denver, Colorado

80218

(303) 831-9378

FAX (303) 831-9379

MARTY ZELLER
President

1 **Design Firm**
Pinkhaus Design Corp.
Designer
Susie Lawson
Client
Charles Crispin
Advertising

2 **Design Firm**
Zauhar Design
Designer
David Zauhar
Client
Scott Gatzke
Photography

3 **Design Firm**
Design Group Cook
Designer
Ken Cook
Client
Hunter Freeman Photography

4 **Design Firm**
David Warren Design
Designer
David Warren
Client
Conservation Partners
Land preservation consulting

1

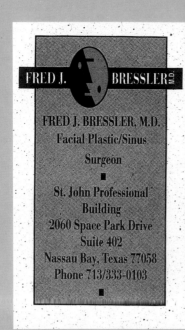

FRED J. BRESSLER, M.D.
Facial Plastic/Sinus
Surgeon

St. John Professional
Building
2060 Space Park Drive
Suite 402
Nassau Bay, Texas 77058
Phone 713/333-0103

2

FRANK WIEDEMANN

GRAPHIC DESIGN

2077 Fulton Street
San Francisco, CA 94117
415 221 0192

3

4

5

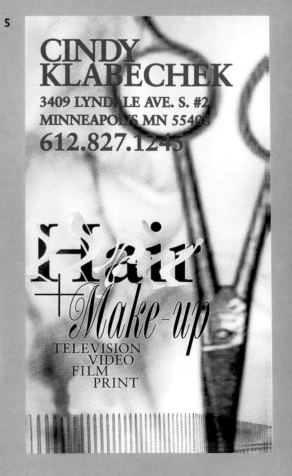

1 Design Firm
MAH Design Inc.
Designer
Mary Anne Heckman
Illustrator
Mary Anne Heckman, Jack Slattery
Client
Fred J. Bressler, M.D.
Facial and plastic surgery

2 Design Firm
Wiedemann Design
Designer
Frank Wiedemann
Photographer
Frank Wiedemann
Client
Self-promotion
Graphic design

3 Design Firm
Zubi Design
Designer
Kristen Balouch
Client
Self-promotion
Design

4 Design Firm
Peterson & Company
Art Director
Bryan L. Peterson
Designer
Bryan L. Peterson
Illustrator
Jan Wilson
Client
John Wong Photography

5 Design Firm
Stress Lab
Designer
Lizz Luce
Client
Cindy Klabechek
Hair and makeup stylist

1

MICHAEL BOYD
MUSIC

Michael Boyd

Two Gravatt Drive
Berkeley CA 94705

Ph 510 849 3554

Fx 510 540 5412

2

Charlotte Schiff-Jones
President

830 Lincoln Road, Miami Beach
Florida 33139

Miami
Tel: 305.531.0858
Fax: 305.531.2585

New York
Tel: 212.288.5115

GAMUT MEDIA

3

PHOTOGRAPHIC
SCOTT HUNT
ILLUSTRATION

SCOTT HUNT

10837 RUTH ANN DR.

DALLAS, TEXAS 75228

214.613.0930

4

ſavoirAffair

ANNa Jean HOLLis

846 Monroe Drive, N.E. • Atlanta, Georgia 30308 • 404/872-2768

5

pro
mo
tio
nal.
des
ign

limerock.

drew force

0333 sw flower st.
portland, oregon 97201

503 245 4647

1 Design Firm
Design Group Cook
Designer
Ken Cook
Client
Michael Boyd Music
*Television music and advertising
production company*

2 Design Firm
Pinkhaus Design Corp.
Designer
Todd Houser
Client
Gamut Media
Multi-media productions

3 Design Firm
Sibley/Peteet Design, Inc.
Designer
Derek Welch
Client
Scott Hunt
Photography

4 Design Firm
Two In Design
Designer
Ed Phelps
Client
Savoir Affair
Event planning

5 Design Firm
Drew Force Design
Art Director
Drew Force
Designers
Drew Force, Phil Bradfield
Photographer
Dave Hawkins
Client
Self-promotion,
Graphic design co-operative

I

Anne Semmes

F O O D   C O N S U L T A N T

55 Cambridge Drive ❦ Short Hills, NJ 07078 ❦ 201.376.5595

2

Fischel Consulting
12136 Madeleine Circle
Dallas, Texas 75230
Bert Fischel
(214) 490-5202 / Fax (214) 490-5220

3

Singulis Vitae
H O M E O P A T I A

DAUTO MIZUTANI

AV AÇOCÊ, 249
MOEMA   SP
CEP   04075-021
FONE   884 0242
FAX   884 6782

4

WILSON

FAMILY FUNERAL CHAPEL
"No one will care for your family like our family"

Kim A. Wilson
President

1240 Winton Way at Drakeley Avenue
Atwater, California 95301 • (209) 358-7700 Fax 358-2465

5

LAKE PLACID LODGE

A Classic Adirondack Retreat

I Design Firm
Toni Schowalter Design
Designer
Toni Schowalter
Client
Anne Semmes
Food consulting

2 Design Firm
Peterson & Company
Designer
Dave Eliason
Client
Fischel
Communications consulting

3 Design Firm
Rocha & Yamasaki Arq.E Design
Designer
Mauricio Rocha
Client
Singulis Vitae
Pharmacy

4 Design Firm
ifx Visual Marketing
Designer
James F. Stone, Jr.
Client
Wilson
Family funeral chapel

5 Design Firm
Kaiser Dicken
Art Director
Craig Dicken
Designers
Craig Dicken, Debra Kaiser
Client
Lake Placid Lodge
Adirondack resort

1

Philip Riis-Carstensen Arkitekt MAA
Ved Højen 10 2900 Hellerup 39 61 23 95

1 Design Firm
Vibeke Nodskov
Designer
Vibeke Nodskov
Client
Philip Riis-Carstensen
Architecture

2 Design Firm
Whitney Edwards Design
Art Director
Charlene Whitney Edwards
Designer
Charlene Whitney Edwards
Illustrator
Nancy Kurtz
Client
Paul Baker Touart
Architectural historian

3 Design Firm
Two In Design
Designer
Ed Phelps
Illustrator
Harriet Burger
Client
Westside Stories
Motion picture production

4 Design Firm
Hornall Anderson Design Works
Art Director
Jack Anderson
Designers
Jack Anderson, Heidi Favour, Bruce
Branson-Meyer
Client
Dave Syferd
Marketing and public relations

5 Design Firm
Phoenix Creative
Designer
Ed Mantels-Seeker
Client
Clayco Accurate Construction
Industrial contracting

6 Design Firm
Melissa Passehl Design
Designer
Melissa Passehl
Client
Alumni Real Estate Group

2

PAUL BAKER TOUART
ARCHITECTURAL HISTORIAN

POST OFFICE BOX 5
WESTOVER, MARYLAND
21871

410 651-1094

3

Westside Stories™

1270 WEST PEACHTREE STREET, NW
SUITE 8B
ATLANTA, GEORGIA 30309
TELEPHONE [404] 908-7499
FACSIMILE [404] 881-1078

4

ALISON T. SEYMOUR, INC.
Natural Fiber Floor Coverings

Alison T. Seymour, Inc.
Natural Fiber Floor Coverings

Voice
206.935.5471

Facsimile
206.935.6409

5423 West Marginal Way SW
Seattle, WA 98106 USA

5

Dale Robertson
Millwright General Foreman

4124 North Broadway
St. Louis, Missouri 63147
314 241-5444 Office
618 541-8614 Mobile
314 855-6172 Beeper
314 356-9775 Home

6

ALUMNI REAL ESTATE GROUP

POST OFFICE BOX 6952
SAN JOSE, CA 95150
408 226-7653

KARL A. DUMAS

1

JIM COX
ACOUSTIC AND ELECTRIC BASS
PRIVATE PARTIES • MUSIC CONSULTATION

PHONE 708.329.1213

2

Andrew Greenberg • 5454 Broadway • Oakland, CA 94618 • Fax 510 420 1574

Greenberg Qualitative Research • 510 420 1514

3

The Herrington

CINDY PEPPLE
ASSISTANT HOTEL MANAGER

15 SOUTH RIVER LANE
GENEVA, ILLINOIS 60134
7 0 8 • 2 0 8 • 7 4 3 3

4

D E S I G N • I L L U S T R A T I O N

Michael Lenn

Mi'sha

1638 Commonwealth Av. • Suite 24 • Boston, MA 02135 • Tel. 617.277.7765 • Fax 617.277.3538

1 Design Firm
JOED Design Inc.
Designer
Joanne Rebek
Client
Jim Cox
Musician

2 Design Firm
Stowe Designer
Designer
Jodie Stowe
Client
Greenberg Qualitative
Research

3 Design Firm
Associates Design
Designer
Jill Arena
Client
The Herrington
Bed and breakfast

4 Design Firm
Misha Design
Designer
Michael Lenn
Client
Self-promotion
Design and illustration

1

Sandy Williamson

(206) 784-7996

1737 NW 56th St.

Suite 101

Seattle, WA 98107

Fax 784-1264

Williamson Landscape
Architecture, LLC

WILLIAL055BF

1 **Design Firm**
Michael Courtney Design
Designer
Michael Courtney
Illustrators
Michael Courtney, Nita Williamson,
Donna Baxter
Client
Williamson Associates
Landscape architecture

2 **Design Firm**
Marc English Design
Designer
Marc English
Client
Swept Away
Cleaning services

WILLIAMSON LANDSCAPE ARCHITECTURE

— ■ —

Design & Construction

Sandy Williamson

(206) 784-7996

1737 NW 56th St.

Suite 101

Seattle, WA 98107

Fax 784-1264

Williamson Landscape
Architecture, LLC

WILLIAL055BF

WILLIAMSON LANDSCAPE ARCHITECTURE

— ■ —

Design & Construction

2

CLEANING SERVICES

SWEPT AWAY

CHRISTINE BLOMQUIST

49 PLEASANT STREET
EPPING, NEW HAMPSHIRE
03042
TELEPHONE (603) 679 - 2989

1

COMPANY
Acme Rubber Stamp

NAME
Julie Paquette

TITLE
Artistic Director

STREET
3102 Commerce

CITY
Dallas STATE **TX** ZIP **75226**

PHONE
(214) 748-4707 FAX **1-800-580-6275**

LOCAL FAX
(214) 748-2263

◄ STAMP HERE ►

RUBBER
ACME
STAMP

2

3

WА
WellerArchitects

Tel 505-255-8270

Fax 505-255-8830

401 Alvarado Drive SE

Suite D Albuquerque, New Mexico 87108

4

REDSTONE

RICH VLIET
President

DESIGN
DEVELOPMENT
————
144 N. MOSLEY

WICHITA, KS 67202

TEL 316 263 2711

FAX 316 263 4711

5

Christian Posch

bG

Tel. 06542   4331-58 Fax. 06542/4331-55

A-5700 Zell am See, Auerspergstraße5 GRAFIK DESIGN

GREENBOX

1 Design Firm
Peterson & Company
Art Directors
Dave Eliason, Bryan L. Peterson
Designer
Dave Eliason
Client
ACME Rubber Stamp Company

2 Design Firm
Vaughn Wedeen Creative
Designer
Rick Vaughn
Client
Rippelstein's
Men's clothing store

3 Design Firm
Vaughn Wedeen Creative
Designer
Rick Vaughn
Client
Weller Architects

4 Design Firm
Greteman Group
Art Directors
Sonia Greteman, James Strange
Designer
James Strange
Client
Red Stone
Design development

5 Design Firm
Greenbox Grafik
Designer
Christian Posch
Client
Self-promotion
Graphic design

1

DAVE SYFERD

☐ **SUN VALLEY**
207 Aspen Dr.
Ketcham, Idaho
83340
208 726 8837

☐ **BOISE**
350 N. 9th St.
P.O. Box 8283
Boise, Idaho
83707
208 342 0925

☐ **SEATTLE**
8006 Avalon Pl.
Mercer Island,
Washington
98040
206 232 3103

2

monica *Lytjana* GÖTZ

322 E 89 APT 4A
NEW YORK NY 10128
212 534 1559

3

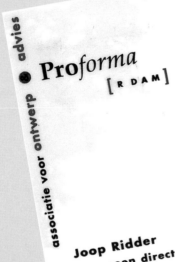

advies ● **Proforma** [R DAM]
associatie voor ontwerp

Joop Ridder
algemeen directeur

Slepersvest 5-7
3011 MK Rotterdam
(010) 411 27 22

advies ● **Proforma** [R'DAM]
associatie voor ontwerp

Els van Klinken
communicatieadviseur

Slepersvest 5-7
3011 MK Rotterdam

4

ARTEFAB

ALAIN LAUZON
Président
Directeur général

3820 E, rue Isabelle
Brossard, Québec
Canada, J4Y 2R3

Tél.: (514) 444 2224
Téléc.: (514) 444 2122

1 Design Firm
Hornall Anderson Design Works
Art Director
Jack Anderson
Designers
Jack Anderson, Heidi Favour,
Bruce Branson-Meyer
Client
Dave Syferd
Marketing and public relations

2 Design Firm
Monica Gîtz Design
Designer
Monica Gîtz
Client
Self-promotion
Graphic design

3 Design Firm
Proforma, Association of
Designers & Consultants
Art Director
Aad Van Dommelen
Client
Self-promotion
Design

4 Design Firm
D2 Design
Designer
Dominique Duval
Client
Artefab
*Opera and theatre
set construction*

1

Etienne Bresson

• d e s i g n e r • s t y l i s t •

213 656 1229

2

Lance Lichter   W62 N551   414.375.6868 *p*
President   Washington Ave. 414.375.6869 *f*
                     Cedarburg, WI
                     53012

WAVE
Property Management

~

3

G. Stephen McCrocklin, Director

THE LANGSFORD CENTER
LEARNING TO EXCEL

4

214 Albany Avenue

Louisville, Kentucky 40206

(-   )6-1818

Bruce Carnahan Landscape Design

1

DONNA L. ROBINSON

Certified Public Accountant

TEL 404·423·9997
FAX 404·427·5819
1256 COBB PARKWAY N.
MARIETTA, GA 30062

CERTIFIED PUBLIC ACCOUNTANTS

PATRICK
W
LACEY
PC

DEDICATED TO EXCELLENCE

2

JOHN WAGNER

PHOTOGRAPHY

212 THIRD AVENUE NORTH SUITE 380
MINNEAPOLIS MINNESOTA 55401
TELEPHONE 612-330-0946 FAX 612-330-0035

3

GEORGIE MEL B. RACELA
Certified Public Accountant
CERTIFICATE NO. 88266

535 Gen. Luis Street
Novaliches
Quezon City

Telephone : 936-2440

4

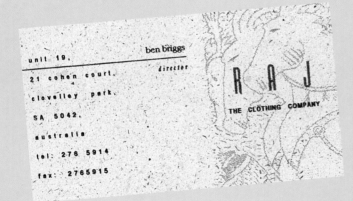

unit 19,
21 cohen court,
clovelley park,
SA 5042,
australia
tel: 276 5914
fax: 2765915

ben briggs
director

R A J

THE CLOTHING COMPANY

5

900 Lay Road

St. Louis, MO 63124

Telephone

314-991-0005

Facsimile

314-991-1512

Community School

Chris Green

6

JAM STREET WEAR

SAM LEE

51, CECIL STREET,
HAMILTON,
WAIKATO AREA,
NEW ZEALAND
TEL: 8490113 FAX: 8492313

1 Design Firm
Wages Design
Designer
Rory Myers
Client
Patrick W. Lacey
Certified public accountant

2 Design Firm
Stress Lab
Designer
Lizz Luce
Client
John Wagner
Photography

3 Design Firm
Design Source, Inc.
Designer
Robert Salazar
Client
Georgie Racela
Certified public accountant

4 Design Firm
Isheo Design House
Designer
Ishmael Sheo
Client
RAJ - The Clothing Company
Boutique

5 Design Firm
Kiku Obata & Company
Art Director
Amy Knopf, Kiku Obata
Designer
Amy Knopf
Illustrator
Sara Love
Client
Community School
Private elementary school

6 Design Firm
Isheo Design House
Designer
Ishmael Sheo
Client
JAM - Street Wear
Clothing maufacturing

1

GREG COLEMAN
Director of Marketing
Tel. 612.339.5218

RETIREMENT AND ESTATE ADVISORS

1320 Metropolitan Centre Minneapolis, Minnesota Fax 612. 337.5070
333 South 7th Street Zip 55402

2

INVESTMENT
······· AGE ·······
PUBLISHING

KATE LINDE
President

17008 Island View Drive
Huntersville, NC 28078
Telephone 704/896-9631

3

S·T·E·V·E·N C.
O·N·E·A·L, M.S.

O

Consultant

3500 CROSSTREE COURT

HORTICULTURE

COLUMBUS, OH 43221

& LANDSCAPE

(614) 777-1615

4

S.E. TARRAF

President

WALL STREET ADVISORS

950 Interchange Tower

600 South Hwy 169

Minneapolis, Mn 55426

Pho 612-546-5657

800-359-6078

Fax 612-546-5672

1 Design Firm
Design Center
Art Director
John Reger
Designer
Sherwin Schwartzrock
Client
Retirement & Estate Advisors
Financial planning

2 Design Firm
Mervil Paylor Design
Designer
Mervil M. Paylor
Client
Investment Age Publishing
Investment texts publishing

3 Design Firm
Robbins Design
Designer
Tom Robbins
Client
Steven C. O'Neal
Horticulture and landscape
architecture

4 Design Firm
Design Center
Art Director
John Reger
Designer
Todd Spichke
Client
Wall Street Advisors
Financial planning

1

Beatty Levine Inc. EVENT PRODUCTION & DESTINATION MANAGEMENT

VICKI EMERICK
DIRECTOR OF
PROGRAM FINANCE

4100 Newport Place
Suite 220
Newport Beach
California 92660
714.251.1111
Fax 714.251.1137
LA 310.598.0085

2

415 574 5894

TRAVIS POWELL

EVENT / MEDIA
PRODUCER

FULL PRODUCTION MANAGEMENT
• EVENTS
• VIDEO
• PRINT

37 TWELFTH AVENUE
SAN MATEO, CA 94402
FAX 415 574 5894

3

PREC**I**SION

Lisa Whitaker
President

Precision Sampling
Incorporated
958 San Leandro Avenue
Suite 900
Mountain View, CA 94043
415 967 8717
FAX 962 0612

4

Aspen Grove

Craig Williams

Post Office Box 98
Gallatin Gateway, MT 59730
406-763-5044

5

Luma

at THE BROADMOOR

1 Design Firm
Vaughn Wedeen Creative
Art Director
Rick Vaughn
Designer
Dan Flynn
Client
Beatty Levine Inc.
*Event production and
destination management*

2 Design Firm
Stowe Designer
Designer
Jodie Stowe
Client
Travis Powell
Event/media production

3 Design Firm
Curtis Design
Designer
David Curtis
Client
Precision Sampling Inc.
Soil sample drilling

4 Design Firm
Palmquist & Palmquist Design
Designers
Kurt Palmquist, Denise Palmquist
Illustrators
Jim Lindquist, Kurt Palmquist
Client
Aspen Grove B & B
Bed and breakfast

5 Design Firm
Marsh, Inc.
Designer
Greg Conyers
Client
Luma
Handmade objects gift shop

1

Joan Deccio Wickham
Food Stylist & Culinary Instructor

P.O. Box 442
Vashon, WA
98070
206-463-3647
Fax 206-463-9223

2

CMO
CUSTOM FLORAL
formerly
Country Maid Originals
Custom
Floral Decorating
Specialty Gifts
CONNIE HITE
Proprietor, Floral Designer
6 8 9 - 4 9 9 1
5963 Jefferson St.
Burlington, KY 41005
Located In Tousey House c.1822

3

Elaine Gantz Wright

∞

5552 Belmont Avenue, Dallas, Texas 75206-6724
214.821.3375 fax 214.942.0878

PHILANTHROPIC PARTNERS

Building Business Through Community Investments

4

DELANEY MATRIX
organizational strategies

Michael Delaney, MHSL

1272 West Palo Alto
Fresno, California 93711-1489
209.439.5158
Fax 209.439.9203

1

Lester Childres

The Pretty Penny, Inc.

14534 Memorial Drive

Houston, Texas 77079

Phone 713/493-2430

Fax Line 713/493-5553

2

J o a n P i e k n y

A r t D i r e c t o r /

G r a p h i c D e s i g n e r

o f f i c e : 2 1 2 / 5 4 6 - 3 2 1 0

s t u d i o : 2 1 2 / 2 4 2 - 3 8 7 8

3

ARVIN & ARVIN

a partnership

SCOTT ARVIN
LUCY ARVIN

2025 N. Broadmoor
Suite Number 182
Wichita, KS 67206

Tel 316 686 0178

Fax 316 686 5865

4

COMMUNITY
REHABILITATION
CENTERS, INC.

Beth Irtz
*Director of
Rehabilitation Services*

Cherry Creek Place I
3131 S. Vaughn Way, Suite 405
Aurora, Colorado 80014

303 • 369 • 9685

F A X 303 • 369 • 0609

5

650

VENICE BLVD.

VENICE, CA

90291

JUSTIN MENCHEN
TEL: 310 827-9666
FAX: 310 827-3397

PJ GRAPHICS

1 Design Firm
MAH Design Inc.
Designer
Mary Anne Heckman
Client
The Pretty Penny, Inc.
Gift store

2 Design Firm
Joan Piekny
Designer
Joan Piekny
Illustrator
Paul Shaw
Client
Self-promotion
Graphic design and art direction

3 Design Firm
Greteman Group
Designer
Sonia Greteman
Client
Arvin & Arvin
Motivational speakers

4 Design Firm
Vaughn Wedeen Creative
Art Director
Steve Wedeen
Designer
Dann Flynn
Client
Horizon Health Care
Rehabilation centers

5 Design Firm
PJ Graphics
Art Directors
Justin Menchen, Paula Menchen
Client
Self-promotion
Graphic design

1

From I-95 Traveling North
• Exit 33. Straight onto Bridgeport Avenue.
• Continue over Devon Bridge.
• Go to second traffic light, Ormond Street.
• Building on left/Parking in rear.

From I-95 Traveling South
• Exit 34. Right onto Bridgeport Avenue.

OPERATED BY CUGINI, INC.

LA CUCINA
PIZZA, PASTA & MORE

RESERVATIONS
203·874·0387

HOME DELIVERY
203·874·5300

128 BRIDGEPORT AVENUE
DEVON, CONNECTICUT 06460

2

ORLAND PARK
REALTORS

BILL CALDWELL
sales manager

ORLAND PARK REALTORS IS A KLISCHUK SUBSIDIARY

9439 West
144th Place
Orland Park
Illinois 60462

ph
708 873 1400

pgr
708 569 5835

3

LANDSCAPE
SANCTUARIES

*Landscape Design, Organics &
Integrated Pest Management Solutions*

George Morris
704.663.0378

4

OCCASIONAL
OCCASIONS
by Carlton

CATERING WITH CONTEMPORARY ELEGANCE

Ronald J. Ross · Director of Marketing · (404) 413–9325

5

COSMED

...ation

Chairman of the Board and
Chief Executive Officer

12360 Manchester Road
Suite Number 204
St.Louis, Missouri 63131
314 I 966.6131
FAX I 966.8148

1 Design Firm
KMC Design
Designer
Kimberly McCoy
Client
La Cucina Restaurant

2 Design Firm
Athanasius-Design
Designer
Jeffrey Wallace
Client
Orland Park Realtors
Real estate

3 Design Firm
Steven Morris Design
Designer
Steven Morris
Client
Landscape Sanctuaries
*Natural and organic
landscaping*

4 Design Firm
The Design Company
Art Director
Marcia Romanuck
Designer
Fran McKay
Client
Occasional Occasions
Catering

5 Design Firm
Phoenix Creative
Designer
Ed Mantels-Seeker
Client
CosMed Corporation
*Cosmetic and specialized
medical service*

1

DOUGLAS MANNING

MANNING PRODUCTIONS, INC.

300 WEST WASHINGTON STREET

SUITE 706 CHICAGO, ILLINOIS 60606

P 312.782.2700   F 312.782.2783

2

BOISÉ
MONT-ROLLAND

ROGER CHARTIER
Conseiller

Boisé Mont-Rolland Inc.
960 rue des Geais Bleus
Mont-Rolland, Québec
J0R 1G0
Téléphone
(514) 623-6345

3

ED LINSTROM
Complete Landscape Maintenance

16011 Winterbrook Road
Los Gatos, CA 95032
(408)356-8418

4

♥ fawbush's

3420 Galleria, Edina, MN 55435 612.922.5717

5

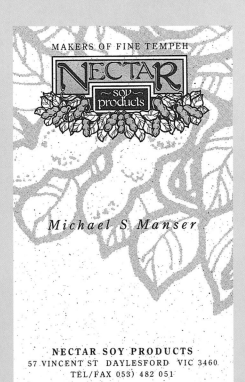

MAKERS OF FINE TEMPEH

NECTAR
~ soy products

Michael S. Manser

NECTAR SOY PRODUCTS
57 VINCENT ST DAYLESFORD VIC 3460
TEL/FAX 053) 482 051

1 Design Firm
JOED Design, Inc.
Designer
Edward Rebek
Client
Manning Productions Inc.
Video production

2 Design Firm
D2 Design
Designer
Dominique Duval
Client
Boisé Mont-Rolland
Land developers

3 Design Firm
JWK Design
Art Director
Jennifer Kompolt
Designers
Jennifer Kompolt,
Melissa James
Client
Ed Linstram
Landscaping and maintenance

4 Design Firm
Tilka Design
Art Director
Jane Tilka
Designer
Jane Tilka
Illustrator
Stan Olsen
Client
Fawbush's
Women's clothing retail

5 Design Firm
Mammoliti Chan Design
Art Director
Tony Mammoliti
Designer
Chwee Kuan Chan
Illustrator
Chwee Kuan Chan
Client
Nectar Soy Products
Soy tempeh manufacturers

1

SOON EVERY CHILD WILL WHISPER THE MAGIC OF TUMBLE DRUM

2

GRENE
CORNEA

CORNEA, CATARACT &
REFRACTIVE EYE SURGERY

MARK WELLEMEYER, M.D.

8020 East Central
Wichita, KS 67206
Tel 316-636-2010
Fax 316-636-5174
1-800-788-3060

3

Keller Groves, Inc.

Herman J. Keller
PRESIDENT

P.O. BOX 2468
WAUCHULA
FLORIDA, 33873
813.773.9411

TUMBLE
DRUM SM

JACQUELINE SWARTZ

Mid-Rivers Plaza
5849 Suemandy Drive
St. Peters, Missouri 63376
Tel 314-397-7700

4

Donna Hall

Consultant

104 Randi Drive

Madison, CT 06443

tel 20

fax 20

DONNA HALL

H

1 Design Firm
Greteman Group
Designers
Sonia Greteman,
Bill Gardner, James Strange
Client
Tumble Drum
Children's recreational center

2 Design Firm
Greteman Group
Designer
Sonia Greteman
Client
Grene Cornea
*Cornea, cataract,
and refractive surgery*

3 Design Firm
JOED Design, Inc.
Designer
Edward Rebek
Client
Herman Keller
Orange grower

4 Design Firm
Greteman Group
Designers
James Strange, Sonia Greteman
Client
Donna Hall
Health care consultant

5 Design Firm
Eat Design
Art Director
Patrice Eilts-Jobe
Designers
Patrice Eilts-Jobe, Kevin Tracy
Illustrator
Kevin Tracy
Client
St. Paul's Episcopal Day School

5

KAREN MONSEES
DIRECTOR OF ADMISSIONS

ST·PAUL'S
EPISCOPAL
DAY SCHOOL

4041 MAIN STREET
KANSAS CITY, MO 64111
SCHOOL OFFICE 816-931-8614
SCHOOL FAX 816-931-6860

Mark J Laughlin

617 437 1356
617 437 1406 Fax

LAUGHLIN
Winkler

Marketing + Design

4 Clarendon Street
Boston Massachusetts
02116 6117

MARiaS SAM

g·r·a·p·h·i·c d·e·s·i·g·n

3310 Thompson Street
Richmond, Va. 23222
(804) 321-4866

2

3

10284 ROYAL ANN AVENUE

SAN DIEGO

CALIFORNIA · 92126

TEL 619.578.8799

FAX 619.578.8799

STEVEN
MORRIS
DESIGN

5

TONI · VOSS

COPYWRITER
CREATIVE THINKER

455 HUNTERS RIDGE
SALINE · MI 48176
TEL 313 · 944 · 0024
FAX 313 · 944 · 0190

4

KoLibri
CREATIV HAIRSTYLING

Andrea Neher
A-6774 Tschagguns 487, Tel. 05556/3920

1 Design Firm
Laughlin/Winkler Inc.
Designers
Mark Laughlin, Ellen Winkler
Client
Self-promotion
Graphic design and marketing

2 Design Firm
Maria Sams Graphic Design
Designer
Maria Sams
Client
Self-promotion
Graphic design

3 Design Firm
Steven Morris Design
Designer
Steven Morris
Client
Self-promotion
Graphic design

4 Design Firm
Grafik Design Ganahl Christoph
Designer
Ganahl Christoph
Client
Kolibri
Hair salon

5 Design Firm
el Design
Art Director
Lynn St. Pierre
Designer
Lynn St. Pierre
Illustrator
Kevin Ewing
Client
Toni Voss
Copywriter

a Cat's Garden

1

Red Rhinoceros

WILLIAM KOLBER
Vice President

1466 BROADWAY SUITE 808

NEW YORK NEW YORK 10036

TELEPHONE (212) 764 5100

FAX (212) 764 5213 / 5231

3

JEWEL RUFFIN

131 Jasper Drive

Amherst, NY 14226

716 · 838 · 0553

CHAMELEON
DESIGN LIMITED

a Cat's Garden

4

TWO BEARS DANCING   1920 ABRAMS PARKWAY

TRADING COMPANY   SUITE 367

                                                              DALLAS, TEXAS

SUE SWIGART   75214

PRESIDENT   214 733 9884

5

Lead Dog
COMMUNICatiONS

33 BEVERLY ROad

KENsingTON

CA 94707

☎ 510 525 3053

fax 510 525 6425

LEAD dog THE VIEW NEVER CHANGES.

IF YOU'rE NOT THE

1 Design Firm
Hixson Design
Designer
Gary Hixson
Illustrator
Public Domain Engraving
Client
A Cat's Garden
Gift retail

2 Design Firm
Patricia Spencer Advertising & Design
Designer
Patricia Spencer
Client
Red Rhinoceros
Men's sportswear design

3 Design Firm
Chameleon Design Ltd.
Designer
Jewel Ruffin
Client
Self-promotion
Graphic design

4 Design Firm
Joseph Rattan Design
Designer
Joseph Rattan
Illustrator
Greg Morgan
Client
Two Bears Dancing
Trading Company
*Native American jewelry
manufacturing*

5 Design Firm
Lead Dog Communications
Designer
Suzanne Jacquot
Illustrator
Cliff Jew
Client
Self-promotion
Design and communications

1

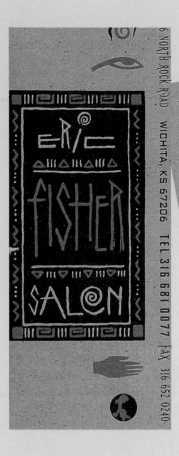

6 NORTH ROCK ROAD   WICHITA, KS 67206   TEL 316 681 0077   FAX 316 652 0240

YOUR NEXT APPOINTMENT

This time is reserved exclusively for you. 24 hours notice
is appreciated if you are unable to keep your appointment.

2

1528 Providence Road

Charlotte, NC

28207

704 364-262:

Thomas & Debra George
Proprietors

3

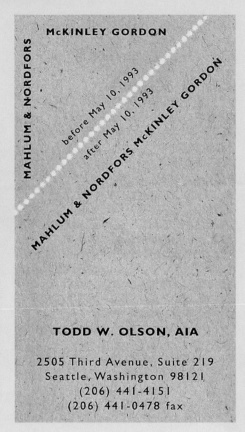

McKINLEY GORDON

MAHLUM & NORDFORS

before May 10, 1993

after May 10, 1993

MAHLUM & NORDFORS McKINLEY GORDON

TODD W. OLSON, AIA

2505 Third Avenue, Suite 219
Seattle, Washington 98121
(206) 441-4151
(206) 441-0478 fax

4

Creating

Success

Through

Strategic

Marketing

WINNING
VISIONS

Richard Winn
President

807 N. Waco, Suite 23
P.O. Box 48127
Wichita, KS 67201
Tel 316 263 2185
Fax 316 265 5943

1 Design Firm
Greteman Group
Designers
Sonia Greteman, Bill Gardner
Client
Eric Fisher Salon
Hair sylist

2 Design Firm
Mervil Paylor Design
Art Director
Mervil M. Paylor
Designers
Mervil M. Paylor, Brady Bone
Illustrator
Gary Palmer
Client
Pasta & Provisions
Pasta, wine and sauce retail

3 Design Firm
Hornall Anderson Design Works
Art Director
Jack Anderson
Designers
Jack Anderson, Scott Eggers,
Leo Raymundo
Client
Mahlum & Nordfors
McKinley Gordon
Architecture

4 Design Firm
Greteman Group
Art Director
Sonia Greteman
Designers
Sonia Greteman, Jo Quillin
Client
Winning Visions
Strategic marketing

1

ROBERT WYLIE

MALABAR
C O A S T

2032 Broadway, Santa Monica, California 90404
Telephone: 310.264.7702 Fax: 310.264.7704

2

SPLENDIDO
Biscotti

Celeste de Tessan

P.O. Box 1347 Glen Ellen, CA 95442
707-939-8656

3

3

PENNY IVANOVIC

VIAGGIO
RISTORANTE MEDITERRANEO

14550 BIG BASIN WAY • SARATOGA, CALIFORNIA 95070 • TEL 408.741.5300

4

Care that Starts from the Heart

Health Strategies Plaza
551 N. Hillside, Suite 410
Post Office Box 47668
Wichita, KS 67201-7668

Betsy Babcock
Chief Executive Officer

• • • • • • •

Telephone 316-684-3838
Toll Free 1-800-657-7250
Facsimile 316-688-9183

Galichia Medical Group P.A.

1 Design Firm
Curtis Design
Art Director
David Curtis
Designer
Joan Bittner
Client
Malabar Coast
Furniture importing

2 Design Firm
Holden & Company
Designer
Cathe Holden
Client
Splendido Biscotti
Bakery

3 Design Firm
THARP DID IT
Art Director
Rick Tharp
Designers
Laurie Okamura, Rick Tharp
Client
Viaggio
Mediterranean restaurant

4 Design Firm
Greteman Group
Art Director
Sonia Greteman
Designers
Sonia Greteman, James Strange
Client
Galichia Medical Group
*Heart surgeon and
general practitioners*

1

FITZHUGH L. STOUT
& ASSOCIATES

FITZHUGH L. STOUT, MAI
Real Property Appraiser
and Consultant

505 East Boulevard
Charlotte, North Carolina 28203
704·376·0295
Facsimile 704·342·3704

2

Charles Shields

415 East Olive Avenue
Fresno, California 93728
209-497-8060
FAX: 209-497-8061

3

HORTICA
URBAN GARDENS

Judith L. Musick
566 Castro Street
San Francisco 94114
tel 415.863.4697
fax 415.863.1024

4

SUITE 102

A FULL DAY SPA

DORA TEMPLES
6201 ANTIOCH ST. SUITE 102
OAKLAND, CA 94611
415 / 339-8181

YOUR NEX
APPOINTMEN

DATE

TIME

5

1 **Design Firm**
Mervil Paylor Design
Designer
Mervil M. Paylor
Client
Fitzhugh L. Stout & Associates
Real estate appraisal

2 **Design Firm**
Shields Design
Designer
Charles Shields
Client
Self-promotion
Advertising and graphic design

3 **Design Firm**
Barry Power Graphic Design
Designer
Barry Power
Client
Hortica Urban Gardens
Flower nursery

4 **Design Firm**
B3 Design
Designer
Barbara B. Breashears
Client
Suite 102
Spa

5 **Design Firm**
Mitsuta
Art Director
Shiann-juh Lai
Designer
Pey-yng Lin
Illustrator
Shiann-juh Lai
Client
Shui-Li Snake Kiln
Ceramics Cultural Park

1

John D. Beckelhymer del Valle
President

WORLD-WIDE ASSET LOCATORS, INC.

1319 Rosario Street
Laredo, Texas 78040-8838
U.S.A.
512.727.3743
fax 512.791.2264

2

MACCO *Systems*

medical & dental
practice management systems

amar patel

457 W. ALLEN AVE. *suite* 117 SAN DIMAS, CA. 91773
fon 909.394.7288 *fax* 909.394.7290

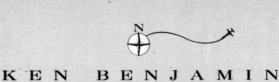

3

THE GARRETT
H O T E L   G R O U P

DAVID W. GARRETT
President

166 BATTERY STREET
BURLINGTON, VERMONT 05401
802-865-0053   802-865-3146 FAX

1 Design Firm
Marc English Design
Designer
Marc English
Client
World-Wide Asset Locators, Inc.
Purchasing brokerage

2 Design Firm
Jeff Labbé Design 0950
Designer
Jeff Labbé
Client
Macco Systems
Medical software development

3 Design Firm
Kaiser Dicken
Art Director
Craig Dicken
Designer
Debra Kaiser
Client
The Garrett Hotel Group
Exclusive hotel developers

4 Design Firm
Vaughn Wedeen Creative
Designer
Steve Wedeen
Client
Juniper Learning
Educational and teacher's aids

5 Design Firm
THARP DID IT
Art Director
Rick Tharp
Designers
Jana Heer, Rick Tharp
Client
Ken Benjamin
Wildlife photography

5

K E N   B E N J A M I N
PHOTOGRAPHER

211 Alexander Avenue • Los Gatos, CA 95030 • 408·354·8626

4

KATHY L. JAHNER

Juniper Learning

POST OFFICE DRAWER O · ESPAÑOLA, NEW MEXICO 87532
TEL 505.753.7410 · TOLL FREE 800.456.1776
FAX 505.747.1107

1

△ R T I S T
J O D I L. Y △ N < E Y

615 552 2570
P.O. BOX 2344
< L △ R K S V I L L E , TN 37042

2

Marc English

Design

**37 Wellington Avenue
Lexington MA
02173-7110
617 : 860 : 0500 phone | fax**

3

PRODUCTIONS di ROSSI

GABRIELLA ROSSI
4 1 5   8 5 1   4 4 3 8
1879 ANAMOR STREET
REDWOOD CITY, CA 94061

Judy Merrill
415 965 7452

4

Merrill Communications
100 E. Middlefield Road, Suite 1-D
Mountain View, CA 94043
Fax 415 965 7475
MCI Mail 443 4229
CompuServe 72634,44
Internet merrill@svpal.org

5

CAROL VALMY-MERCHANT

COPYWRITING *for*
CREATIVE MARKETING
COMMUNICATIONS

3565 RIPPLETON ROAD
CAZENOVIA, NEW YORK 13035

315-655-8532

1 Design Firm
Jodi L. Yancy, Artist
Designer
Jodi L. Yancy
Client
Self-promotion
Fine art and illustration

2 Design Firm
Marc English Design
Designer
Marc English
Client
Self-promotion
Design consulting

3 Design Firm
Stowe Designer
Designer
Jodie Stowe
Client
Productions di Rossi
Production art

4 Design Firm
Stowe Designer
Designer
Jodie Stowe
Client
Merrill Communications
Promotion and marketing

5 Design Firm
Jowaisas Design
Designer
Elizabeth Jowaisas
Client
Carol Valmy-Merchant
Copywriter

Design Firm
MC Studio/Times Mirror Magazines
Art Director
Paul Kelly
Designers
Kirsten Heincke, Paul Kelly
Client
Self-promotion
Graphic design

monica götz
art director

212 779 5080

two park avenue, new york, ny 10016 fax 779 5577

a division of times mirror magazines, inc.

a division of times mirror magazines, inc.

a division of times mirror magazines, inc.

a division of times mirror magazines, inc.

a division of times mirror magazines, inc.

1

Geek Squad
computer support services
212 Third Avenue North, Suite 579
Minneapolis, Minnesota 55401

Robert C. Stephens
geek-squad@bitstream.mpls.mn.us
tel. 612.751.6205
fax. 612.288.9983

Geek
Squad

2

MIM'S BAKERY

let 'em
eat cake
let 'em
eat cake
let 'em
eat cake

890 HUMBOLDT AVE
CHICO, CA 95928
916 345 3331

3

ART
SPACE

REGAN
JACKSON

ART DIRECTION

TEL: 310.841.6061
FAX: 310.841.0350

3111 S. LA CIENEGA BLVD. LOS ANGELES, CA 90016

ORCHIDS PUEBLO 3111-3117

4

REAL
FAST
DELIVERY!

QUALITY DOESN'T COST! *IT PAYS!*

WURTSBAUGH
SPECIALTY MARKETING SERVICES

731 Carman Meadows Drive
Manchester, Missouri 63021
☎ **(314)227-5615** ☎

MARTHA WEGMANN, PRESIDENT

CALL US
TODAY!

ALMOST
ANY
PLACE!

YOU CAN'T
LOSE!

1 **Design Firm**
Stress Lab
Designer
Chuck Hermes
Client
Geek Squad
Computer support services

2 **Design Firm**
Wiedemann Design
Designer
Frank Wiedemann
Client
Mim's Bakery

3 **Design Firm**
13th Floor
Art Director
Regan Jackson
Designer
Eric Ruffing
Client
Regan Jackson
Art direction

4 **Design Firm**
Phoenix Creative
Designer
Eric Thoelke
Client
Wurtsbaugh
Specialty marketing services

1

2

3

4

Julie Cascioppo Cabaret & Jazz Vocalist 206.547.1150

5

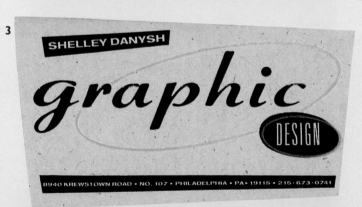

1 Design Firm
Jeff Labbé Design 0950
Designer
Jeff Labbé
Client
Conn Quigley
Shoe repair

2 Design Firm
V. Allen Crawford Design
Designer
V. Allen Crawford
Client
Victoria Sadowski
Independent metalsmith

3 Design Firm
Shelley Danysh Studio
Designer
Shelley Danysh
Client
Self-promotion
Graphic design

4 Design Firm
Giorgio Davanzo Design
Designer
Giorgio Davanzo
Client
Julie Cascioppo
Cabaret and jazz vocalist

5 Design Firm
Jeff Labbé Design 0950
Designer
Jeff Labbé
Client
Ron Perry
Photography

1

OUNG JU LEE

GRAPHIC
DESIGN
212.546.3482
516.767.8440

2

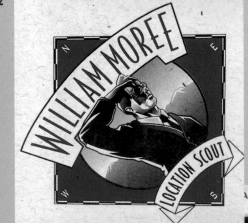

WILLIAM MOREE
LOCATION SCOUT

...ALL A SCOUT

800
MOREE
WT

FAX 617-423-3769 MIAMI 305-226-...

354 CONGRESS ST. BOSTON MA 02210

BOSTON LOCAL 617-426-7378

3

梅 **Billy Moy**

2002 Park Road
(Rib Mt. State Park)
Wausau, WI 54401

715.359.5830
1.800.290.6650
414.321.1818 *fax*

MOY'S
Rib Mountain Ginseng™

梅 氏 劲 山 花 旗 蔘

梅 英 福

1.800.290.6650

RICK WAS BORN IN 1952 IN MANSFIELD, OHIO.
...HEN HE WENT TO COLLEGE AT MIAMI UNIVERSI...
...NOT IN FLORIDA). AND AFTER THAT HE CAME...
...ALIFORNIA AND OPENED A SMALL DESIGN STUDI...
...ALLED THARP DID IT. HE NOW HAS FIVE OR...
...IX OTHERS DOING IT WITH HIM. SOMETIMES T...
...WIN AWARDS CERTIFICATES FOR THE STUFF THE...
...O, (USUALLY NOT ON **A** COMPUTER), AND HAN...
...HEM ON A CLOTHESLINE ACROSS THE STUDIO. T...
...WON A CLIO ONCE, BUT CAN'T FIND IT. RICK...
...NON-CORPORATE IDENTITY, PACKA...
...THAT GET INTO THE SMITHSONIAN...
...Y OF CONGRESS. BIG DEAL YOU SAY?...
...HER STUFF TOO. LIKE SKI, IRON...
...PE. HE DISLIKES WHINERS, UPC...
...MOST SOFTWARE PROGRAMS EXCE...
...OR A COUPLE OF EASY ONES. H...
...IAS ANOTHER OFFICE IN PORTL...
...REGON WITH A CREATIVE DIREC...
...RIEND. HE DOESN'T HAVE ANY...
...KIDS THAT HE KNOWS OF. THIS...
...S PRINTED BY WATERMARK PRES...

#!@*

4

rick tharp

1 Design Firm
YoungJu Lee
Designer
YoungJu Lee
Client
Self-promotion
Graphic design

2 Design Firm
Paratore Hartshorn Design
Designer
Paratore Hartshorn Design
Client
William Moree
Location scout

3 Design Firm
Becker Design
Art Director
Neil Becker
Designer
Neil Becker, Terry Lutz
Client
Moy's Rib Mountain Ginseng
Ginseng mail order sales

4 Design Firm
THARP DID IT
Art Director
Rick Tharp
Photographer
Franklin Avery
Client
Self-promotion
Graphic design

1

MICHAEL JEFFCOAT

FAB REP

301 East 7th Street
•
Suite 203
•
Charlotte, NC 28202
•
Facsimile: 704.342.0044
•
Telephone: 704.342.0000

1.800. $F_3 A_2 B_2 R_7 E_3 P_7$.

2

EAT DESIGN

4 1 1 1   B A L T I M O R E
K A N S A S   C I T Y
M I S S O U R I   6 4 1 1 1
T E L E P H O N E
8 1 6 . 9 3 1 . 2 6 8 7
F A C S I M I L E
8 1 6 . 9 3 1 . 0 7 2 3

PATRICE EILTS

1 Design Firm
Mervil Paylor Design
Designer
Mervil M. Paylor
Client
FabRep
Furniture and fabric representative

2 Design Firm
Eat Design
Art Director
Patrice Eilts-Jobe
Designer
Toni O'Bryan
Client
Self-promotion
Graphic design and advertising

3 Design Firm
High Techsplanations
Designer
Mike James
Client
Leaping Lizards
Volleyball team

4 Design Firm
Elton Ward Design
Art Director
Steve Coleman
Designer
Chris De Lisen
Client
Self-promotion
Design

5 Design Firm
Barry Power Graphic Design
Designer
Barry Power
Illustrator
Everett Ching
Client
Everett Ching
Illustration

3

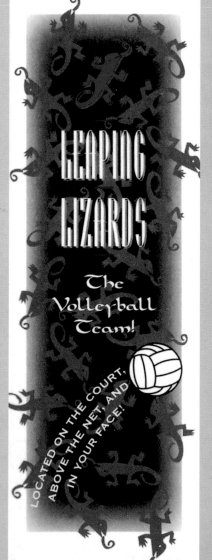

4

STEVE COLEMAN
DIRECTOR

ELTON WARD

FOUR GRAND AVENUE
PARRAMATTA NSW 2124
AUSTRALIA, PO BOX 802
TELEPHONE (02) 635 6500
FACSIMILE   (02) 635 3436

5

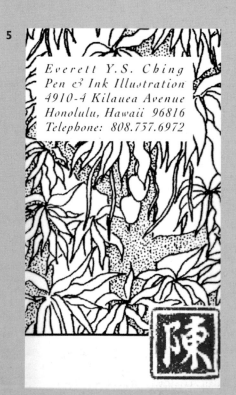

*Everett Y.S. Ching
Pen & Ink Illustration
4910-4 Kilauea Avenue
Honolulu, Hawaii 96816
Telephone: 808.737.6972*

1

ART KANE STUDIO, INC.
568 BROADWAY • NY, NY 10012 • TEL. 212 925 7334

2

Rex Stocklin
Chief Designing Officer

13603 Marina Pt. Dr C421 • Marina del Rey, Ca 90292 • p 310-577-4956 • f 310-577-4958

4

CARL R. KOHLER, A.I.A.

3011 Dent Place, N.W.
Washington, D.C. 20007
(202) 338-0986

3

41

L I Z   O ' B R I E N
41 WOOSTER STREET • NEW YORK, N.Y. 10013
2 1 2 • 3 4 3 • 0 9 3 5

5

MIRES DESIGN INC
2345 KETTNER BLVD SAN DIEGO CA 92101
PHONE: 619 234 6631 FAX: 619 234 1807
E MAIL: MIRES@MIRESDESIGN.COM

1 Design Firm
Mike Quon Design Office
Designer
Mike Quon
Client
Art Kane Studio, Inc.
Photography

2 Design Firm
Paradigm Design
Designer
Rex Stocklin
Client
Self-promotion
Graphic design

3 Design Firm
Eric Kohler
Designer
Eric Kohler
Client
"41"
1940s furniture gallery

4 Design Firm
Eric Kohler
Designer
Eric Kohler
Client
Carl R. Kohler
Architecture

5 Design Firm
Mires Design, Inc.
Art Director
John Ball
Designer
John Ball
Client
Self-promotion
Graphic design

6 Design Firm
Choplogic
Designer
Walter McCord
Client
Axiom
Photography

6

A X I O M
I N C
1 2 0
S O U T H
B R O O K
S T R E E T
L O U I S V I L L E
K E N T U C K Y
4 0 2 0 2
5 0 2
5 8 4
7 6 6 6

1

SAWDUST PENCIL CO.

Charles Maguire
Plant Manager

44 National Road
Edison, New Jersey 08817
908•248•9088 Fax 908•248•9425

2

Nicola Stranieri
musicista
via Emanuelli 15
28100 Novara, Italia
telefono 0321 450 726

batterista

3

WAYNE GUSTAFSON

JULIAN'S SANTA FE

221 SHELBY • SANTA FE, NEW MEXICO 87501 • 505.988.2355

4

619-225-2276

Keri Sims
W R I T E R
*2060 Catalina Boulevard
San Diego, California 92107*

5

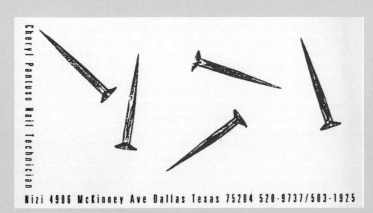

Cheryl Pantuso Nail Technician

Nizi 4906 McKinney Ave Dallas Texas 75204 520-9737/503-1925

6

PROMO
INTERNATIONAL

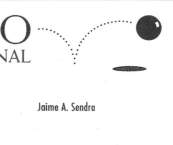

5622 Dyer Street

Dallas, TX 75206

214.360.8788

214.361.4835 fax

Jaime A. Sendra

---

1 Design Firm
Shelley Danysh Studio
Designer
Shelley Danysh
Client
Sandust Pencil Company
Pencil and marker manufacturing

2 Design Firm
Tangram Strategic Design
Designer
Antonella Trevisan
Client
Nicola Stranieri
Drummer

3 Design Firm
Cisneros Design
Designer
Fred Cisneros
Client
Julian's
Italian restaurant

4 Design Firm
Linnea Gruber Design
Designer
Linnea Gruber
Client
Keri Sims
Writer

5 Design Firm
Gibbs Baronet
Art Directors
Willie Baronet, Steve Gibbs
Designer
Willie Baronet
Illustrator
Willie Baronet
Client
Cheryl Pantuso
Manicurist

6 Design Firm
Advance Design Center
Designer
Bryan Rogers
Client
Promo International
Promotional items production

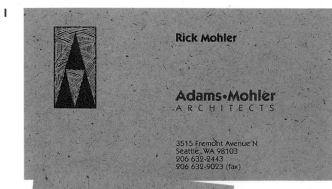

Rick Mohler

Adams•Mohler
A R C H I T E C T S

3515 Fremont Avenue N
Seattle, WA 98103
206 632-2443
206 632-9023 (fax)

Adams•Mohler
A R C H I T E C T S

2

ARTURO

(617)497-7270
40 LINNAEAN STREET APT. 11
CAMBRIDGE, MA 0 2 1 3 9

3

A DIVISION OF CONSOLIDATED MANAGEMENT CO.

H
U
N
G
R
Y

2894 106TH STREET SUITE 104

DES MOINES, IOWA 50322

OFFICE PHONE: (515) 278-9774

HOME PHONE: (303) 936-3827

MIKE ANDERSON
DIRECTOR OF CAMP SERVICES

C
A
M
P
E
R

1 Design Firm
Robert Williamson
Designer
Robert Williamson
Client
Adams-Mohler
Architecture

2 Design Firm
Karyl Klopp Design
Designer
Karyl Klopp
Client
Arturo
Holistic counseling

3 Design Firm
Sayles Graphic Design
Designer
John Sayles
Client
Hungry Camper
Resort food service

4 Design Firm
Cisneros Design
Designer
Fred Cisneros
Client
Custom Properties of Santa Fe
*Commercial and
residential building*

4

CARLA HILEY
office manager

CUSTOM PROPERTIES
OF SANTA FE
...a general contracting firm

1494 St. Francis Drive
Santa Fe, New Mexico 87501
505-982-8824
FAX: 505-989-3669

1 Coffee, Tea Espresso & Gifts

Ross Davidson

510-339-8187
5772 Thornhill Drive
Oakland, CA 94611

2 GREENACRES

TELEPHONE 316 634 1500

8141 EAST 21ST WICHITA, KS 67206-2903

A Natural Foods Market

3 MICHAEL ABELL

322 SO. BROADWAY
WICHITA, KANSAS
ZIP 67202 4304
TEL 316 263 6939
FAX 316 265 0081

ABELL PEARSON
PRINTING COMPANY

4 LOS GATOS BAR & GRILL

MARK HACKER
proprietor

15½ NORTH SANTA CRUZ
LOS GATOS, CALIFORNIA 95030
TELEFAX 408.366.2222
TELEPHONE 408.399.LGBG

1 Design Firm
Visible Ink
Designer
Sharon Howard Constant
Client
Albuquerque Connection
Coffee house

2 Design Firm
Greteman Group
Designer
Sonia Greteman
Client
Green Acres
Natural foods market

3 Design Firm
Greteman Group
Designer
Sonia Greteman
Client
Abell Pearson
Printing

4 Design Firm
THARP DID IT
Art Director
Rick Tharp
Designers
Laurie Okamura, Rick Tharp
Illustrators
Jana Heer, Laurie Okamura
Client
Los Gatos Bar and Grill

5 Design Firm
B3 Design
Designer
Barbara B. Breashears
Client
Apple Lane Baker

5

GOURMET FRUIT TARTS

APPLE, CHERRY,
PUMPKIN, LEMON,
STRAWBERRY / RHUBAR.
IN SEASON

▼

SUGAR FREE
WHEAT FREE
LOW CHOLESTEROL
LOW FAT
ELEGANT AND DELICIOU.

▼

LYNDA BROCKMANN
PRESIDENT

▼

121 PONDEROSA LANE
WALNUT CREEK, CA 94595
RING 510/932-8283
FAX 510/935-8934

1 Design Firm
13th Floor
Designer
Eric Ruffing
Client
Cyan Video Production
Music and video production

2 Design Firm
Blue Sky Design
Designers
Robert Little, Joanne Little,
Maria Dominguez
Client
Self-promotion
Graphic design

3 Design Firm
Peat Jariya Design/Metal Studio
Art Director
Peat Jariya
Designer
Peat Jariya Design Staff
Client
Self-promotion
Graphic design

4 Design Firm
13th Floor
Designer
Eric Ruffing
Client
Susan Frank & David Frisch
Furniture design and fabrication

5 Design Firm
Marise Mizrahi
Designer
Marise Mizrahi
Client
Self-promotion
Consulting

1

[cyan]

STEVE CRIST

4 4 7 0
SUNSET BLVD
SUITE 300
LOS ANGELES
CALIFORNIA
9 0 0 2 7

FAX 213 481 1900
TEL 213 481 2500

2

Blue Sky Design

JOANNE C. LITTLE
Vice President & Creative Director

10300 Sunset Drive, Suite 353, Miami, Florida 33173
Telephone 305·271·2063   Facsimile 305·271·2064

3

[metal] Studio Inc. 13164 Memorial Drive #222, Houston, Texas 77079

Peat Jariya

[metal]

713.523.5177

4

furniture
DESIGN
fabrication
SUSAN FRANK + **DAVID FRISCH**
1928 echo park av, los angeles, ca 90026
TEL. 213.   FAX 213.644.0496
644.0495

5

Design
Art

Marise Mizrahi

212.   274.8663

74 Leonard St. #6A New York, NY 10013

Photography

1

PURPLE SEAL GRAPHICS

D E S I G N

I L L U S T R A T I O N

LIM·HO YEN

P.O. BOX 3041

CARBONDALE

ILLINOIS 62902

EFFECTIVE
VISUAL
COMMUNICATION

林和源
紫篆
廣告
設計

▶ ▶ ▶ **618** ☼ **453·3489** ◑ **549·6537**

2

STEIN

Architects

29 Commonwealth Ave
Boston, MA 02116
Tel 617.437.9458
Fax 617.421.9567

3

Lynn Parker
Principal

Parker LePla

Brand Development
Public Relations

4464 Fremont Ave. N.
Suite 210
Seattle, WA 98103
(206) 633-1951
Fax (206) 633-2036
Email:74217,2415
@ compuserve.com

4

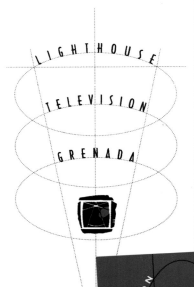

LIGHTHOUSE

TELEVISION

GRENADA

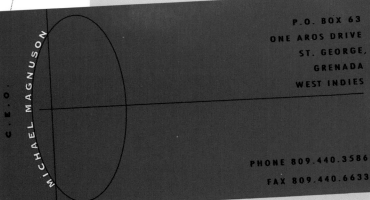

MICHAEL MAGNUSON

C.E.O.

P.O. BOX 63
ONE AROS DRIVE
ST. GEORGE,
GRENADA
WEST INDIES

PHONE 809.440.3586
FAX 809.440.6633

1 Design Firm
Purple Seal Graphics
Designer
Lim-Ho Yen
Client
Self-promotion,
Graphic design

2 Design Firm
Clifford Selbert
Design Collaborative
Art Director
Clifford Selbert, Robin Perkins
Designer
Robin Perkins
Client
Stein Architects

3 Design Firm
Walsh & Associates, Inc.
Designer
Miriam Lisco
Client
Parker LePla
*Brand development
and public relations*

4 Design Firm
Pinkhaus Design Corp.
Designer
Claudia DeCastro
Client
Lighthouse TV Grenada
Caribbean television station

1 Design Firm
Zedwear
Art Director
John Klaja
Designer
John Klaja
Photographer
Stuart Diekmeyer
Client
Self-promotion
T-shirt design and distribution

2 Design Firm
Sommese Design
Designer
Lanny Sommese
Client
Self-promotion
Design and illustration

3 Design Firm
Mike Quon Design Office
Designer
Mike Quon
Client
CD 101.9
Radio station

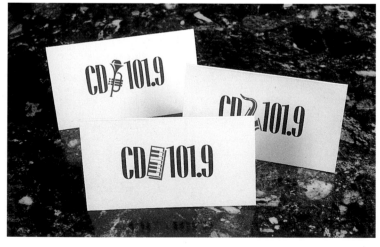

1 **Design Firm**
David Warren Design
Designer
David Warren
Client
Aspects of Vail
Crystal glass retail

2 **Design Firm**
Jeff Labbé Design 0950
Designer
Jeff Labbé
Client
Self-promotion
Design

3 **Design Firm**
Daniel Bastian
Designer
Daniel Bastian
Client
Gattfried von Einem
Radio producion

4 **Design Firm**
Wages Design
Art Director
Bob Wages
Designer
Lionell Ferreira
Client
Axcess Marketing Group
Interior industry marketing

1 Design Firm
Animus Comunicação
Art Director
Rique Nitzsche
Designer
Rique Nitzsche,
Felício Torres
Client
Less Money
Shoe retail

2 Design Firm
One & One Design
Consultants Inc.
Designer
Dominick Sarica
Client
AMS Woodcrafts
Woodworking

3 Design Firm
Maximum
Art Director
Ed Han
Designer
Deirdre Boland
Illustrator
Deirdre Boland
Client
The Chicago
Bicycle Company
*Hand-crafted
bike manufacturing*

4 Design Firm
Blink
Designer
Scott Idleman
Client
Self-promotion
Graphic design

1

KELLY SHAW

business
[403] 762 · 0243
facsimile
[403] 762 · 4046
residence
[403] 678 · 6004

NUMBER FIVE HAWK AVENUE INDUSTRIAL COMPOUND BOX 2560 BANFF CANADA

TANYA DOELL

business
[403] 762 · 0243
facsimile
[403] 762 · 4046
residence
[403] 762 · 4302

DARREN DELICHTE

business
[403] 762 · 0243
facsimile
[403] 762 · 4046
residence
[403] 762 · 8359

1 Design Firm
Geo Graphics—Banff
Designers
Darren Delichte, Tanya Doell
Client
Self-promotion
Graphic design

2 Design Firm
Mike Quon Design Office
Designer
Mike Quon
Client
The Spot
Hair salon

THE SPOT
521 MADISON AVENUE
NEW YORK, NY 10022
TEL. 212-688-4450

2

THE SPOT

CHU-LI

521 MADISON AVENUE
NEW YORK, NY 10022
TEL. 212-688-4450

THE SPOT

ANDRÉ TAVERNISE

521 MADISON AVENUE
NEW YORK, NY 10022
TEL. 212-688-4450

1

2

3

4

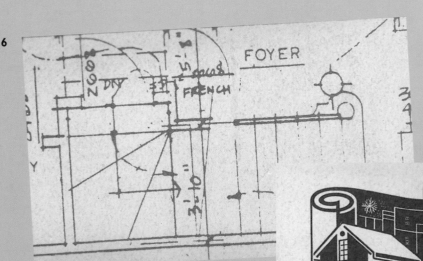

5

6

1

MEN at WORK

DALE RICH
PROPRIETOR
375-2316
PAGER NO.
383-7569

2

Margaret Fisher

C R E A T I V E
O P T I O N S
I N
M A R K E T I N G
P R O M O T I O N S

PH 075 75 5297

3/129
SUNSHINE BLV
MERMAID WATERS
QLD 4218

3

KAMEHACHI
café

1400 NORTH WELLS ▸ SECOND FLOOR
CHICAGO IL 60610

TEL. 312-664-1361
TUESDAY - SUNDAY UNTIL 2:00 AM

FOR LATE NIGHT
SUSHI & SPIRITS

4

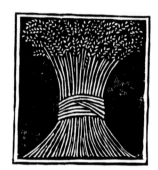

JANET MILLER
Food Stylist
Home Economist

310 · 459 · 9139

5

GREG STEWART

EVOLUTION

FILM & TAPE, INC.

5358 CARTWRIGHT AVENUE

NORTH HOLLYWOOD, CA 91601

PHONE: 818.505.0333 FAX: 818.505.1333

1 Design Firm
Vibeke Nodskov
Designer
Vibeke Nodskov
Client
Groupvision (Nordic)

2 Design Firm
Blue Sky Design
Designer
Maria Dominguez
Client
Nicole Bailey
Design consulting

3 Design Firm
Catalina Communications
Designer
Marji Keim-López
Client
Self-promotion
Environmental graphic design

4 Design Firm
Becker Design
Designer
Neil Becker
Illustrator
Deborah Hernandez
Client
Instinct Art Gallery

1

2

3

4

1

CARLO CAPRARO

15466 LOS GATOS BLVD
SUITE 105
LOS GATOS, CA 95030

TEL 408.358.0107
FAX 408.358.8207

2

Design • Illustration
415 • 626 • 1523

CARLO
PERSONAL
FITNESS
TRAINING

3

JERRY ROBINSON

CONSTRUCTION
DESIGN
CONSULTING

P O BOX 691246

WEST HOLLYWOOD, CA 90069

TELEPHONE 310 652 7656

4

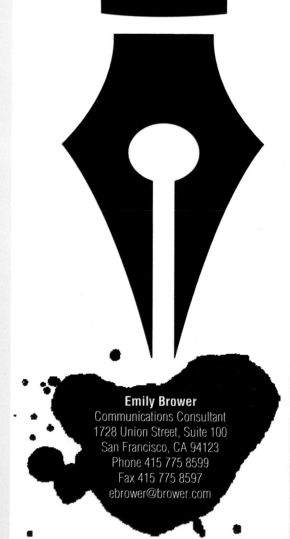

Emily Brower
Communications Consultant
1728 Union Street, Suite 100
San Francisco, CA 94123
Phone 415 775 8599
Fax 415 775 8597
ebrower@brower.com

5

DAM
SITE
DESIGN

DOUGLAS F. WOLFF, IDSA
PRESIDENT

161 S. 12 MILE RD
CERESCO, MICHIGAN
49033-0106
TEL: 616-979-1221
FAX: 616-979-3720

1 Design Firm
JWK Design
Art Director
Jennifer Kompolt
Designers
Jennifer Kompolt,
Patrick Keller
Illustrator
Patrick Keller
Client
Carlo
Personal fitness trainer

2 Design Firm
Squeak
Designer
Robin Dick
Client
Self-promotion
Design and illustration

3 Design Firm
Jay Vigon Studio
Art Director
Caroline Plasencia
Designer
Caroline Plasencia
Illustrator
Jay Vigon
Client
Jerry Robinson
*Construction,
design, and consulting*

4 Design Firm
Stowe Designer
Designer
Jennifer Lloyd
Client
Emily Brower
Communications consulting

5 Design Firm
Dam Site Design
Art Director
Douglas Wolff
Designer
Stacy L. Wolff
Client
Self-promotion
*Product design and
prototype/model making*

1

FILM & VIDEO
COMMUNICATIONS

MIRA

crea
tive
gr
oup

BOB O'DONNELL
creative director

1200 NW FRONT AVE • SUITE 200

PORTLAND, OREGON 97209

TELE:503•464•0630

FAX:503•464•0782

2

IMPORTER AND REPRESENTATIVE OF AFRICAN
TEXTILES • TRADITIONAL CLOTHINGS • ART • ARTIFACTS
WHOLESALE INQUIRIES WELCOME.

FEMI BANJO
Merchant

78 Upper A

4765

AFRICAN PRIDE
AT UNDERGROUND ATLANTA

3

PAPER
POST

1145 Lindero Canyon Rd., #D3
Thousand Oaks, CA 91362
818·865·0702

4

MARILYN WORSELDINE ◆ MARKET SIGHTS INC
3040 CAMBRIDGE PLACE NORTHWEST WASHINGTON DC 20007
TELEPHONE 202-342-3853 OR FAX 202-337-7851

5

LOS GATOS CYCLERY

FOR THE TOWN
FOR THE TRAIL

THYRA STEVENSON

15954 LOS GATOS BLVD. • LOS GATOS, CA 95032 • FAX 408.356.7092 • TEL 408.356.1644

FOR THE TOWN

1 Design Firm
Oakley Design Studios
Designer
Tim Oakley
Client
Mira Creative Group
Film and video communications

2 Design Firm
Two In Design
Designer
Ed Phelps
Client
African Pride
*Traditional African
merchandise retail*

3 Design Firm
SND, Sue Nan Designs
Designer
Sue Nan Douglass
Client
Paper Post
*Art, rubber stamps
and unusual paper store*

4 Design Firm
Market Sights, Inc
Designer
Marilyn Worseldine
Client
Self-promotion
Graphic design

5 Design Firm
THARP DID IT
Art Director
Rick Tharp
Designers
Laurie Okamura, Rick Tharp
Client
Los Gatos Cyclery
Bicycle retail

1

743 East Lake St.
Wayzata, Minn. 55391
Ph:(612)473-2940

Black's Ford

Ruth Whitney Bowe

2

ELLINGTON RUCKSACK CO.

ALECIA ELSASSER

0112 SW Hamilton   Portland, OR 97201
800-736-1222   503-223-7457 tel   503-223-7453 fax

4

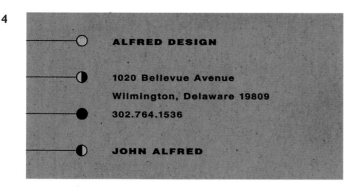

ALFRED DESIGN

1020 Bellevue Avenue
Wilmington, Delaware 19809

302.764.1536

JOHN ALFRED

3

MELISSA PASSEHL DESIGN

5

glen rogers perrotto

18595 ralya court
cupertino, california
95014

408.446.5401

1 Design Firm
Tilka Design
Art Director
Jane Tilka
Designer
Anne Koenig
Illustrator
Mike Reed
Client
Black's Ford
Specialty restaurant

2 Design Firm
Robert Bailey Incorporated
Designer
Ellen Bednarek
Client
Ellington Rucksack Co.
*Leather rucksacks, bags,
and wallet manufacturer*

3 Design Firm
Melissa Passehl Design
Designer
Melissa Passehl
Client
Self-promotion
Graphic design

4 Design Firm
Alfred Design
Designer
John Alfred
Client
Self-promotion
Graphic design

5 Design Firm
Melissa Passehl Design
Designer
Melissa Passehl
Client
Glen Rogers Perrotto
Print-making and fine art

1 Design Firm
John Evans Design
Designer
John Evans
Client
Self-promotion
Graphic design

2 Design Firm
desasterD.
Designer
Daniel Bastian
Client
IMP International
Music tour booking agency

3 Design Firm
Phoenix Creative
Designer
Ed Mantels-Seeker
Client
Self-promotion
Graphic design

4 Design Firm
Mires Design, Inc.
Art Director
José Serrano
Designer
José Serrano
Client
Vanderschuit Studio, Inc.
Photography

1

John Evans Design

2200 North Lamar

Suite Number 220

Dallas, Texas 75202

Tel 214.954.1044

Fax 214.922.9390

2

imp international
music
promotion
GmbH

Uwe Lohse
Kurtis Young

2800 Bremen 1
Grundstraße 39
Germany
Telefon
49 421 70 66 71/72
Fax
49 421 70 66 73

3

Steve Springmeyer

President

Phoenix Creative

611 North Tenth

Seventh Floor

Saint Louis

Missouri 63101

314 | 421-5646

FAX | 421-5647

PHOENIX

4

Carl VanderSchuit

VanderSchuit

Studio Inc.

751 Turquoise

San Diego

California

92109-1034

Telephone

619-539-7337

Facsimile

619-539-2081

V
A
N
D
E
R
S
C
H
U
I
T

1

2

WCVB TV
BOSTON

Marc English
Design Shaman

5 TV Place
Needham Heights, MA
02194-2303

617.433.4386
617.449.0260 fax

Amy Wong-Freeman
architect

M A H L U M
& N O R D F O R S
M c K I N L E Y
G O R D O N

2505
Third Avenue
Suite 219
Seattle, WA
98121

206 441 4151

3

THE WYANT SIMBOLI GROUP, INC.

JULIA WYANT

DESIGN
MULTIMEDIA
VIDEO

•

96 EAST AVENUE
NORWALK, CT 06851

TEL:203.838.0191 FAX:203.853.3125
WSGrp@aol.com

4

Via Emanuelli 15, 28100 Novara, Italia
0321 450 726
C.F. TRVNNL62M42B885O
P. IVA 01321610030

Antonella Trevisan
Graphic Designer

5

MICHEAL DOSS: STUDIO TELEPHONE: 206-270-9185

A R C H I T E C T U R E

119 W. DENNY WAY

SEATTLE, WA 98119

T: 206 - 270 - 9185

F: 206 - 270 - 9287

MICHEAL O. DOSS

1 Design Firm
Purple Seal Graphics
Designer
Lim-Ho Yen
Client
Self-promotion
Graphic design

2 Design Firm
WCVB TV Design
Designer
Marc English
Client
Self-promotion
Television station

3 Design Firm
The Wyant Simboli
Group Inc.
Art Director
Julie Wyant
Designer
Kristen Kiger
Illustrator
Kristen Kiger
Client
Self-promotion
Graphic design

4 Design Firm
Tangram Strategic Design
Designer
Antonella Trevisan
Client
Antonella Trevisan
Graphic design

5 Design Firm
Purple Seal Graphics
Designer
Lim-Ho Yen
Client
Debra Jones
Fine art and jewelry design

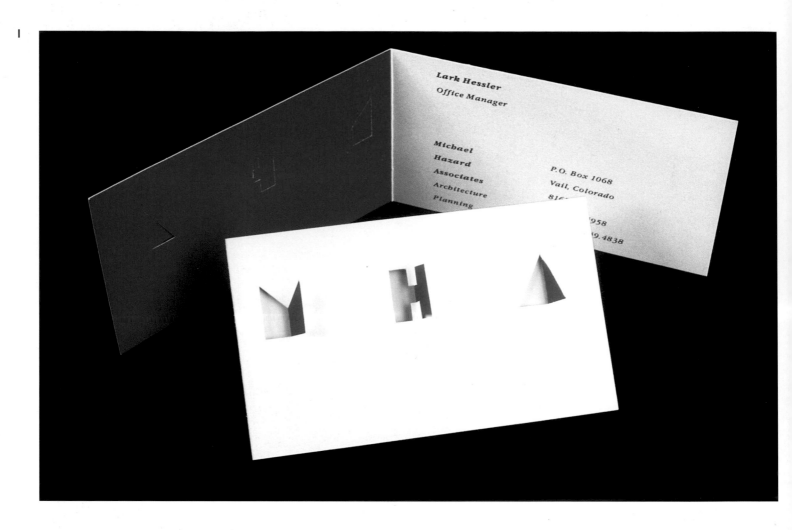

1

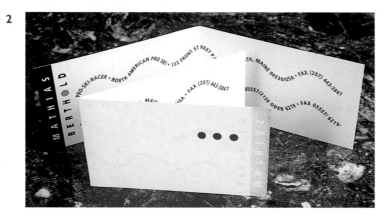

2

3

4

1 Design Firm
David Warren Design
Designer
David Warren
Client
Michael Hazard Associates
Architecture

2 Design Firm
Grafik Design Ganahl Christoph
Designer
Ganahl Christoph
Client
Mathias Berthold
Professional ski racer

3 Design Firm
Regate Communication
Designer
Bob Kasper
Client
New Media
Marketing

4 Design Firm
David Warren Design
Designer
David Warren
Client
Self-promotion
Design

1
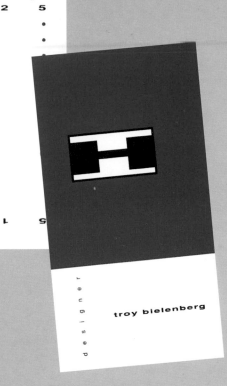

2

3

George Gruber

612-430-9824
fax 612-430-0423

10823 Pawnee Avenue North
Stillwater, Minnesota 55082

4

1 Design Firm
Idea Haus
Art Director
Troy Bielenberg
Designer
Erik Weber
Illustrator
Erik Weber
Client
Self-promotion
Graphic design

2 Design Firm
Minkus & Associates
Designer
Nikolas Pfendner
Client
Matt Chapman
Explosive aerobatics

3 Design Firm
Gruber Hill Design
Art Director
Beth Hanson
Designer
Peter Hill
Illustrator
Peter Hill
Client
Self-promotion
Design

4 Design Firm
Mires Design, Inc.
Art Director
Scott Mires
Designer
Scott Mires
Illustrator
Tracy Sabin
Client
Ear to Ear
Music production

1 Design Firm
Peggy Groves Design
Designer
Peggy Groves
Client
Self-promotion
Art and graphic design

2 Design Firm
Jay Vigon Studio
Designer
Jay Vigon
Client
Bedford Falls
Film production

3 Design Firm
Walsh & Associates, Inc.
Art Director
Miriam Lisco
Designer
Miriam Lisco
Calligrapher
Glenn Yoshiyama
Client
Fran's Chocolates
*Hand-wrapped
chocolate manufacturing*

4 Design Firm
Leslie Kane Design
Designer
Leslie Kane
Client
Self-promotion
Graphic design and lettering

5 Design Firm
Monroy & Cover Design
Designer
Gail Cover
Client
Amanda Pirot
*Marketing and
project management*

1

PEGGY GROVES

1388 Lincoln Park West

CHICAGO, ILLINOIS 60614

TELEPHONE 312.482.9661

2

Jay Vigon

B E D F O R D   F A L L S

1419 Second Street
Santa Monica, Ca. 90401
Tel: 310 · 395 · 3553
Fax: 310 · 394 · 2512

3

Fran Bigelow

Fran's™

CHOCOLATES, LTD.

CORPORATE / LABORATOIRE DU CHOCOLAT
1300 EAST PIKE STREET · SEATTLE WA 98122
206/322-0233 · FAX 206/322-0452
800-422-3726

4

Leslie A. Kane
•graphic design•

4909 69th Street
Urbandale, IA 50322
(515) 278-8449

5

AMANDA PIROT

Marketing and Project Management For Designers
San Francisco, California Tel/Fax 415•474•3702

1 Design Firm
The Bradford Lawton
Design Group
Art Directors
Brad Lawton,
Jennifer Griffith-Garcia
Designer
Brad Lawton
Illustrator
Brad Lawton
Client
Dr. Scheel Nayar
Obstetrics and gynecology

2 Design Firm
Peggy Groves Design
Designer
Peggy Groves
Client
Kamehachi Cafe
Late night Japanese restaurant

3 Design Firm
Yaba (Yeh!) Design
Designer
Yael Barnea-Givoni
Client
Self-promotion
Tile design and painting

4 Design Firm
GN Design Studio
Designer
Glenda S. Nothnagle
Client
Dori
*Residential and
commercial cleaning*

1

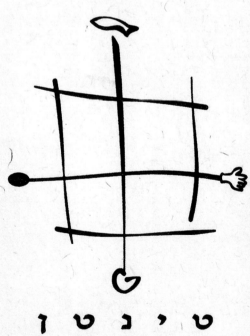

DR. SCHEEL NAYAR
OB/GYN
7355 Barlite
San Antonio
Texas 78224
Tel. 210-921-BABY
Fax 210-921-2360

2

KAMEHACHI
Japanese Restaurant & Sushi Bar

亀
八

1400 North Wells
Chicago, IL 60610
312.664.3663

3

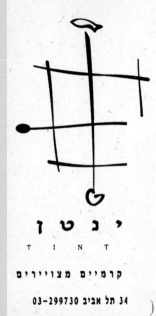

י נ ט ן
T I N T
קרמיים מצויירים
34 תל אביב 03-299730

4

Dori
Residential & Commercial Cleaning
Voice Mail
&
234-5101

ט י נ ט ן
T I N T A N
אוייחים קרמיים מצויירים
שינקין 34 תל אביב 03-299730

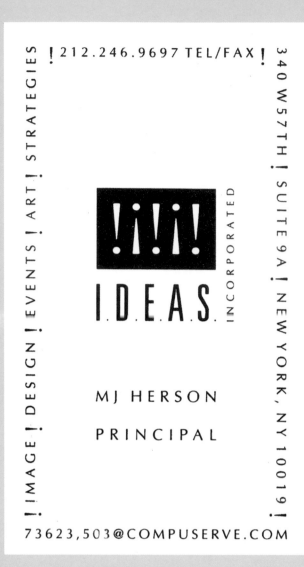

!212.246.9697 TEL/FAX!

340 W 57TH! SUITE 9A! NEW YORK, NY 10019!

!IMAGE! DESIGN! EVENTS! ART! STRATEGIES

INCORPORATED

I.D.E.A.S.

MJ HERSON

PRINCIPAL

73623,503@COMPUSERVE.COM

STAN **BAROUH**

PHOTOGRAPHY

704 SLIGO CREEK

PARKWAY

TAKOMA PARK

MARYLAND

2 0 9 1 2

T 202-265-7035

P 202-837-7946

F 202-265-8128

117 W 13TH ST #5 NYC 10011

KAY WAKABAYASHI

212·989·0166

GRAPHIC DESIGN

MARIO FINOTTI

FOTOGRAFO

VIA XIII MARTIRI 12
28070 GARBAGNA NOVARESE
ITALIA
0321/845192

PARTITA IVA 00408960037
CCIAA NOVARA 128911

1 Design Firm
Mo Viele, Inc.
Designer
Mo Viele
Client
I.D.E.A.S.
Communications and design

2 Design Firm
Market Sights, Inc
Designer
Marilyn Worseldine
Illustrator
Norman Ramock
Client
Barouh Photography

3 Design Firm
Tangram Strategic Design
Designer
Enrico Sempi
Client
Mario Finotti
Photography

4 Design Firm
Kay Wakabayashi
Designer
Kay Wakabayashi
Client
Self-promotion
Graphic design

1

Steven Abrahams
Landscape Works
207 Dolores Street
San Francisco
CA 94103-2211
Tel. 415.626.8021

2

BLACK SHEEP STUDIO

ILLUSTRATION & DESIGN

NINE WHITE BIRCH ROAD

STANHOPE, NJ 07874

SUSAN MARX
(201) 691-7657

3

BROWNE
PRODUCTION GROUP

———————

Eric Browne
3429 Airport Way S.
Seattle, WA 98134
(206) 329-4947
Studio - 382-0591

4

HARRY'S DOVE
Ceramic Sculpture

JENNIFER WALKER
(510) 339-3431

5

good food – good price

Ken Takahashi
(good boy)

the Dog House Waikiki

Sit: King's Village
131 Kaiulani Avenue
Speak: (808) 923-7744
Fetch: (808) 574-2052

1 Design Firm
Barry Power Graphic Design
Designer
Barry Power
Client
Steven Abrahams
Landscape Works
Landscape design

2 Design Firm
Black Sheep Studio
Designer
Susan Marx
Client
Self-promotion
Design and illustration

3 Design Firm
Walsh & Associates, Inc.
Designer
Michael Stearns
Client
Browne Production Group
Photography and film

4 Design Firm
Visible Ink
Designer
Sharon Howard Constant
Client
Harry's Dove
Ceramic sculpture

5 Design Firm
Voice
Designer
Clifford Cheng
Client
The Dog House
Waikiki snack shop

1 Art Director
Vanessa Eckstein
Designer
Vanessa Eckstein
Client
Fernando Arrioja
Mexican filmmaker

2 Design Firm
Tangram Strategic Design
Designer
Antonella Trevisan
Client
Logos Consulenza,
*Employment
placement agency*

3 Design Firm
Kaiser Dicken
Art Directors
Debra Kaiser, Craig Dicken
Designer
Debra Kaiser
Illustrator
Debra Kaiser
Client
Brad Rabinowitz Architect

4 Design Firm
THARP DID IT
Art Director
Rick Tharp
Designers
Amy Bednarek,
Laurie Okamura, Rick Tharp
Client
Self-promotion
*Corporate identity
and brand packaging design*

5 Design Firm
Glazer Graphics
Designer
Nancy Glazer
Client
Self-promotion
Illustration

6 Design Firm
Covi Corporation
Designer
Ursula Loepfe
Client
Self-promotion
Graphic design

1

FILM MAKER   8 1 8   7 9 2   6 2 4 3

FERNANDO ARRIOJA

628 E CALIFORNIA BLVD
PASADENA
91106 CA

8 1 8   7 9 2   6 2 4 3

2

Antonella Boggio

Logos Consulenza
Logos Consulenza s.n.c.
Viale Roma 43a, 28100 Novara
Telefono 0321 459830 R.A.
Fax 0321 458082
Partita IVA 01289840033

3

200 Main Street
Burlington, Vermont 05401
(802) 658-0430

B R A D   R A B I N O W I T Z   A R C H I T E C T

*Architecture
Space Planning
Interior Design*

4

408.354.6726   ⒯

☎

6

COVI Corporation

USA
5850 OBERLIN DRIVE
SUITE 310
SAN DIEGO, CA 92121
PHONE: 619/481-6566
FAX: 619/792-5426

MONA HOWELL

SWITZERLAND
ROSACKERSTR. 18
CH-4573 LOHN
TEL: 065/47 25 19
FAX: 065/47 26 41

COVI

CORPORATE VISUAL IDENTITY

5

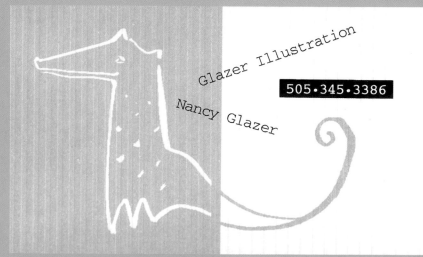

Glazer Illustration
Nancy Glazer
505•345•3386

1

Paperworks design

Graphic Design • Advertising • Photography • Printing

Logos • Brochures • Advertising
Publications • Trade Show Design
Packaging • Environmental Graphics

300 SW Second Street
Corvallis, OR 97333
USA, Planet Earth

503.753.4003
fax 503.754.1006

2

RON ZAHURANEC
PO BOX 65
TUSTIN CA
92681 0065
909 735 7435

3

LEE ANN RHODES
Graphic Designer

105 DUMBARTON RD.
SUITE D
BALTIMORE, MD
21212

4

SHARON STOKES
EXECUTIVE VICE PRESIDENT

1051 SERPENTINE LANE
PLEASANTON, CA 94566

RING 510/426•6155 FAX 510/426•9797

5

SONG MART
PRODUCTIONS

CHAS YOUNG
14 CASA DEL ORO LOOP
SANTA FE, NM 87505

505 • 466 • 0818

6

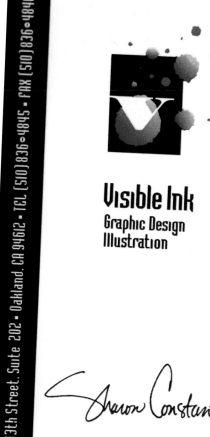

678 13th Street, Suite 202 • Oakland, CA 94612 • TEL (510) 836-4845 • FAX (510) 836-4846

Visible Ink
Graphic Design
Illustration

Sharon Constant

1 Design Firm
Paperworks Design
Art Director
Joanne McLennan
Designer
Sue Crawford
Client
Self-promotion
Design

2 Design Firm
Z Works
Designer
Ron Zahuranec
Client
Self-promotion
Graphic design

3 Design Firm
Lee Ann Rhodes Design
Designer
Lee Ann Rhodes
Client
Self-promotion
Graphic design

4 Design Firm
B3 Design
Designer
Barbara B. Breashears
Client
Class Connection
School fund-raising

5 Design Firm
Glazer Graphics
Designer
Nancy Glazer
Client
SongMart Productions
Music publishing

6 Design Firm
Visible Ink
Designer
Sharon Howard Constant
Client
Self-promotion
*Graphic design
and illustration*

1 Design Firm
Holden & Company
Designer
Cathe Holden
Client
Ducks in a Row
Interior decorating and creative services

2 Design Firm
Gabriella Hajdu-Advertising/Design
Designer
Gabriella Hajdu
Client
Self-promotion
Advertising and design

3 Design Firm
Tilka Design
Art Director
Jane Tilka
Designer
Wendy Ruyle
Client
Grape Vine Catering

4 Design Firm
Jay Vigon Studio
Art Director
Fred Eric
Designer
Jay Vigon
Producer
Caroline Plasencia
Client
Vida
Restaurant

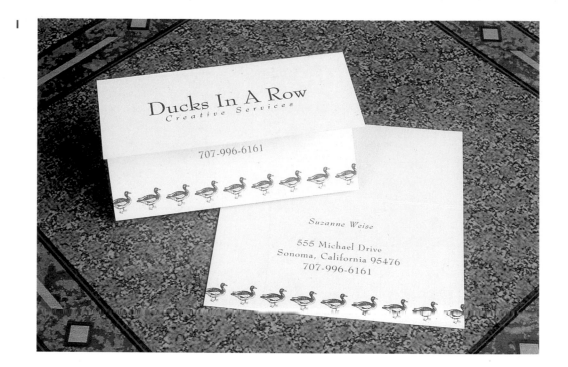

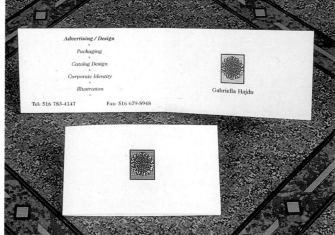

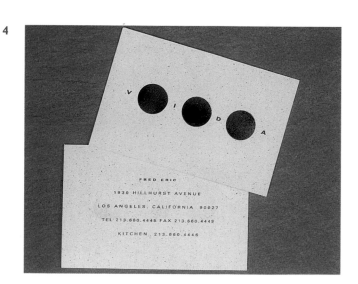

I

1 Design Firm
Gibbs Baronet
Art Directors
Steve Gibbs, Willie Baronet
Designer
Steve Gibbs, Willie Baronet, Kelly Kimball
Client
Self-promotion
Graphic design

2 Design Firm
Hornall Anderson Design Works
Art Director
Jack Anderson
Designers
Jack Anderson, Julie Keenan
Illustrator
George Tanagi
Client
Rod Ralston Photography

Jonathan Ingram

GIBBS BARONET

2200 North Lamar

Suite 201

Dallas Texas 75202

214.954.0316

214.855.0460 fax

Bronson Ma

GIBBS BARONET

2200 North Lamar

Suite 201

Dallas Texas 75202

214.954.0316

214.855.0460 fax

2

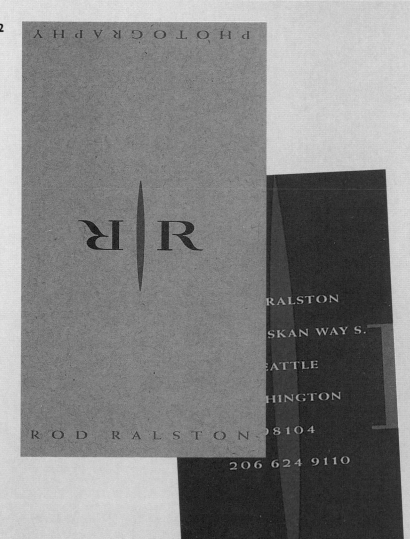

Meta Johnson Newhouse

GIBBS BARONET

2200 North Lamar

Suite 201

Dallas Texas 75202

214.954.0316

214.855.0460 fax

Tanya Lutz

GIBBS BARONET

2200 North Lamar

Suite 201

Dallas Texas 75202

214.954.0316

214.855.0460 fax

1 Design Firm
Pinkhaus Design Corp.
Designer
Todd Hauser
Client
Challenge Promotions, Inc.
Public relations

2 Design Firm
Peterson & Company
Art Director
Bryan L. Peterson
Designer
Scott Paramski
Illustrator
Scott Paramski
Client
Rocky Powell
Photography

3 Design Firm
One & One Design
Consultants Inc.
Designer
Dominick Sarica
Client
AMS Woodcrafts
Woodworking

4 Design Firm
Modelhart Grafik Design
Designer
Herbert O. Modelhart
Client
Self-promotion
Graphic design

5 Design Firm
Gibbs Baronet
Art Directors
Willie Baronet, Steve Gibbs
Designer
Jonathan Ingram
Illustrator
Jonathan Ingram
Client
Customwerx
*Custom cabinetry and
woodworking*

1

director
Roberto L. Silva
601 Brickell Key Drive
Suite 1020
Miami, Florida
33131
☎ 305 381 7899
FAX 305 381 9298

2

PRODUCTIONS

₀CKY POWELL **2205** COMMERCE DALLAS TEXAS
ZIP 75201 **TEL** 214.744.4242 **FAX** 214.748.8762

3

T 206 654 5300
F 206 382 6615
COMPUSERVE: 74603,2713
INTERNET: davidh@xactdata.com
DIRECT: 206 382 6606

XACTDATA C
COLUMBIA S
701 5TH AVE
SEATTLE WA

K.C. ALY
PRESIDENT

X·ACT
DATA

4

Herbert O. Modelhart
Grafik-Design

Pöllnstraße 19 · A-5600 St. Johann / Pg.
Tel. 0 64 12 / 84 66 o. 63 64 · Fax 84 66-4

5

JIM MORSE
CUSTOMWERX · 1594 HART ST
SOUTHLAKE TEXAS 76092
817.481.2677 · Fax 817.488.1738

Reiseburo Stranger

Petra Stranger

Inh. Petra Stranger · A-5600 St. Johann im Pongau · Hauptstraße 41 · PF39
Tel.: 0 64 12 /5757 · Fax: 0 64 12 / 57 57-20

Barry Power Graphic Design

logos / advertising
personalized greetings
business cards / more

3921 19th Street, San Francisco, California 94114 415.863.5085

MUSTARD (SEED)

ENTERPRISES

·ILLUSTRATION·

KAREN L. NAILE
PO Box 932
No. Chatham, NY 12132

(518) 766-2965

JOHN CRAMES

1260 NORTH BROAD STREET

HILLSIDE NEW JERSEY 07205

PHONE 908-353-1644

FAX 908-353-1644

FERNANDO MAGALHÃES PINTO

AV. RIO BRANCO, 12/20° ANDAR
CEP 20090-000 - CENTRO
RIO DE JANEIRO - RJ - BRASIL
TEL.: (021) 263-9179 - 233-6356
FAX.: (021) 233-8152

1 Design Firm
Modelhart Grafik Design
Designer
Herbert O. Modelhart
Client
Reisebüro Stranger
Travel agency

2 Design Firm
Barry Power Graphic Design
Designer
Barry Power
Client
Self-promotion
Graphic design

3 Design Firm
Mustard Seed Enterprises
Designer
Karen L. Naile
Client
Self-promotion
Illustration

4 Design Firm
Pisarkiewicz & Company
Art Director
Mary F. Pisarkiewicz
Designer
Joseph Dzialo
Illustrator
Jennifer Harenberg
Client
Rubber Duck Car Wash

5 Design Firm
Animus Comunicaçáo
Art Director
Rique Nitzsche
Designer
Rique Nitzsche, Felício Torres
Illustrator
Felício Torres
Client
Bras Bike
Bicycle retail and trade

1

k a t y   s u l l i v a n

general fine artist
4 2   g r a n d v i e w   a v e .   c o r n w a l l   o n   h u d s o n ,   n y .   1 2 5 2 0
9 1 4 . 5 3 4 . 8 4 9 2

1 Design Firm
Katy L. Sullivan
Designer
Katy L. Sullivan
Client
Self-promotion
Fine art

2 Design Firm
Cisneros Design
Art Director
Fred Cisneros
Designers
Fred Cisneros, Jim Price
Client
Price Printing
Commercial printing brokerage

3 Design Firm
Isheo Design House
Designer
Ishmael Sheo
Client
Joshua Race Ministry
Music company

4 Design Firm
Shields Design
Art Director
Charles Shields
Designer
Charles Shields
Illustrator
Doug Hansen
Client
The United States Chart Company
Commodities chart service

2

James Price
P.O. Box 16403
Santa Fe, New Mexico 87506
(505)473-9332

3

JOSHUA RACE ✦ MINISTRY

KELVIN LIM

KINGDOM
H E R I T A G E   Block A, 01-06-15 Brem Park, Jalan Selesa 2, Happy Garden, 58200 Kuala Lumpur.
Tel: 7800842 (h) 7175716 (Off) Fax: 2983670 Pager: 2932000 – 11207

4

Chuck Crane
PRESIDENT

333 S.W. 5th Street   ✦   Grants Pass, Oregon 97526
503-955-2885   ✦   Fax: 503-955-2889

1

600 CHANEY ST.

LAKE ELSINORE

CALIFORNIA 92530

DELEO CLAY TILE
SINCE 1984
QUALITY CRAFTSMANSHIP

TEL 714-674-1578

FAX 909-245-2427

1-800-654-1119

2

CHIP LERWICK, *President*

SINCE 1993
HEARTLAND
FUTONS   FIBERS
SAINT LOUIS, MISSOURI

800 239-8022
tel. 314 231-8022
fax 231-8104

*Manufacturers of the
highest-quality
futons, made with a 100%
recycled fiber core.*

*2107 Lucas Avenue
Saint Louis
Missouri 63103*

3

Pitchfork Development, Inc.

Post Office Box 2370

572 Park Avenue

Park City, Utah 84060

Telephone: (801)649-3900

Facsimile: (801)649-3757

James W. Lewis
President

1 Design Firm
Mires Design, Inc.
Art Director
Jose Serrano
Designer
Jose Serrano
Illustrator
Nancy Stahl
Client
Deleo Clay Tile Company
Clay roofing tile retail

2 Design Firm
Phoenix Creative
Art Director
Eric Thoelke
Designer
Eric Thoelke
Client
Heartland Futons
Recycled-fiber futon retail

3 Design Firm
The Weller Institute for
the Cure of Design
Designer
Don Weller
Client
Pitchfork Development Inc.
*Real estate development
and construction*

TIMELESS IMAGES

DENNIS R. HOWE
PHOTOGRAPHER

(708) 433

STUDIO OR LOCATION

320 GREENBAY ROAD, HIGHWOOD, IL

H O W E H STUDIOS

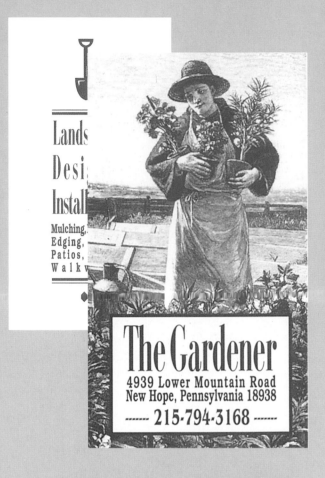

Lands
Desi
Instal

Mulching,
Edging,
Patios,
Walkw

The Gardener
4939 Lower Mountain Road
New Hope, Pennsylvania 18938
------- 215·794·3168 -------

3

TASARIM ILLUSTRASYON   0 · 212 273 18 01

KAGAN ATSÜREN

YAŞARBEY SK. 9/8 80310 MECİDİYEKÖY İSTANBUL

1 Design Firm
Teslick Graphics
Designer
Julie L. Teslick
Client
Howe Studios
Photography

2 Design Firm
Full Moon Creations, Inc.
Art Director
Frederic Leleu
Designer
Lisa Leleu
Illustrator
Lisa Leleu
Client
The Gardener
*Landscape design and
installation*

3 Design Firm
Propaganda
Designer
Kagan Atsüren
Client
Self-promotion
Freelance illustration and design

4 Design Firm
Leslie Chan Design Co., Ltd.
Designer
Leslie Chan Wing Kei
Client
Topline Communication Inc.
Production

4

林 欽 賢 藝術指導
STEVEN LIN Art Director

T O P L I N E

經典集國際廣告有限公司

經典集國際廣告有限公司
台北市敦化南路一段236巷31號 5 樓
TOPLINE COMMUNICATION INC.
5F. No. 31, Lane 236, Tun Hua S. Road, Taipei, Taiwan.
Tel: (02)731-6666 Fax: (02)751-1522

1

TOD ERNST

Planet Hair

316 267 8000

504 E. DOUGLAS   WICHITA KS 67202

2

Baillie Gerstein

2107 GREENFIELD AVE

LOS ANGELES, CA 90025

TEL. 310.477.5242

FAX. 310.479.7609

3

ELLEN
KNABLE
&ASSOC
INCORPORATED

1 2 3 3

SOUTH

LA CIENEGA BLVD.

LOS ANGELES

CALIFORNIA

9 0 0 3 5

TELEPHONE

310 855 8855

F A X

310 657 0265

1 Design Firm
Greteman Group
Art Director
Sonia Greteman
Designers
Sonia Greteman, Karen Hogan
Client
Planet Hair
Hair salon

2 Design Firm
Jay Vigon Studio
Art Director
Jay Vigon
Designer
Caroline Plasencia
Producer
Caroline Plasencia
Illustrator
Jay Vigon
Client
Baillie Gerstein
Commercial voice-over specialist

3 Design Firm
Jay Vigon Studio
Designer
Jay Vigon
Client
Ellen Knable & Associates
Artists' representitive

1

SUSAN WRIGHT ★ TELEPHONE 316 945 8000

WICHITA, KANSAS 67215 ★ 3500 S. HOOVER RD.

HEARTH & HOME

2

ASTRONOMICAL
SOCIETY OF
KANSAS CITY

P. O. BOX 400
BLUE SPRINGS
MISSOURI 64013
889-STAR X5400

JACKIE
WADE
PRESIDENT

11305 KING
OVERLAND PARK
KANSAS 66210
913.469.0135

ELMCREST
OBSERVATORY

POWELL
OBSERVATORY

3

MOONLIGHT DESIGNS

Kim Beaty

1025 Ashworth Road, Suite 314, West Des Moines, Iowa 50265
Phone: 515-222-9990   FAX: 515-222-9989

1 Design Firm
Greteman Group*
Designers
Sonia Greteman, Bill Gardner,
James Strange
Client
Hearth & Home
Fireplace retail

2 Design Firm
Eat Design
Art Director
Patrice Eilts-Jobe
Designers
Patrice Eilts-Jobe, Toni O'Bryan
Client
Jackie Wade
Astronomer

3 Design Firm
Moonlight Designs
Designer
Kim Beaty
Client
Self-promotion
Graphic design

SAGE BRUSH DESIGN

DANIELLE BEWER

403 West Channel Road
Santa Monica, California 90402
Tel. 310·459·7487 Fax 310·459·5508

1 **Design Firm**
Sage Brush Design
Designer
Danielle Bewer
Client
Self-promotion
Art and graphic design

2 **Design Firm**
Phoenix Creative
Designer
Ed Mantels-Seeker
Client
Art Company London
Antique painting reproduction
and wholesale

3 **Design Firm**
Phoenix Creative
Designer
Ed Mantels-Seeker
Client
The Gifted Gardener
Gardening gifts, accessories, and
furniture retail

Art Company London

Michael J. Goodson
PRESIDENT

Eleven East Wisconsin
Suite 200
Trenton, Illinois 62293
618 224-9435
FAX:
618 224-9296

THE
GIFTED
GARDENER

8935 Manchester
Saint Louis
Missouri 63144

Telephone: 961-1985
Area Code 314

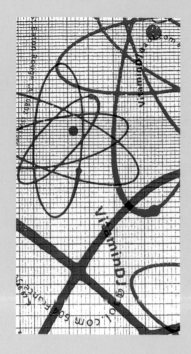

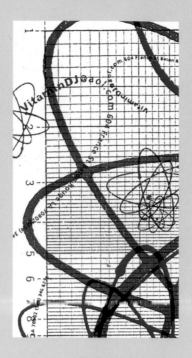

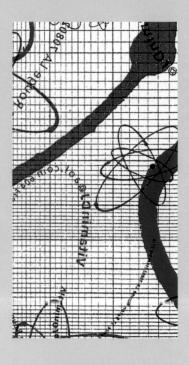

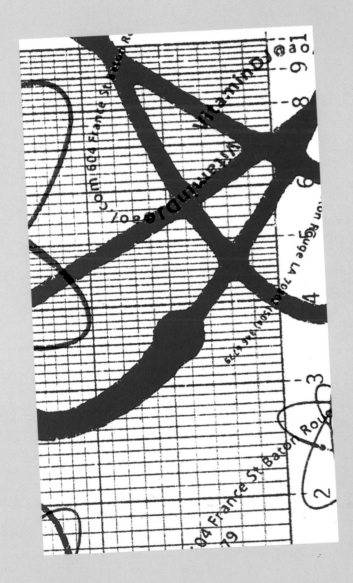

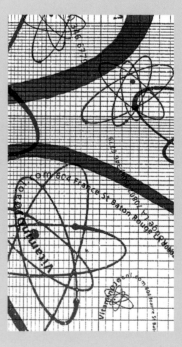

Design Firm
Paper Shrine
Designer
Paul Dean
Client
Vitamin DJ
Disc jockey

Design Firm
Kaiser Dicken
Art Director
Debra Kaiser
Designer
Debra Kaiser
Illustrator
Craig Dicken
Client
Imagine Books
Antique book retail

Boulevard
A 92101
, 229, 237, 264, 310,
41

Corp.
2nd Street
, NY 10016
174, 256

esign
mmonealth Avenue

MA 02135

a
Lane 138, Sec.1
ng-kung Rd. Taichung
iwan, R.O.C.

le, Inc.
ospect Street
02
NY 14850

hart Grafik Design
dwig Pechstrasse 7
o St. Johann/Pg
a
39

a Götz Design
ast 89th Street, #4A
ork, NY 10128

by & Cover Design
dges Alley
rancisco, CA 94133
30

light Designs
Ashworth Road
314
Des Moines, IA 50265

Design
aelstraat 20
PV Amsterdam
etherlands

er Graphic Design
5, 15-19 Boundary Street
cutters Bay, Sydney, NSW 2011
alia
239, 247

media Asia
Box 18416
ose, CA 95158

ard Seed Enterprises
ox 932
hatham, NY 12132

rny Design
5 Charles Plaza
e 930
ha, NE 68114

cy Stutman Calligraphics
3 Rana Court
sbad, CA 92009

cy Yeasting Design & Illustration
o Monmuth Avenue
couver, BC V59 5R9
ada
, 246

to Maki
Ramona Avenue, #2
Francisco, CA 94103

Nesnadny + Schwartz
10803 Magnolia Drive
Cleveland, OH 44106
67

New Idea Design, Inc.
3702 S. 16th Street
Omaha, NE 68107
268

Niehinger & Rohsiepe
Pulverstrasse 25
D-44869 Bochum
Germany
herbert.rohsiepe@gelson.net
9

O2 Design
Tanner Place
54-58 Tanner Street
London SE1 3HP
England
102

Oakley Design Studios
519 SW Park Avenue
Suite 521
Portland, OR 97205
213, 324

(ojo)2
Calle 64 No. 4-85 (208)
Bogotá
Columbia
172

Olive Tree
12 Glen Court
Coorparoo, Qld. 4151
Australia
263

On The Edge
505 30th Street
Suite 211
Newport Beach, CA 92663
170, 238, 257

One & One Design Consultants, Inc.
25 West 43rd Street
New York, NY 10036
318, 338

One, Graphic Design & Consulting
812 Gloucester Ferry Road
Greenville, SC 29607
235, 246

Opera Grafisch Ontwerpers
Baronielaan 78
NL-4818 RC Breda
The Netherlands
operath@knoware.nl
18, 28, 44, 61, 108

Palmquist & Palmquist Design
P.O. Box 325
Bozeman, MT 59771
291

Paper Power
53 Warwick Road
Ealing, London W5 5P2
England
272, 273

Paper Shrine
604 France Street
Baton Rouge, LA 70802
346

Paperworks Design
300 SW 2nd Street
Corvallis, OR 97333
335

Paradigm Design
13603 Marina Pointe Drive, #C421
Marina Del Ray, CA 90292
310

Paratore Hartshorn Design
354 Congress Street
Boston, MA 02210
308

**Patricia Spencer
Advertising & Design**
205 E. 78th Street
New York, NY 10021
298

Peat Jariya Design/Metal Studio
1210 W. Clay
Suite 13
Houston, TX 77019
314

Peggy Groves Design
1906 Lincoln Park West
Chicago, IL 60614
321, 330, 331

Pen Ultimate
83 Windwhisper Lane
Annapolis, MD 21403
272

Peter Comitini Design
611 Broadway
New York, NY 10012
231

Petter Frostell Graphic Design
Roslagsgatan 34
11355 Stockholm
Sweden
petter.frostell@tella.com
96

Peterson & Company
2200 North Lamar
Suite 310
Dallas, TX 75202
280, 282, 286, 338

Pfeiffer plus Company
1910 Pine Street
Suite 515
St. Louis, MO 63103
103

PhD
427 Shawmut Avenue
Boston, MA 02118
278

Phillips Design Group
25 Drydock Avenue
Boston, MA 02210
221

Phoenix Creative
611 N. 10th Street
St. Louis, MO 63101
208, 213, 226, 238, 276, 283, 294,
305, 326, 341, 345

Pinkhaus Design Corp.
2424 South Dixie Highway
Miami, FL 33133
279, 281, 315, 338

Pisarkiewicz & Company
34 West 22nd Street
New York, NY 10010
339

PJ Graphics
650 Venice Boulevard
Venice, CA 90291
293

Prestige Design
602 Johns Drive
Euless, TX 76039
187

**Proforma, Association
of Designers & Consultants**
Slepersvest 5-7
3011 MK Rotterdam
The Netherlands
287

Propaganda
Inönücaddesi 53/13 Ayazpasa
Taksim 34504 Istanbul
Turkey
342

Purple Seal Graphics
P.O. Box 3041
Carbondale, IL 62902
315, 327

pw design graphics
2040 York Avenue
Suite 215
Vancouver, BC VGJ IE7
Canada
168, 185

R & M Associati Grafici
Traversa Del Pescatore 3
80053 Castellammare Di Stabia
Italia
info@rmassociati.com
10, 16, 58, 91

Ralph Huss
Budapesterstrasse 25
20359 Hamburg
Germany
239

Ramona Hutko Design
4712 South Chelsea Lane
Bethesda, MD 20814
153

Raven Madd Design
P.O. Box 11331 Wellington
Level 3 Harcourts Building
Corner Gray Streer and Lambton
Quay
New Zealand
248

Redgate Communication
221 Main Street
Suite 480
San Francisco, CA 94105
328

**Ricardo Mealha Atelier
Design Estrategico**
Av. Eno Duarte Dachelo
Torre2
Piso 2 Sazas 9 & 10
Portugal
140, 141

Rick Eiber Design (RED)
31014 SE 58th Street
Preston, WA 98050
186, 210, 216, 241, 252, 260, 269

Ringo W.K. Hui
Rm 404, Wo Hui House
Wo Ming Court
Tseung Kwan o
Hong Kong
77

Robbins Design
1018 Birchmont Road
Columbus, OH 43220
290

Robert Bailey Incorporated
0121 SW Bancroft Street
Portland, OR 97201
325

Robert Williamson
4602 14th Street NW
Seattle, WA 98107
312

Rocha & Yamasaki Arq.E Design
Rua Dos Franceses, 470.C/Ap.164
01329-010 Sao Paulo SP
Brazil
282

Roger Gefvert Designs
4282 Highway 89 South
Livingston, MT 59047
269

S & S Design
Francisco de Toledo 241La
Virreyna
Lima 33
Peru
sanfarmo@comercio.com.pe
45

Sackett Design Associates
2103 Scott Street
San Francisco, CA 94115
132

Sage Brush Design
403 W. Channel Road
Santa Monica, CA 90402
321, 345

Sagmeister, Inc.
222 West 14th Street
New York, NY 10011
ssagmeiste@aol.com
180, 184, 192, 199, 201, 211, 229

Sandy Gin Design
329 High Street
Palo Alto, CA 94301
177, 184

Sayles Graphic Design
3701 Beaver Avenue
Des Moines, IA 50310
156, 157, 166, 175, 185, 192, 200, 241,
263, 312, 320

Sb design
Rua Furriel Luiz A. Vargas
#380/203
90470-130 Porto Alegre RS
Brazil
sbdesign@myway.com.br
90, 131

Second Floor
443 Folsom Street
San Francisco, CA 94105
design@secondfloor.com
32, 137

Shelley Danysh Studio
8940 Krenstown Road, #107
Philadelphia, PA 19115
307, 311

Shields Design
415 East Olive Avenue
Fresno, CA 93728
198, 292, 301, 340

Sibley Peteet Design
3232 McKinney, #1200
Dallas, TX 75204
rhonda@spddallas.com
8, 133, 274, 281

Siebert Design Associates
1600 Sycamore
Cincinnati, OH 45210
178

Sivustudio
Tontunmaentie 22H
0220 Espoo
Finland
234, 261

Skarsgard Design
807 Hutchins Avenue
Ann Arbor, MI 48103
skarsgard@bigfoot.com
154

SND, Sue Nan Designs
1145 Lindero Canyon Road
Thousand Oaks, CA 91362
324

Solo Grafica
11251 Caminito Rodar
San Diego, CA 92126
243

Sommese Design
481 Glenn Road
State College, PA 16803
316

Spectrum Graphics Studio
2860 Carpenter Road
Suite 100B
Ann Arbor, MI 48108
49

Spin Productions
620 King Street West
Toronto, Ontario M5V1M6
Canada
norm@spinpro.com
146

Squeak
14851 Summerbreeze Way
San Diego, CA 92128
320, 323

Stang
Gedempte Zalmhaven 835
3011 BT Rotterdam
Holland
stang@ipr.nl
47, 61

Stefan Dziallas Design
Olbersstrasse 9
28307 Bremen
Germany
262

Stephen Peringer Illustration
17808 184th Avenue NE
Woodinville, WA 98072
173, 271

Steve Trapero Design
3309-G Hampton Point Drive
Silver Spring, MD 20904
255

Steven Morris Design
10284 Royal Ann Avenue
San Diego, CA 92126
294, 297

Stewart Monderer Design, Inc.
10 Thacher Street
Boston, MA 02113
sm@monderer.com
96

Storm Design &
Advertising Consultancy
174 Albert Street, Prahran
Victoria 3181
Australia
194, 242

Stowe Design
125 University Avenue
Suite 220
Palo Alto, CA 94301
185, 228, 284, 291, 303, 323

Stress Lab
212 3rd Avenue N, #385
Minneapolis, MN 55401
280, 289, 305

Studio Boot
Brede Haven
8A's-Hertogenbosch
The Netherlands
69, 79, 87, 109, 112, 113, 121, 124, 149

Suburbia Studios
53 Tovey Crescent
Victoria, BC V9B 1A4
Canada
195

Sullivan Perkins
2811 McKinney
Suite 310 LB111
Dallas, TX 75204
274, 292, 320

Sunny Shender Design
2865 S. Atlantic Street
Seattle, WA 98144
275

Susan Guerra
30 Gray Street
Montclair, NJ 07042
166, 215

Tanagram
855 W. Blackhawk Street
Chicago, IL 60622
174, 196, 254

Tangram Strategic Design
Via Negroni 2
28100 Novara
Italy
311, 327, 332, 334

Teikna
366 Adelaide Street East
Suite 541
Toronto, ON M5A 3X9
Canada
212, 223, 244

Teslick Graphics
41 Elm Avenue
Highwood, IL 60040
342

Tharp Did It
50 University Avenue
Suite 21
Los Gatos, CA 95030
206, 233, 235, 276, 300, 302, 308,
313, 324, 334

"That's Nice" l.l.c.
1 Consulate Drive, #3N
Tuckahoe, NY 10707
84

The Bradford Lawton
Design Group
719 Avenue E
San Antonio, TX 78215
277, 331

The Design Company
3103 East Shadowland Aveunue
Atlanta, GA 30305
203, 212, 251, 294

The Eikon Marketing Team
901 Pine
Rolla, MO 65401
266

The Hive Design Studio
10 Jackson Street, #204
Los Gatos, CA 95032
amyb13@aol.com
23, 38, 78

The Home Studio
3105 Moss Side Avenue
Richmond, VA 32222
229

The Paul Martin Design Co.
32 Dragon Street
Petersfield, Hampshire GU31 4JJ
England
270

The Puckett Group
7521 Buckingham Drive, #2W
St. Louis, MO 63105
candy_freund@simmons-
durham.com
134

The Riordon Design Group
131 George Street
Oakville, ON L6J 3B9
Canada
group@riordondesign.com
6, 7

The Running Iron Studio
726 Long Drive, #26B
Sheridan, WY 82801
227

The Weller Institute for
the Cure of Design, Inc.
P.O. Box 518
Oakley, UT 84055
chachaw@allwest.net
29, 341

The Woldring Company
306 West Michigan Avenue
Kalamazoo, MI 49007
306, 321

The Wyant Simboli Group, Inc
96 East Avenue
Norwalk, CT 06851
327

Tilka Design
1422 West Lake Street, #314
Minneapolis, MN 55408
295, 325, 336

Tim Kenney Design Partners
3 Bethesda Metro Center
Suite 630
Bethseda, MD 20814
135

Toni Schowalter Design
1133 Broadway, 1610
New York, NY 10010
218, 182

Total Creative, Inc.
8360 Melrose Avenue, 3rd Floor
Los Angeles, CA 90069
105

Tower of Babel
24 Arden Road
Asheville, NC 28803
226, 235

Tracy Design
5638 Holmes
Kansas City, MO 64110
197

Transparent Office
Overgadeau O.Vandet 54 A2
DK-1415 Cph.K
Denmark
247

Treehouse Design
10637 Youngworth Road
Culver City, CA 90230
tr_treehouse@pacbell.net
14, 145

Troller Associates
12 Harbor Lane
Rye, NY 10580
55

twenty2product
440 Davis Court
Apt. 509
San Francisco, CA 94111
terry@twenty2.com
34

Two In Design
1270 West Peachtree Street NW
Suite 8B
Atlanta, GA 30309
281, 283, 324

Underdog Design
4147 49th Avenue SW
Seattle, WA 98116
320

Urbangraphic
3165 Kershawn Place
Escondido, Ca 92029
urbangraph@aol.com
68

V. Allen Crawford Design
25 Locust Lane
New Egypt, NJ 08533
307

Val Gene Associates
5208 Classen Boulevard
Oklahoma City, OK 73118
197, 258, 259

Vanessa Eckstein
12 Charles Street, #3C
New York, NY 10014
334

Vaughn Wedeen Creative
407 Rio Grande NW
Albuquerque, NM 87104
286, 291, 293, 302

Veronica Graphic Design
Suite 67 Isle of Capri
Commercial Centre QLO. 4217
Australia
321

Vestígio
Rua Chaby Pinheiro, 191-2°
P-4460-278
Sra. da Hora
Portugal
info@vestigio.com
29, 83, 135

Via Vemeulen
William Boothlaan 4
Rotterdam
The Netherlands
viarick@ipr.nl
36

Vibeke Nødskov
Overgaden Oven Vandet 54A2
DK-1415 Copenhagen
Denmark
239, 283, 322

Visible Ink
678 13th Street
Suite 202
Oakland, CA 94612
274, 313, 333, 335

Visser Bay Anders Toscani
Assumburg 152, Postbus
P.O. Box 71116
1008 BC Amsterdam
Holland
75, 155

Visual Advantage
13080 Woodlands Parkway
Clive, IA 50325
274

Visual Marketing Associates
322 S. Patterson Boulevard
Dayton, OH 45402
info@vmai.com
100, 143

Voice Design
1385 Alewa Drive
Honolulu, HI 96817
voice@lava.net
66, 150, 333

Vrontikis Design Office
2021 Pontius Avenue
Los Angeles, CA 90025
200, 221, 224

Wages Design
887 W. Marietta Street
Studio 5-111
Atlanta, GA 30318
289, 317

Wallace/Church
330 E. 48th Street
New York, NY 10017
wendy@wallacechurch.com
33

Walmsley Design
40 Hobbs Brook
Weston, MA 02193
320

Walsh and Associates, Inc.
1725 Westlake Avenue North
Suite 203
Seattle, WA 98109
269, 292, 315, 330, 333

Watts Graphic Design
79-81 Palmerston Crescent
South Melbourne 3205
Australia
233

WCVB TV Design
5 TV Place
Needham Heights, MA
327

WDG Communications
3011 Johnson Avenue NW
Cedar Rapids, IA 52405
213

Whitney Edwards Design
14 West Dover Street
Easton, MD 21601
283

Widmeyer Design
911 Western Avenue, #305
Seattle, WA 98104
165, 182, 206, 214, 215, 232, 2?
244

Wiedemann Design
227 Shipley Street
San Francisco, CA 94107
280, 305

Witherspoon Advertising
1000 West Weatherford
Fort Worth, TX 76102
271

Yaba (Yeh!) Design
5 Bialik Street
Tel Aviv, Israel 63324
331

YoungJu Lee
2 Kaywood Road
Port Washington, NY 11050
308

Z Works
P.O. Box 65
Tustin, CA 92681
335

Zappata Designers
Lafayette 143, Anzures
C.P. 11590 Mexico City
Mexico
221

Zauhar Design
510 1st Avenue N, #405
Minneapolis, MN 55403
279

Zedwear
1718 M Street NW
Suite 1010
Washington, DC 20036
316

Zeigler Associates
107 E. Cary Street
Richmond, VA 23219
zeiglera@erols.com
27, 97

Zeroart Studio
P.O. Bos 71466, Kowloon
Central Post Office
Hong Kong
zeroart@netvigator.com
127, 216

Zubi Design
57 Norman Avenue, #4R
Brooklyn, NY 11222
280